MILTON AND THE BAROQUE

MILTON AND THE BAROQUE

Murray Roston

University of Pittsburgh Press

© Murray Roston 1980

Published in Great Britain 1980 by
The Macmillan Press Ltd

Published in the U.S.A. 1980 by
THE UNIVERSITY OF PITTSBURGH PRESS,
Pittsburgh, Pa. 15260

Printed in Great Britain by
UNWIN BROTHERS LIMITED
The Gresham Press
Old Woking Surrey

Library of Congress Cataloging in Publication Data

Roston, Murray.
  Milton and the baroque.

  Includes bibliographical references and index.
  1. Milton, John, 1608–1674. Paradise lost.
  2. Milton, John, 1608–1674—Style. 3. Baroque
literature—History and criticism. 4. Art, Baroque.
  I. Title.
  PR3562.R6   821'.4   79–21611
  ISBN 0–8229–1138–8

FOR MY MOTHER

Contents

List of Plates

Acknowledgements

I should like to express my thanks to two colleagues who were kind enough to read this book in manuscript and to make a number of helpful comments: to Professor Harold Fisch for the literary aspects, and Professor M. Barasch for the art history.

The quotations from *Paradise Lost* are from the edition by Merritt Y. Hughes (New York, 1962) and appear by courtesy of the Odyssey Press.

The Research Committee of Bar-Ilan University assisted me with a grant to cover the cost of typing and the preparation of illustrations, and I am grateful for their help.

Finally, a very special word of thanks to my wife Faith, who accompanied me on my summer tours through the art centres of Europe and, by her own deep love of art and her wide knowledge of its history, made those explorations a shared experience long to be remembered.

M. R.

1 The Baroque Vision

The placing of Milton within a baroque setting is, in itself, no longer a novelty. Since historians began (a little reluctantly perhaps) to acknowledge that literature cannot be isolated from the dominant artistic movements of each era, the relationship between *Paradise Lost* and the continental baroque has become widely recognised. The authoritative assertion of theme, the adoption of a 'Grand Style', and the monumentality of the work as a whole provide at least initial evidence of a connection with that European mode; and the perceptive studies by Wylie Sypher and Roy Daniells have in recent years made the baroque attribution an integral part of the Milton scene.

Nevertheless, the reader intent on the epic itself may well ask what has been gained by that knowledge. It may be of some historical interest to know that Milton was not alone in his artistic endeavours, that contemporary architects and painters were also creating works in the Grand Style; but for literary purposes, such information would appear to be merely academic, a further footnote added to the lengthy list of possible sources or parallels to the poem. The complaint is, I think, justified, for the most stimulating part of such comparative investigation linking literature with the visual arts is not in the establishing of these larger period settings, but in the stage beyond that. It occurs when this contact between the arts sets off a flash of recognition, a realization that the way a painter solved a problem posed by his era can throw fresh light on the writer's technique too. And conversely, when the writer solves the problem differently from the painter, we may through that change be made aware of some basic element distinguishing the verbal art of poetry from the visual effect of a canvas. In either instance, we return to the literary work with an understanding which could not easily have been obtained within the exclusively literary sphere.

Any theory generated by such art parallels is, of course, valueless until it has been substantiated by a careful re-reading of the literary texts. Literary problems require finally the tools of literary analysis; but such comparative study can at the very least provide a refreshingly new vantage-point. By moving away into the adjacent field of art history and viewing *Paradise Lost* as part of the broader landscape of the era, we may from that distance discern new avenues of approach to old topics, at a time when some of the previously used paths are beginning to look a little worn.

The purpose of this book, therefore, is not to argue for the baroque attribution once again but to go beyond, and to explore what insights that knowledge can offer into some of the central problems raised in twentieth-century Milton criticism. One inherent disadvantage of such a study is that those primarily interested in poetry may in the opening section wonder when Milton will finally appear. Clearly, some detailed analysis of the baroque as an art form must precede any attempt to apply its principles to literature, particularly when a rather new interpretation of that mode is being suggested; but if the reader will bear with me, I can at least promise that Milton will not be forgotten in the subsequent discussion.

(i)

Only a few decades ago, the baroque style had fallen into such low repute that Benedetto Croce could declare categorically: 'Art is never baroque, and the baroque is never art.'[1] That view, which regarded it as merely a degeneration of the Renaissance ideal has now, mercifully, been discarded, and the authenticity of the baroque as an independent art form is no longer the subject of debate. The reasons for its condemnation in that earlier period are, however, easy enough to understand. At their worst, baroque painting and sculpture are more stridently offensive to the sensitive viewer than the inferior art of other eras. The minor painters of the eighteenth-century rococo, for example, are merely ineffective in a quiet and untroublesome way, while in baroque *kitsch* the over-dramatised gestures, the exaggerated piety, and the gory martyrdoms cry out for attention, and hence impinge more deeply on the memory. Yet no art movement should be judged by its worst practitioners, and at its best, as in the majestic interior of S. Andrea al Quirinale, the rich vitality of a Rubens painting, or the breathing statuary of Bernini, the baroque attains an aesthetic integrity rivalling the finest achievements of the Gothic or Renaissance traditions.

On the other hand, if the baroque has now won recognition as an art form in its own right, the source of its aesthetic impulse remains in dispute. Art historians continue to offer conflicting theories of its basic motivation and of the cultural changes to which it was responding. In the Renaissance, the connection between art and the philosophy of the era emerges with greater clarity. It requires little scholarly effort to perceive in the circular form of Bramante's Tempietto or in the slender, rounded arches of Brunelleschi's Foundling Hospital the current Neoplatonic belief in the perfection of the circle and the harmony of the spheres; but such relationships have proved more difficult to establish for the succeeding era.

In the mid-sixteenth century, a new mood had begun to make itself felt in all the arts, a striving after magnificence and splendour. Originating in Rome and spreading swiftly across all Europe, it aimed at evoking from the spectator a more intense emotional response, at arousing feelings of rapture, devotion or awe. In architecture, the more austere classical style of church was replaced by a huge structure, imposing in appearance and crowned by a massive dome. The interiors became jewel-like, richly ornamented with coloured marble, onyx, porphyry and lapis lazuli, and surmounted by a wealth of stucco decoration. There was a tendency to theatricality which broke down the traditional divisions between the arts. Sculpture, metalwork, and coloured glass were combined with painting and fresco to create such dazzling scenes as the Cornaro Chapel in S. Maria della Vittoria, where the *Ecstasy of S. Teresa* was presented at the height of her sensuous vision as a stage piece witnessed by noblemen seated in boxes at either side. On the professional stage too, music, drama, dance, and spectacle merged with extravagantly constructed scenery to inaugurate the new genre of Italian opera.

The two most widely held theories explaining the origin of this baroque impulse and of the extraordinarily variegated style it produced are in their own ways persuasive at first sight. Carl J. Friedrich, in a broadly ranging study of the period, has argued that behind the grandeur of the baroque lies an exaggerated belief in man himself. It was a belief, he maintains, which found its political expression in the emergence of monarchal absolutism throughout the European states, and in the growing fascination with what Hobbes in his *Leviathan* called the ' . . . general inclination of all mankind, a perpetuall and restlesse desire of Power after Power, that ceaseth only in Death'.[2] This drive for power, coupled with an unlimited self-confidence created the urge in architects, sculptors, painters, poets, and musicians ' . . . to accomplish the impossible in *all* directions'. Sumptuous palaces arose, set within artificially created parks and gardens, with huge piazzas before them containing sculpted fountains, obelisks, and colonnades. They were designed to set off dramatically the buildings themselves, symbolising the strength and dignity of the monarch. Lavish court festivities were held, of which the new opera formed part, and in the ornate salons to which the regal stairways led would be depicted in allegory the apotheosis of the king, for whose honour it was all intended.

There is much to justify the attribution of this style to the growth of monarchal absolutism, and there is at the very least some profound interaction between them. However, as Friedrich himself admits, his theory leaves unanswered certain features central to the growth and development of the movement.[3] Whatever changes may have occurred in the palatial residences constructed by the secular heads of state in this period, it has always been acknowledged that the fullest flowering of the baroque is to be found primarily within the great Catholic churches of the late sixteenth and seventeenth centuries. It was this which introduced a new dimension into the architecture of the time, and in many respects provided the initiative and model for the splendour of the courtly palaces. To give but one example, the centrality of Bernini in the development of the Italian baroque cannot be questioned, and yet the overwhelming majority of his work was clearly religious in character, not merely in its papal patronage but in its intrinsic quality as the creation of a personally devout Catholic.[4] His interior of St. Peter's, his S. Andrea and *S. Teresa* could hardly be said to express the materialism of a Hobbesian philosophy or, in fact, any undue faith in worldly or human potential. In its initial impulse, therefore, one must assume that the baroque is a phenomenon which is at the very least closely connected with the religious movements of the age. To identify it as originating from political changes in the secular sphere or from the new recognition of man's grasping after worldly power would leave unexplained the distinctly religious fervour animating so much of the early movement.

The more established view places the emphasis firmly on the religious side. It traces the baroque directly to the church itself and, more specifically, to the belated attempts of the Catholic church to stem the alarmingly swift tide of Protestantism from spreading across all Europe. The Council of Trent, meeting intermittently between 1545 and 1563 was not one of the more creditable episodes in ecclesiastical history. The unseemly bickering and concern with petty internal politics which marred its sessions seemed often to obscure the urgency of its task and the magnitude of the threat it was facing. In the decisions which were eventually reached, however, it is possible to discern two major lines of policy, internal and external, which were to be pursued throughout the following decades. That duality in the strategy of the church—to some extent self-contradictory since at one level it acknowledged the strictures of Luther while at another it denied them—proved in practice a remarkably effective prescription. Within the Catholic church itself there arose a quiet recognition that the Protestant charges of corruption and moral laxity had not been entirely unfounded, and the Council wisely set about correcting those abuses from within. Bishops were ordered to reside within their dioceses in order to care personally for the spiritual welfare of their charges, the office of *praestor* or 'indulgence collector', which had originally ignited the rebellion, was now abolished, lax monastic orders were reformed by a stricter enforcement of their regulations and, while the adoration of saints' relics was formally confirmed, strict instructions were issued to cleanse such worship of the folkloristic or idolatrous additives which had accrued in the course of time.

Such was the internal effect of the Reformation on the Catholic church. For the outside world, however, a more assertive and even aggressive policy was adopted. The authority of the Pope was now strengthened by the newly devised catechism, the doctrine of transubstantiation denied by the Protestants was declared central to the Catholic faith and, above all, the church embarked on a vigorous offensive intended to halt the inroads of Protestantism. It is in this latter context that the rise of baroque art and architecture has generally been placed. The massivity of the baroque structure and the sumptuousness of its ornamentation are seen in that historical setting as intended to crush, as if by sheer visual weight, any possible questioning of papal infallibility, and to intimidate the Protestant rebel by its proud assertion of ecclesiastical power. The Jesuits, together with the reformed Carmelite order, founded as part of this more aggressive policy, were enormously active during the latter half of the sixteenth century, sending their emissaries abroad to infiltrate into the Protestant countries, often at the risk of their lives, exploiting political rivalries to play off one kingdom against another, encouraging the practice of Loyola's *Spiritual Exercises*, setting up educational institutions, and using every means at their disposal to loosen the hold of the Reformation and confirm the faith of the Catholic communities. The Jesuits, it is argued, initiated the new baroque style, incorporating it within their mother church Il Gesù, and ensuring by their own efforts that its message should be transmitted throughout Catholic Europe until every city should boast its own architectural testimony to the triumph of Rome.

The problem here, as Rudolf Wittkower has rightly pointed out, is chronological. The high point of the baroque occurred unquestionably in the period between 1630 and 1660, when the three greatest figures in the Italian movement—Bernini, Borromini, and Pietro da Cortona—were at the zenith of their powers. But by then the Counter-Reformation had already lost its force. It had completed its major work and, at least within the Catholic countries, had succeeded in restoring the security of papal rule. By the end of the sixteenth century, the great leaders of that movement were already dead, and the church was settling back to routine. In fact, after the lengthy process of investigation which necessarily precedes beatification, twenty years or more after their deaths the church, on one single day in 1622, formally canonised Ignatius Loyola, Teresa of Avila, Philip Neri, and Francis Xavier, as though to proclaim to the world at large that the task of spiritual regeneration was over, and Catholicism had been saved from its enemies.[5] It would be strange, to say the least, if the fullest flowering of baroque art and architecture should have coincided with the decline or even the termination of the movement to which its origins are attributed, rather than with the period of its greatest vigour nearly a hundred years earlier.

On the other hand, if neither monarchal absolutism nor the Counter-Reformation provide in themselves satisfactory explanations for the rise of the baroque, any other theory suggested for its source must be sufficiently broad to embrace both the secular and religious manifestations of the movement. It would need to explain too the extraordinary variety of its stylistic components over and above the massivity and sumptuousness. There is, for example, the new sense of spatial dynamism in the sculpture of this period. Where Michelangelo's *David* had been relaxed, classically posed, sensitive, and quietly self-confident, Bernini's *David* is caught at the moment of action, the muscles taut and straining, the body twisted in movement, and the face distorted by the grimace of physical effort as he pits himself against his enemy. Although the figure stands alone, we are (in contrast to Michelangelo's version) here made acutely aware of the presence of Goliath at a fixed point before him. Space has become actualised and activated. Then there is the new use of light in painting, not only in the chiaroscuro technique of contrasting illumination and darkness, as in the works of Caravaggio, but more strikingly in the radiant blaze of energy which seems to dazzle the eye. Yet above all these, there is in so much painting of the era a new impression of limitless power, of myriad figures bursting atectonically out of the frame of frescoes and paintings, or soaring heavenward in a way which cannot be satisfactorily explained by the traditional attribution of the baroque either to man's lust for material power in this world or to the anti-Protestant reactions of the Catholic church. The very multiplicity of these artistic changes and the remarkable range they cover suggest that the source is to be found not in any sectarian or political change in the era, but rather in some fundamental upheaval in man's concept of himself, a revolution of larger proportions, producing repercussions in all areas of human activity, whether religious, political, or aesthetic.

There was indeed such an upheaval in human thought at this time. It began comparatively quietly in 1543 with the publication of Copernicus' astronomical treatise *De Revolutionibus Orbium Coelestium*. He died soon after writing it, some say on the very day of its publication, but the ideas he had promulgated gradually gathered momentum until by the early seventeenth century their rumblings reverberated far beyond the confines of astronomical debate. By challenging the traditional Ptolemaic view of the universe where sun, moon, and stars revolved concentrically about a fixed earth, and replacing it with a cosmos in which the spinning globe of earth itself rotated about a larger sun, the movement to which Copernicus gave rise not only eventually dislodged man from his position of centrality in the universe but, by implication, cast doubt upon some of his most cherished beliefs. The old system had posited an overall hierarchical order, harmoniously reflected in all its lesser parts. God ruling majestically over his archangels and angels, with the heavenly spheres orbiting in due order of precedence below, formed the model and the moral sanction for the hierarchies established in church and society. From that great chain of being Renaissance man had derived many of his ethical and political imperatives, not least the divine right of kings and the rigid class divisions of society. If Copernicus proved correct and the cosmic hierarchy was shown to be an antiquated illusion, by what justification could a king demand obedience from his subjects, or a father claim respect from his son?

By 1611 the new 'philosophy' or cosmology had begun to spell for John Donne the collapse of the old dispensation. The discovery of new planets in the firmament, the altered relation of sun to earth, and the discarding of belief in an area of fire beyond the air—all intrinsic to the Copernican movement—had disrupted the established order of man's world, and in its place he saw only a bewildering moral chaos:

> And new Philosophy calls all in doubt,
> The Element of fire is quite put out;
> The Sun is lost and th' earth, and no mans wit
> Can well direct him where to looke for it.
> And freely men confesse that this world's spent,
> When in the Planets, and the Firmament
> They seeke so many new; then see that this
> Is crumbled out againe to his Atomies.
> 'Tis all in peeces, all cohaerence gone;
> All just supply and all Relation;
> Prince, Subject, Father, Sonne are things forgot . . . .[6]

This revolution in human thought and the challenge it posed to the era has a more intimate connection with the rise of the baroque than has been recognised. Certainly the Counter-Reformation movement as well as the growth of monarchal absolutism did in the course of time foster the artistic development of the mode by adapting it to suit their own needs; but they did so as part of their own response to this broader innovation, as they attempted to salvage their own beliefs or to find suitable replacements when they had to be discarded.

Moreover, there is a significant chronological factor to be considered. The impact of Copernicanism swept through Europe in two main waves. The first was felt towards the latter part of the sixteenth century when Copernicus' thesis was slowly gaining adherents as a yet unproven theory casting doubt on the accepted Ptolemaic view. Then in 1610 Galileo sighted through his newly developed telescope twin satellites revolving around the planet

Jupiter, thereby disproving for all time the belief that the heavenly spheres orbit concentrically about the earth. If this thesis connecting the baroque with Copernicanism is correct, it may explain what has puzzled art historians for so long: why the initial impulse of the baroque is so clearly discernible in the later sixteenth century (at the time, for example, of the building of Il Gesù between the years 1568 and 1584), while the second and major impulse made itself felt much later in the 1630s under the direction of Bernini and Borromini. As reactions occurring some little time after each discovery had been publicised and imaginatively absorbed, the rise of the baroque and the later surge into the High Baroque correspond closely to these intellectual changes, and strengthen the likelihood of their interdependence.

These innovations in man's conception of the cosmos did not come full-grown into the world but proceeded by stages. The initial response to Copernicus' theory was much milder than might have been expected from so seminal a work. It was, one should recall, a technical treatise seeking to solve anomalies in astronomical measurement and, although astronomy occupied a more important place in public interest at that time because of its connection with astrological prediction, as well as the determination of time and navigational bearings, the treatise was intended primarily for the specialist. Moreover, it was written with considerable caution, the caution not only of a responsible mathematician but also of a Christian fully aware of the dangers of heresy in the age of the Inquisition, as the dedication of the work to Pope Paul III makes clear.

One leading scholar in the history of ideas has rightly pointed out that those elements in the treatise which were to have so far-reaching an effect in that era are to be found less in what Copernicus actually wrote than in what his theory implied.[7] Copernicus, for example, did not make any claim for the infinity of the universe nor for the plurality of worlds inhabited by creatures similar to man. Yet the consideration of such problems followed as a natural corollary of his thesis. For a contemporary of Copernicus, nurtured on the geocentric Ptolemaic system, the very positing of the theory that the earth revolves about the sun demanded a realignment of thought. Instead of imaginatively viewing the planets from a settled earth he must now adopt a new intellectual mobility, visualising, for example, how the sun would appear at certain seasons in relation to the earth when viewed from the vantage-point of Venus. Such

relativism of viewpoint, which accorded no special validity to any
one vantage-point, led to a sense of equality between the planets.
They were no longer to be seen as they had been in the old
dispensation as celestial spheres composed of some incandescent
heavenly substance and moved by the divine love of angelic
Intelligences, but as physical masses essentially similar to the earth
and driven by the same mechanistic forces. The belief that only the
'sublunary' world was subject to change and that all the universe
beyond the moon's sphere was eternal and unchanging was to be
disproved in 1572 when Tycho Brahe sighted a new star in the
firmament; but the discovery had been prepared for by the very
notion of the entire universe operating under the same physical laws
as earth.

The idea of an infinite universe was also in men's minds long
before Giordano Bruno published his *Of the Infinity of the Universe* in
1584. Once the Ptolemaic system with its belief in an outer sphere
enclosing the created universe had been challenged, the possibility
of infinity was inevitably to be considered. One may note that
Copernicus, while he makes no explicit claim for such infinity,
comes remarkably close within the *De Revolutionibus* itself. At the
conclusion to chapter VI, in describing the magnitude of the
universe, he uses the ambiguous term *indefinitam*, which in Latin
may mean either 'undefined' or 'unlimited'; and the following
sentence leaves the matter open. The reader, presumably, was to
take his choice: 'What follows from this demonstration is the
undefined (?) magnitude of the heavens in comparison to the earth.
How far this immensity extends we little know.'[8] How the
contemporary reader did interpret the term is indicated by two
sources which have chanced to survive. We know from the *Dialogue
of Guy de Bruss against the New Academies* that in 1557, long before
Bruno's work, a group of scholars discussing Copernicus assumed
without question that the infinity of the heavens formed an integral
part of his theory.[9] Then again, in 1576 Thomas Digges appended
to a revised version of his father's almanack an enthusiastic and
more popular account of Copernicanism, consisting largely of a free
translation. In the course of it he too assumed that infinity was
intrinsic to the theory. We are only able, he writes, to see those stars
relatively near to us, but beyond them there are further ranges of
stars ' . . . till our sight, being not able farther to reach or conceive,
the greater part rest, by reason of their wonderful distance, invisible
unto us. And this may well be thought by us to be the glorious court

of the great God, whose unsearchable, invisible works we may partly by these His visible conjecture, to whose infinite power and majesty such an infinite place surmounting all others both in quantity and quality only is convenient.'[10]

These changes in human thought, therefore, were spreading across Europe from the time of Copernicus onwards, and they involved not merely a new astronomical theory but a basic reappraisal of the nature of the universe and man's place within it. Medieval man, as C. S. Lewis has remarked, had believed in the immensity of the heavens but never in their infinity; just as he preferred to live within a walled city, so he had the comforting feeling that the universe, however large it might be, was still a closed and hence imaginable entity. When Dante or his contemporaries write of the heavens, there is never a hint there of Pascal's terror at *le silence éternel de ces espaces infinis*.[11] The difference is substantial. Within the latter part of the sixteenth century, man's habitation, on which he had been settled in comparative security for so long, had been thrust into an awesome and dynamic setting. It had become a spinning globe, hurtling through the regions of space among innumerable planetary systems and galaxies which stretched further than the mind could ever conceive. As Bruno mused in extending Copernicus' theory of the solar system into a multiple form:

> Why, indeed, may not all the stars be themselves suns, and each sun appear to itself the centre of the universe? Where, then, are its limits? Has it limits? Is it not rather infinite, an infinity of worlds like our solar system? There must be hundreds of thousands of suns, and about them planets rolling, each one, perhaps, inhabited by beings, possibly better, possibly worse than ourselves. Throughout, nature must be the same, everywhere the centre, everywhere and nowhere . . . .[12]

Before entering into any detailed examination of the relationship between the new cosmic theories and their artistic manifestation, one general point needs to be made. No complex mode in art can ever be pinned down to a single theme or idea. Any initial impulse inevitably becomes ramified in its forms, and even the most major changes in human history have joined with subsidiary or parallel movements to be modified or diverted by them. However, insofar as there is any common denominator uniting the manifold and varied forms of the baroque, both secular and religious, that denominator is, I would suggest, to be found in the new sense of vastness, magnificence, and boundless energy such as had never existed in the predominantly man-centred ethos of the High Renaissance. It is not, as has been argued, that man attained in the baroque age an exaggerated sense of *his own* potential, but that the perspective of the world and of his place within it had been drastically altered.

Within the secular sphere the effect of this cosmic enlargement was profound. On the one hand, man, dwarfed by the magnitude of the universe, was forced to surrender the idea of the Renaissance that he was the measure of all things. Yet the change produced was two-directional. In a sense, by his very presence among the whirling planets, he was a participant in this vast interaction of cosmic forces. His conception of celestial energy expanded as he began to visualise the enormous forces at work in the heavens, and this expanded view he began to apply to his own activities. On the political scene, there arose a new fascination with the absolutism of power, the monarch imaginatively arrogating to himself some portion of that unbounded cosmic strength. Cortona's ceiling fresco in the Palazzo Barberini or Rubens' *Apotheosis of James I* in the Banqueting House at Whitehall were allegories whereby the ruling families saw themselves metaphorically projected into the heavens, vicariously enjoying celestial dominion. The seventeenth-century monarch began to visualise himself as an all-powerful figure, whose satellites revolved subserviently around him as he dispensed light and wealth to all. It was a concept which reached its culmination in that most baroque of all absolutist monarchs, Louis XIV, the builder of Versailles. Was it pure chance that he took as his title *Le Roi Soleil*, as though in public acknowledgement of the Copernican source of his inspiration? The palaces these rulers built, such as the Villa Aldobrandini, no longer had small formal gardens attached but, on the model of the new cosmos, were placed within spacious parks, with long avenues of trees radiating from them, and smaller buildings erected at some distance to emphasise, like minor planets, the majestic centrality of the main residence itself.

Within the religious setting, however, the impact was even more pronounced. For the sixteenth-century Christian, the new theory of the heavens was potentially shattering in its implications, posing a threat to the very foundations of his belief. In ancient Greece, the shape of the universe or the process of its initial formation had been of little more than academic interest; but within the Bible the order and purpose of creation formed a cornerstone of the Hebraic and, later, of the Christian faith. In the opening chapters of Genesis it was assumed that all creation—the earth, the heavens, the sun and moon—had been formed solely as a setting for that climactic moment when God should determine to make man in his image, after his own likeness. This new creature was to have dominion over the earth, the sun providing him with light and with seasons, while his moral task, choosing between good and evil, was to be the ever-present and intimate concern of his Creator. The salvation or damnation of man's eternal soul was, it was assumed, the justification for the existence of the entire universal system, and if in later years commentators would from time to time hint at the possibility of other inhabited worlds,[13] such thoughts had never distracted from the central concern with man's place on this earth as the testing-ground for his fate in the world to come.

Now, suddenly, he found himself dislodged from his position of eminence and, it would appear, reduced to the status of a microscopically small insect crawling over the surface of a spinning earth in a vast and indifferent universe. It was soon realised that in fact the Copernican theory implied even more than the nullification of man's centrality; it gave rise also to the suggestion that God himself might be superfluous in the mechanistically conceived universe. Astronomers were now becoming capable of plotting the precise course of the planets, predicting their locations at specific times and explaining the workings of the cosmic system in accordance with fixed laws which precluded the necessity of divine intervention, and perhaps even of divine supervision. In the face of this major threat to traditional belief (the church's first potential clash with the empirical sciences), its success in surmounting or avoiding that challenge forms a remarkable chapter in ecclesiastical history. The various eddies and streams which together contributed to achieving this success are too numerous and complex to be easily classified; but it is possible at least to distinguish two main currents, apparently contradictory in direction but in fact complementing each other in their final effect.

One response within the church was closely identified with the introspective, meditative tradition reinstituted by Ignatius Loyola and reflected predominantly in the mannerist forms of religious art and literature in this period. There the sensitive Christian intellectual, appalled by the implications of scientific discoveries which he must of necessity acknowledge as authentic, responded by limiting their significance. These discoveries, he noted, applied only to the physical world, and accordingly he looked elsewhere for his solutions. Within his spiritual meditations he imaginatively transcended that world, projecting himself into the eternal life of the soul beyond, and assigning to that the ultimate validity. In the paintings of Tintoretto and El Greco the firm perspective of the Renaissance becomes suddenly elasticised, stretching and shrinking in accordance with the inner vision of the meditator. The canvas as a whole vibrates with the passionate conviction of a viewer concerned only with the miraculous or sacramental implications of the scene and scorning the objective or empirical actuality. Hence the weird, phosphorescent colours of a dream-like world. Hence also the remarkable imagery of contemporary metaphysical poetry in which love, both sacred and profane, transcends the limitations of time and space to contract the world into an eye, or enlarge one second into eternity.[14]

The second response, which forms the theme of this present book, moved in a different direction, and suggests why there was so little confrontation between the church and the cosmologists in the sixteenth century despite the potential challenge implicit in their theories. For the response of the church here, as in its earlier treatment of pagan folklore and local deities, was to conquer not by hostility but by a process of gradual assimilation and sanctification. Instead of being intimidated by the discoveries of science, the church welcomed them as positive findings, absorbing them into its theological system, and pointing to them triumphantly not as contradictions, but as splendid corroborations of religious belief. For, it was argued, if the astronomers had thrust back the limits of the Ptolemaic universe to reveal countless stars whirling through space in dazzling array, yet held in intricate patterns by a powerful interplay of forces, what magnificent testimony that was to the omnipotence of the Supreme Creator, who had formed each one of those innumerable stars, hurled its huge mass into space, and held it there in mobile equilibrium. In effect, the church did not so much absorb the New Philosophy as enormously enlarge its own conceptions to include the infinitude that had been revealed to it.

At first sight it might appear that the traditional theological system would need to crack or split wide open in order to accommodate this new, limitless world. But it was soon realised that, as one looked far back, beyond Renaissance and even medieval Christianity towards the original biblical world, particularly as it appears in the Old Testament setting, there was the baroque vision waiting, as it were, to be revitalised. The Psalmist had gazed in wonder at the heavens whose daily revolutions testified to the glory of their Maker, and had visualised God supreme above the created universe, radiant in power and majesty:

> . . . who coverest thyself with light as with a garment; who stretchest out the heavens like a curtain: who layeth the beams of his chambers in the waters: who maketh the clouds his chariot: who walketh upon the wings of the wind: who maketh his angels spirits; his ministers a flaming fire: who laid the foundations of the earth, that it should not be removed forever. (Ps. 104: 2–5).

In the subsequent history of the church, the omnipotence of the divine was never, of course, denied nor even challenged, and it therefore remained an essential attribute of God. What did change was the way that attribute was conceived. For such church fathers as Augustine, it no longer conjured up a vision of boundless might but became rather a formal tenet within a theological system from which ideas could be philosophically derived. In his *City of God*, he discusses the often paradoxical implications: 'God is rightly called omnipotent, even though He is unable to die and be deceived. We call him omnipotent because He does whatever He wills to do and suffers nothing that He does not will to suffer. He would not, of course, be omnipotent if He had to suffer anything against His will. It is precisely because He is omnipotent that for Him some things are impossible.'[15] In medieval drama too, although the plays often begin with a formal, didactic reminder of God's all-powerful nature, the description recalls the solemn 'pantocratic' figure appearing so often in medieval book illuminations, with one hand raised emblematically in blessing, in accordance with the semi-oriental Byzantine tradition. There is no dynamism, no wielding of immense power. In the Chester cycle, God announces on his entry:

> I am Alpha and Omega,
> Foremost and noblest,
> Being my will it should be so
> It is, it was, it shall be thus.
> I am great and gracious God that never had any beginning;
> The whole substance of begetting lies in my essence.

Within the plays themselves, Deus becomes a white-robed, school-masterly figure reproving his disobedient children. He is only slightly larger than man-size in conception. In subsequent years, God grew in proportion as man's concept of himself grew, and the depiction of God in Michelangelo's *Creation of Adam* is certainly more impressive. On the other hand, as the Renaissance adapted Christianity to fit the rationalism of Neoplatonic philosophy, God, now identified with the Beautiful-and-Good, became in effect the passive apex of a static hierarchy of ideas rather than a vigorous and awesome Creator. Although, then, the omnipotence of God had been theologically and formally affirmed throughout the ages, the dynamic infinitude of the baroque God did constitute a break-away from established convention. Yet it aroused little alarm or opposition within the church, since it was authenticated by its return to the original Old Testament view of an all-powerful Creator in personal and active control of the heavens.

In the same way as this enlarged vision of God found its natural place within Christianity despite its innovative features, so it was more easily to be reconciled with the scientific view than might at first be imagined. The New Philosophy of the sixteenth century was not, like modern scientific thought, so dedicated to the principle of objective analysis as to be in direct conflict with the religious beliefs of the era. We are still comparatively close to the age of a Thomas Huxley or Freud, welcoming the evidence of Darwinism and psychology as final proofs that religion was a primitive superstition haunting man with baseless illusions of life after death. In fact, the cosmologers of the sixteenth century were very different in their approach. Although, as we have seen, some contemporaries of Copernicus and Galileo were quick to discern the challenge to traditional Christianity implicit in the new theories, the discoverers themselves were far from any feeling of deliberate iconoclasm. On the contrary, there is in their own writings a sense of mystical faith, as they unveil the new universe; and their fervour accorded well with the positive, devotional response of the Christian baroque. Copernicus, for example, at the high point within his *De Revolutionibus*, when he revealed for the first time his theory of a heliocentric system, declared with lyrical awe:

> . . . in the middle of all stands the sun. For who in our most beautiful temple could set this light in another or better place, than that from which it can at once illuminate the whole? Not to

speak of the fact that not unfittingly do some call it the light of the world, others the soul, still others the monarch. Trismegistus calls it the visible God, Sophocles' Electra, the All-Seer. And in fact does the sun, seated on his royal throne, guide his family of planets as they circle round him.

Similarly, Tycho Brahe in his *De Nova Stella* of 1573 tells with bated breath of his discovery of a new star in the firmament, even though all philosophers and theologians had been agreed until then that in the ethereal regions of the celestial world no change either of generation or corruption was possible. It is, he says, '. . . a miracle indeed, either the greatest of all that have occurred in the whole range of nature since the beginning of the world, or one certainly that is to be classed with those attested by the Holy Oracles, the staying of the Sun in its course in answer to the prayers of Joshua, and the darkening of the Sun's face at the time of the Crucifixion'. For Bruno, the multiplicity of solar systems was far from being a denial of God's might. On the contrary, he wrote: 'This is the excellence of God magnified and the greatness of his Kingdom made manifest; he is glorified not in one, but in countless suns; not in a single earth, but in a thousand, I say in an infinity of worlds.'[16] Even Kepler, whose identification of the elliptical orbits of the planets was to shatter for ever the supposed harmony of their perfect circles, writing in a letter to Johann Herwart in 1598, remained close to Christian sources in describing the implications of his research:

> It is no small comfort when I reflect that we should not so much marvel at the vast and almost infinite breadth of the most distant heavens but much more at the smallness of us manikins, and the smallness of this our tiny ball of earth and also of the planets. To God the world is not immeasurable, but we are exceedingly small compared with this world. . . . However, we must not reason from size to special significance. For God, who dwells on high, still looks down upon the humble.

These quotations are not exceptions, but typify the spiritual fervour with which the cosmologists responded to the discoveries, and in another letter to Herwart written in the same year, Kepler records with pride the sacredness of his task: 'Enough for me is the honour of guarding, with my discovery, the door of God's temple, in which

Copernicus serves before the high altar.' The church's absorption of the New Philosophy into its own theological and aesthetic patterns was in this respect, then, a smoother process than has often been thought.

On the other hand, one must never forget that the church did formally resist the Copernican view as contradicting, at the most literal level, the biblical account of a four-cornered and immobile earth. The Scriptures could not be conveniently altered to accommodate the cosmographers. Giordano Bruno was burnt at the stake for obstinately maintaining his heretical views, and Galileo was forced publicly to recant, and then confined under house arrest for many years. There was, however, a large gap between formal acceptance and what was, in fact, a tacit admission that the concept of the heavens had been radically changed, and even these famed instances of the persecution of cosmologers by the church do not, under closer examination, point quite so unequivocally in the direction of a major conflict between science and religion. Bruno, as has recently been discovered, had really aroused the ire of the church by certain of his religious beliefs which were quite unconnected with Copernicanism and which arose from his advocacy of the Hermetic philosophy. When he was indicted for his heresies, the charge of unorthodox astronomical views was only added for good measure, and would not in itself have led to his execution or, in all probability, even to a formal arraignment. Similarly, there is the notable fact that Galileo's *Dialogue on the Ptolemaic and Copernican Systems* of 1632, which attempted to reconcile the new cosmological theories with the biblical texts, received no less than four official *imprimaturs* from the church censors before publication. He had promised the Pope that within the book he would always refer to the heliocentric system only as a theory and not as a proven fact, and he had observed the undertaking scrupulously. The treatise was only suppressed subsequently for personal and not theological reasons, when Pope Urbanus detected in it what he regarded as a slight to his own dignity.

Whatever the official viewpoint, therefore, in a larger sense the new cosmos, conceived as boundless and dynamic under the control of a Supreme Creator, proved remarkably congenial to the beliefs and interests of the church itself, despite the technical problems it might raise for a literal reading of certain biblical passages.[17] In that context, then, the baroque should be seen less as a sectarian movement within the church, aimed at blocking the spread of

Protestantism, but rather as universal in its appeal. It served the Jesuits in their Counter-Reformation campaign, but that was not its primary impulse. For even within the Catholic movement, the baroque was aimed at directing the thoughts of the worshipper not to the glory of the Pope or Vatican, but above them to the magnificence of an expanded vision of the divine, a revitalised God who, in a fuller sense than had previously been conceived, can bind the sweet influence of Pleiades or loose the bands of Orion, bring forth the stars in their seasons, know the ordinances of heaven, and set their dominion on earth.

Once the connection has been perceived between this amplified view of the heavens and the baroque mode, its apparently diverse art forms take on a remarkable unity and coherence. Architecture became the dominant genre of the era, and, as might be expected, it was that most characteristically baroque setting, the church interior, which reflected most vividly the Christian response to the changed cosmos. The translation of the vision into stone was a gradual process, developing through the sixteenth and seventeenth centuries as a series of subtle but often far-reaching innovations was introduced. The transformation it effected impressed itself so deeply upon subsequent generations of architects that today it requires a conscious effort to recollect how original it was in the long history of church building. It can, I believe, be shown that for the first time the inside of the church became expressive of the new forces and proportions of the expanded firmament.

In earlier eras, for example, the ceiling of a cathedral or chapel had consisted of simple stone vaulting, of fan tracery, or of patterned ornamentation. On those occasions when mosaics or frescoes were introduced above, they had no specific association with the heavens, and presented general scenes from the Bible or from saints' legends. There was the famed Hell on the ceiling of the Florentine Baptistery, or the series in the Sistine Chapel depicting stories from the early generations of man, the Creation, the Fall, and the Flood, which both by their theme and presentation are more closely to be connected with earth below than with the sky. Now in the baroque, the ceiling and apse take on a totally new quality. The scenes they represent become exclusively celestial – the Ascension of the Virgin, the Trinity in Glory, the apotheosis of a saint (Plate 6). Moreover, where previous frescoes, such as those of the Sistine Chapel, had been placed on the ceiling for reasons not connected with their theme, and any of the scenes would have proved equally effective if transferred to a wall, here the frescoes exploit to the full their positioning above the heads of the spectators, and seem to burst through the roof, taking on the dimensions and spaciousness of the heavens themselves.

Andrea Pozzo's *The Glory of St. Ignatius* (Plate 1), like so many ceiling frescoes of the era, is not merely a scene from heaven painted above. In addition it employs the illusory technique known as *quadratura* (about which he wrote an important treatise), whereby the real walls of the nave are visually extended upwards so that they appear to reach into the distant skies. It is hard to distinguish where the true walls end and the false columns begin, and the imagination is stimulated to follow them as they project into the far regions. Angels float upwards from all directions, helping to obscure the architectural transition and, by their crowding together, to increase the effect of innumerability and hence of limitlessness. As they grow smaller, the immensity of the space they have traversed is subtly conveyed. Everything in the scene is drawn upwards towards a blaze of light at the zenith of the skies, symbolising the newly energised concept of the divine throne. In brief, the airiness and floating spaciousness of the vast heavens in such scenes is made to contrast with the solidity, opulence, and weighty majesty of the area below, where massive pillars, exuberant stucco design, and gilded capitals represent the richly endowed world of man's earthly habitation.

Such frescoes as those by Pozzo or Gaulli (Plate 2) would be less effective were they not supported by contributory elements in the structure of the church itself. Indeed, they were the finishing touches to a church interior, consummating a visual concept which had existed architecturally even without them. A convenient starting-point for understanding the change might be the innovative use of the cornice, the line of stonework above the columns or pilasters. In the classical tradition, the entablature above the capitals of the pillars had culminated in a slightly projecting cornice, functionally supporting the base of a pediment, or meeting the roof of the building. The Renaissance had adopted this classical motif in a subdued, more ornamental form, flattening it out until it became little more than a decorative device to connect the columns with the upper features of the interior. As the period of the baroque approaches, however, the cornice begins to project more boldly, until eventually it juts out sharply from the wall, supporting nothing. The visual effect is extraordinarily important; for as it

continues uninterruptedly around the entire interior, it now seems
to slice the whole church horizontally across, cutting off the lower
'earthly' section from the area above (Plate 3), in a way that has no
precedent. To emphasise the contrast with the heavy materiality of
the earth below, the lower area is now windowless, illuminated only
from above, where hidden or recessed lunettes let in the light from
just below the ceiling. Then there is a further innovation. Between
the main cornice and the 'heavenly' section above, a second, less
prominent cornice is now introduced. Symbolically, the space
between the cornices suggests the gap between earth and heaven.
On that upper cornice, there begin to appear statues of trumpeting
angels or winged cherubs on their way to and from the celestial
regions, to support the impression of a middle space and to widen it
optically.

The main spectacle was reserved for the portion above, and for an
appreciation of the change it introduced, it needs to be compared
with the previous traditions of ecclesiastical architecture. The use of
a dome was not unique to the baroque, even though it was given
renewed prominence in that period; but the way it was exploited
from within was fundamentally different. Romanesque churches,
such as S. Marco in Venice, had also possessed large domes
supported by enormous arches to carry the great weight. Yet there
the arches, as they continue downwards, blend into the side-walls
with only the gentlest of transitions, producing the restful and stable
shape of an inverted 'U', reaching from the dome to the ground.
The golden mosaics, which cover the walls and arches from ceiling
to floor, help to soften their outline and absorb them as integral
parts of the structure. In the following era, when the Renaissance
did use a dome, as in Brunelleschi's S. Spirito in Florence, it was
usually reduced in size to humanistic proportions, and the supporting arches consist in that church of single dark spans set harmoniously against a cool white background. They reflect the
colonnade along the nave which, beneath the cornice, rests on slim
classical columns.

In the baroque church, the arches have changed their visual
function. Boldly cut across by the projecting cornice, the upper
sections of the arches are now marked off as clearly defined semi-
circles; and in contrast to the simple Renaissance form, the
numerous courses of variegated moulding on the surface of each
arch produce a series of countless parallel arcs, giving the single
span an effect of multiplicity and perpetual movement. Large and

small arches, similarly moulded, echo this restless movement on every side, and the emphatic outlining of the horizontal base of the dome, and of the semi-circular recess of the apse, again with multiple moulding, suggest numerous orbits and counter-orbits whirling through the sky.[18] As though to draw attention to their symbolic force, the crowning emblem – introduced specifically by the baroque mode and confirming the centrality of the Copernican universe in that configuration – is a radiant sun now regularly placed above the high altar, its golden beams magically drawing together the entire scene to create the impression of planets circling within the solar system beneath the higher light of the heavens above (see Plate 3).

The sun emblem appears so frequently in the churches of the era as to become a veritable hallmark of the baroque.[19] In the Jesuit churches, the Society's insignia generally appear emblazoned within the sun; elsewhere it is a dove representing the Holy Spirit. Of the latter type, Bernini's version in St. Peter's is certainly the most impressive. There the dove appears in the centre of a 'solar' stained-glass window high above the altar, and the yellow light, pouring through, is caught and reflected by the golden rods emanating from it to create a dazzling effect, as stucco angels and *putti* bask in its glow. How far this Copernican symbolism was conscious on the part of the baroque artist is impossible to say, but the sun emblem suggests that, as in most dominant art forms, the artist was instinctively expressing the conceptions current in his own time. Just as modern man finds it difficult to look at the moon today without thinking of an astronaut landing upon it, so here a seventeenth-century artist could scarcely depict the sun without being conscious at some level of the new theories with which it had become associated, the new sense of celestial dynamism, of enormous forces held by the Creator in harmonious interplay within the distant skies.

There is an interesting facet of this baroque association with Copernicanism. In Renaissance art and architecture there was widespread use of the circle or sphere as the most 'perfect' of geometrical forms, expressing as it did the deeper philosophical tenets of Neoplatonism and the ideal of a form which remains unchanged from whatever angle it is viewed. The circle had dislodged completely the pointed arch of the Gothic, appearing as the dominant motif on façades and interiors, and at times even influencing the structural planning of churches and chapels. To a modern reader Kepler's revelation in 1611 that the heavenly spheres move in elliptical and not circular orbits might appear to be of merely technical interest, but for the era itself it created a revolution in thinking in its disruption of an intellectual system based upon a belief in the harmony of the spheres. Donne (who knew Kepler's work well) was perhaps not actually speaking in the following passage of the discovery of the ellipses; but written in the same year as Kepler's discovery was published it does indicate the growing concern with the effects of the new cosmology. He himself never belonged spiritually or artistically to the baroque mode. More closely allied to the religious mannerists, he saw the empirical world and the new universe it had revealed as a threat to his faith. The appearance of new stars in the firmament, together with Galileo's viewing of the satellites, had given renewed significance to those discrepancies in the measurements of the sun's orbit which had for long seemed to contradict the Ptolemaic concept of circular harmony. For Donne, then, the disintegration of the old system symbolically heralded the collapse of all established values. The sun itself could no longer be trusted:

> For his course is not round: nor can the Sunne
> Perfect a Circle, or maintaine his way
> One inch direct; but where he rose today
> He comes no more, but with couzening line,
> Steales by that point, and so is Serpentine . . .
> So, of the Starres which boast that they doe runne
> In Circle still, none ends where he begun.
> All their proportion's lame, it sinkes, it swells.[20]

The baroque artist, on the other hand, welcoming the new world as revealing the splendour of divine creation, readily incorporated even this shift from circle to ellipse into the church itself. In 1638, a few years after Kepler's ideas had first been promulgated, we find Borromini introducing an innovation into his church of S. Carlo alle Quatro Fontane, in Rome, an oval dome, taking care that its shape should be carried through to the interior, to be clearly visible from within. The church itself won immediate acclaim, and the Procurator General of the Order for which it was built recorded that on its completion numerous foreign visitors had tried to obtain copies of the plans because of its extraordinary artistic merit. The elliptical dome interior occupies a position of especial prominence in this church, since the building itself is entirely windowless below, all light entering from above through a series of small windows in the drum of the dome. The eye, therefore, is invited to gaze upwards at the source of the light, and hence at the oval which dominates the building. Historians, while admiring the ingenuity of the dome's construction, have described it as a mere eccentricity on Borromini's part, a 'bizarre' innovation;[21] but in the context of this association of the upper portion of the baroque church with the celestial spheres, it would seem much more natural to view it as intrinsic to the new conception of the elliptical movements of the heavens.

In isolation, this interpretation of Borromini's dome might appear a little strained, since it could be argued that he adopted the ellipse through the constrictions of the small building-site available. However, there is an even more remarkable instance not merely contemporaneous (it was begun a few years after S. Carlo) but literally a few paces away in the same street. Bernini's S. Andrea al Quirinale is, by general agreement, among the most beautiful of all baroque churches, perhaps because it is one of the very few which was planned and carried through to completion by a single architect. In size it does not compare with such major churches as S. Ignazio, yet within its compact area it conveys an extraordinary sense of majesty, richness, and grandeur. The golden interior of the dome, which here covers the entire church, is in the form of a huge sun, with rays emanating from the centre to the side-walls. But the dome, like the whole church, is in the shape of a large ellipse, with the oval serving as a reiterated motif, reflected in the patterned marble floor, in the side-chapels, and in the concave screen wall counterpointing the oval structure within (Plate 4). Over the high altar presides another oval sun, above which is an elliptical yellow window through which the light filters, and the grey clouds painted around it confirm that a sun emblem is intended both here and on the main ceiling.[22] It would seem, therefore, that the introduction of the ellipse into church architecture a few years after Kepler's epoch-making discovery was not quite so bizarre as has been thought, and it supports the close association suggested here between the baroque and the new cosmology. There is no need to prove a conscious intent on the part of the architect. It is sufficient that he had learned to think of the heavens in terms of ellipses rather than circles, instinctively introducing that form when symbolically depicting the celestial scene in the stone and stucco of the church interior. The extent to which it replaced the traditional circle can be seen not only in the celebrated Piazza which Bernini constructed as the forecourt for St. Peter's in the shape of a huge ellipse, but also in the oval chapel which he designed for the Louvre a few years later.

It has been rightly said that the baroque was as much an extension of Renaissance concepts as a rebellion against them, and in one major respect the Renaissance and the baroque were of accord. For within the numerous and often complex currents of the Renaissance, one theme had been its growing regard for this temporal world as more than a merely transitory ante-room to eternity. The belief in right reason had evoked a fresh respect for man's ability to observe and deduce logically from the tangible realities about him. The pragmatism of Machiavelli, for all its apparent conflict with the rational morality of the age, was based on a similar regard for the material facts relevant to political and social survival. And perhaps most of all, the embryonic empirical sciences were moving more closely towards a suspicion of doctrines previously accepted on authority, and towards a determination to believe nothing until it had been objectively tested and confirmed. Leonardo da Vinci insisted on a detailed dissection of the human anatomy as a prerequisite for accurate drawing, Montaigne challenged the blind acceptance of established theories on trust, and Bacon warned philosophers that only by combining rational theorising with experimental evidence would they ever attain to truth.

When the baroque welcomed the expanded cosmos, it welcomed with it this Renaissance respect for the authenticity of physical reality, marking a profound change in ecclesiastical thinking. One need hardly point out the vigour with which the medieval church, dominated by Augustine's teachings, had denied the significance of worldly wealth, of earthly power, and indeed of mortal existence. The monastery and a life of ascetic withdrawal from daily concerns had formed the ultimate ideal of the age, reluctantly modified for those too weak to achieve it in full; but even for the layman there were to be insistent reminders of the ephemerality of human existence. As Renaissance this-worldliness gained momentum, so the response of the church had become more strident with, as Emile Mâle has shown, a ghoulish use of skeletons, decaying corpses, and Dances of Death to remind Everyman that nothing but his faith and good deeds would accompany him beyond the grave.[23]

With the coming of the baroque and the acceptance of the more worldly view, the Catholic church, by its very nature, could not desert its call to the monastic life, nor its repeated warnings of an approaching Day of Judgement; but a shift in emphasis occurred nevertheless. The Jesuits, for example, who during the sixteenth century revitalised the medieval monastic tradition in their own lives, no longer withdrew into the cloistered cell like their spiritual forebears, nor devoted themselves as wandering friars exclusively to the poor and needy, but went out to the wealthy princes, to the distant territories of the earth, and to the secular intellectuals of Europe to conquer them for Christianity on their own ground. They established their own schools and colleges to rival the leading educational institutions of the day, adapted opera to their needs, created their own private intelligence system, and became in due course a political force to be reckoned with. In short, instead of rejecting the world, they exploited its resources in order to further their own spiritual ends.

One aspect of that policy was the gathering of substantial donations from the rich patrons they cultivated, in order to construct elaborate churches; and those baroque edifices themselves exemplified this welcoming of the solidity and richness of the physical world as a means of affirming the glory of God. In most eras churches have been built of masonry, and a Gothic cathedral can have weighed no less than a baroque church. But where the master builder of the medieval cathedral had exploited every visual technique to lighten the impression on the eye, the baroque architect did the reverse. The Gothic arches and stained-glass windows are tall, slender, and pointed, carrying the eye up to the delicate fan tracery above. Solid structural columns are deceptively shaped to appear like clusters of thin pipes, and on the outside of the building the spires or pinnacled turrets express artistically the medieval exhortation to raise one's thoughts from this passing world to the eternity above. In contrast, the baroque church overwhelms the viewer with its heavy barrel vaulting, its countless friezes and architraves, and the solidity of the windowless area below. Every inch of space is crowded with niches, arcades, ornamental motifs, marble slabs, and stone balustrades, in an orchestrated, con-trapuntal form reminiscent of some mighty oratorio. Most of all, there is the sense of powerful gravitational forces resisted with difficulty by thick supporting pillars. Marble pediments and overhanging entablatures are set ponderously on columns and pilasters, whose plinths project from their bases as though they needed a broader foundation to bear the great weight resting upon them. Outside, the single dominant dome presses majestically down upon the edifice in final assertion of monumental might.

The façades of these churches display once again this response to the physically conceived cosmos, in their baroque concern with thrust and counter-thrust. Where in the preceding era façades such as Alberti's S. Maria Novella had been composed of variegated light-coloured marble to create symmetrical patterns of circles and scrolls on the flat surface, the baroque façade grows dark and forbidding. The material used is now grey stone, and around the heavy entrance doors a portico juts out, casting its shadow across them. The portico itself is generally enclosed within a second, larger portico, and the deliberate crowding of semi-circular pediment within triangular, often echoed along the windows and doors, produces the tension of an inner modular form seeming to struggle for space against the constricting and enclosing frame. Even the overall form reflects this immobile tension; for the double cornice which, inside the church, splits the interior horizontally, does the same outside, although there it achieves a different effect. Now it is not heaven which is divided from earth. Instead, the cornice separates two entirely independent and weighty façades placed one upon the other, each containing its own complete set of plinths, pillars, niches, pediments, and porticos. It is as though some giant had lifted one whole church from the ground and placed it squarely on top of another. The lower 'church', as in the façade of S. Susanna in Rome (Plate 5), bears the massive weight which has, as it were, descended upon it, and must visually resist its downward pressure. In baroque painting, too, both within the church and without, this rejoicing in the power and solidity of the actual reached a crescendo. On a Rubens canvas, the muscular male figures exult in their own physical prowess, or admire the generous corpulence of their female companions. This is the 'resolution in the flesh' of which we have so often heard, and which forms an integral part of the new acceptance of an energised, tactile world.

Within the secular buildings of the baroque, those elements which distinguish the contemporary church find their parallel, though in a modified form. The expanded universe of the cosmographers, however revolutionary to man's thinking in general, was in the political sphere less a threat than an encouragement to absolutism; and since it aroused no potential antagonism, it produced a quieter and less vigorous response. The sumptuous

palaces erected in this period have similar heavenly scenes on their
ceilings, but their purpose there is primarily ornamental. Pietro da
Cortona's splendid *Allegory of Divine Providence and Barberini Power*
(1633) in the Palazzo Barberini in Rome links the political
absolutism of this powerful family to the augmented magnificence
of the divine, and allows them to share allegorically in this heavenly
power. There is a similar opening up to the boundless heavens as in
a fresco by Gaulli, a similar crowding of numberless figures rising
above the clouds, and a similar radiance marking the apex of the
vision. Yet it remains a coolly decorative, mythological scene
lacking the fervour of its religious counterpart. The eye is allowed to
wander interestedly from the allegorical figure in the lower section
to the emblems of the Barberini family above, whereas the religious
frescoes within the church dazzle us with the concentrated brilliance of the divine light from which all creative power is seen to
emanate, and towards which the angelic host is drawn in adoration.

However, here too there is a chronological difficulty, which
would appear to weaken the theory that the major impact was on
the church and only secondarily on the political scene. If, as I have
argued, the ceiling frescoes of Gaulli and Pozzo are, as it were, the
authentic and most vigorous response to the new infinity, while the
secular palaces offered merely mythological adaptations of it, rather
vaguely extending it to flatter the new monarchs and princes, we
shall need to explain why Cortona's secular Barberini fresco was
painted around 1633 while his remarkable religious frescoes on the
ceiling and apse of S. Maria in Vallicella (Plate 6), which served as
the models for his pupils Gaulli and Pozzo, were begun only in 1647.
One would expect the authentic works to appear first and the
overspill into the secular palace to follow at a later stage.

The answer, in fact, is remarkably simple—that in the earlier
period when they ought to have found their natural place within the
church, such paintings were specifically excluded by the iconoclastic fervour of the early Counter-Reformation. The church of S.
Maria in Vallicella, for example, (more popularly known as the
Chiesa Nuova) had been built in 1575 for the Oratorians, and Philip
Neri, their founder, sensitive to the Protestant charge that the
religious images in Catholic churches had encouraged idolatrous
and superstitious worship, had issued strict instructions at that time
that its walls should remain whitewashed and entirely devoid of
painted figures. Only after the first quarter of the seventeenth
century, when the Counter-Reformation ardour had died down

and the founders of such orders were no longer alive, was the ruling relaxed, and then only gradually. Giovanni Lanfranco then painted in S. Andrea della Valle one of the first of such frescoes, his *Virgin in Glory* (1625–7), which spirals upwards into space and which preceded the Barberini ceiling by almost a decade. But the iconoclastic climate still forced Cortona away from the church into a secular palace, and only in 1647 did he receive his commission for the Chiesa Nuova, which marked the real starting-point for the spread of these 'boundless' ceiling frescoes throughout the baroque churches and palaces of Europe.[24]

These illusionist *quadratura* frescoes may justifiably be regarded, therefore, as belonging intrinsically to the baroque church interiors (where they consummate the celestial devotionalism of the entire architectural design) rather than to the banqueting halls and palatial stairways where their function is primarily decorative. There, as we have seen, they added to the prestige of the monarch and associated him with the heroic or mythological; but the infinitude of the heavens was by no means as central to their purpose as it was within the church. Indeed, these secular versions, because of their ornamental purpose, already show a hint of the late baroque and rococo flamboyance into which they were soon to lead, notably in the lavish theatres and opera houses of Europe.

In summary, then, it would seem that neither the Counter-Reformation nor the rise of political absolutism should be regarded as the main sources of the baroque, however closely it was to become associated with those two movements. They fostered its growth and adopted its forms as their own, but ultimately they were themselves only facets of a much larger concept, to which the source should rightly be attributed. It was a source which in both the religious and secular spheres induced artists to marvel at the vastness, the energy, and the sheer mass of the newly conceived universe, and to exploit visually the expanded panorama it afforded.

(ii)

For a study of Milton there is special importance in recognising this more universal source of the baroque. Any attempt in the past to examine *Paradise Lost* against the background of the art forms dominant in that period has inevitably been hampered, if not disqualified, by an objection which must arise in the mind of the reader, however the critic may try to suppress it or shunt it to one side. If, as has been generally believed, the baroque arose primarily as a propaganda weapon created by the Catholic church to crush the Protestant rebellion, would it not be a little strange, to say the least, that a leading protagonist of an extremist sect within that Protestant rebellion should look to the Counter-Reformation church for his own artistic inspiration? Antagonists, it is true, may sometimes unwittingly adopt a gesture or stylistic trick from their adversaries, but that would hardly explain how Milton could so wholeheartedly adopt basic elements of the baroque style into the very form and character of his own epic work. No-one would question the Protestant character of his great epic, and Maurice Kelley has in fact shown that it presents in poetic form the very themes expounded theologically in his prose treatise *The Christian Doctrine*.[25] To have expressed those Protestant themes in patently Counter-Reformation terms would have been like some avowed vegetarian inscribing his creed on animal parchment. Nor is this merely a matter of 'style' in some vague sense of the word. From the opening moment of the Reformation, Luther had singled out for attack the un-Christian ostentation of the Roman church and the sale of indulgences to pay for the building of an extravagant St. Peter's. When Rome responded by deliberately reaffirming its policies the Reformers grew increasingly vociferous in their condemnation, continuing their attacks on the 'idolatry' of Catholic art throughout the following century. Such hostility would seem, therefore, to disqualify the Jesuit baroque, associated with gilded pillars and jewelled reliquaries, as the mode to be adopted for a specifically Puritan epic.[26]

Once, however, the baroque style is comprehended in less sectarian terms as the response of the era as a whole to man's cosmic discoveries, then *Paradise Lost* can be seen for what it really is—not a derivative of the Catholic Counter-Reformation but a parallel Protestant expression of the new vision of creation, and of the place of the Christian worshipper within it. That does not mean there was no borrowing from the more established mode, but it was a borrowing only of those elements which the Protestant could legitimately admire as part of a shared Christian view. St. Paul's cathedral, rebuilt by Wren after the Great Fire, was also a specifically Protestant creation. In a country which had inherited a wealth of Gothic churches from the Catholic pre-Reformation era, this was to be the great ecclesiastical monument to Anglicanism. Yet like Milton's epic it takes the Italian baroque as its model, with a façade of high stateliness and grandeur, massive two-storeyed porticos, assertive twin towers, and one of the most magnificent domes in all Europe (Plate 7). Wren had originally planned a façade of even more impressive baroque proportions, with colossal pillars rising uninterrupted from the ground to the lofty upper pediment, and the plan was only abandoned when stone blocks large enough for the project proved to be unobtainable. The interior of the cathedral is quieter than the Italian tradition, modified in part by the Protestant preference for austerity, and in part also by the approach of eighteenth-century classicism, since its construction, with numerous alterations in planning, spanned a slightly later period, from 1675 to 1712. The traditional baroque features, however, are still clearly there—the countless pilasters, the double cornice, the contrapuntally varied arches, and even an ornate high altar. In effect, then, while discarding the more flamboyant elements distasteful to the Protestant tradition, Wren quite deliberately borrowed from the Italian baroque the architectural expression it gave to this contemporary awareness of divine grandeur and might, thereby creating in St. Paul's of London a worthy Protestant rival to St. Peter's of Rome.

The Puritans, it is true, were a stage further removed from Catholicism than was the Anglican church, and one might have expected from Milton a sharper antagonism to the Roman baroque. Yet for him the problem proved less acute than might be imagined. Had he been designing a church, he would, in all probability, have found the pressures of continued Protestant attacks on papal opulence edging him, despite his personal preferences, towards the plain style in architecture; if not towards the simple, whitewashed timber buildings adopted by his contemporaries in New England, then at least to some less grandiose style. There is evidence from his writings that his views on church architecture did, in fact, move in that direction. In 'Il Penseroso', written before he held any official position in the Puritan party and was thus free to express his own preferences, he describes with warm affection the religious splendour of such churches as the old St. Paul's, which he knew so well from his schooldays, with its high vaulted roof and weighty pillars. It was not baroque, but was certainly closer to the Catholic tradition in its Gothic splendour and imposing size:

But let my due feet never fail
To walk the studious Cloister's pale,

And love the high embowed Roof,
With antic Pillars massy proof,
And storied windows richly dight,
Casting a dim religious light.

After the years of the Rebellion, when he had served with
distinction as the leading polemicist of the party, he was more
sensitive to doctrinal pressures. In *Paradise Lost*, as the fallen angels
gather their shattered strength to resume their insurrection and set
to work building Pandaemonium in hell, the opportunity is too
good for a Puritan to miss. Milton accordingly depicts the devilish
building as a baroque structure, such as he had seen on his visit to
Italy in 1638–9, lavishly ornamented with pilasters and golden
architrave:

Built like a Temple, where *Pilasters* round
Were set, and Doric pillars overlaid
With Golden Architrave; nor did there want
Cornice or Frieze, with bossy Sculptures grav'n;
The Roof was fretted Gold. Not *Babylon*
Nor great *Alcairo* such magnificence
Equalled in all thir glories, to inshrine
Belus or *Serapis* thir Gods, or seat
Thir Kings, when *Egypt* with *Assyria* strove
In wealth and luxury.

(I, 713–22)

Even here, the condemnation is not total, and one senses a grudging
admiration behind the attack. The building may be luxurious and
ornate but its magnificence, he admits, rivals the most glorious of
pagan temples; and he cannot forbear adding a moment later that
its architect Mulciber had built in heaven before the fall.
Nevertheless, condemn it he does, implying that only God—'the
great Architect' as he calls him elsewhere—or his ministering angels
are entitled to build in such vastness and splendour. The implication is that for the Christian on earth it is more seemly to seek
humility, and hence to avoid the presumptuousness of attempting to
rival the Tower of Babel. For all his sympathies, then, he comes
down at least ostensibly on the side of simplicity and modesty in
church building.

Milton, however, was not designing a church. He was writing a poem, an art form far removed from the vexed history of Reformation attacks on lavish edifices. The Puritan advocated the plain style in literature as well, but its purpose there was practical rather than doctrinal. On the basis of Paul's injunction'. . . except ye utter by the tongue words easy to be understood, how shall it be known what is spoken?', (I Cor. 14, 9), preachers were urged to employ simple language, with plain metaphors drawn from everyday life. William Perkins opposed the use of Latin and Greek quotations in sermons or pamphlets, and insisted that true art lay in the ability to conceal art, so that the result would be easily intelligible to the common people. In the same way, Valentine Marshall recommended that preachers keep close to the language of the Scriptures, on the grounds that '. . . . the Gold upon the Pill may please the eye; but it profits not the patient. The Paint upon the Glass may feed the fancy; but the room is the darker for it.'²⁷ This advice, however, while it may have been valuable for popular preaching, whether by printed tract or word of mouth, was obviously of minimal relevance for a Protestant epic. It was universally acknowledged that the epic was a genre demanding by its very nature loftiness of style and grandeur of theme. Indeed, it may have been partly for that reason that Milton was drawn finally towards the epic form, immune as it was to such demands for plain writing. He was thus free in his poem to parallel what Wren was doing in his cathedral, to incorporate the baroque mode as an artistic response to the new concepts of man's relationship to God, without any feeling of disloyalty to the Puritan ideals of which it was to be the exponent.

Milton's *Paradise Lost* has become so familiar a classic that, like most monuments, its presence can easily be taken for granted. Before we begin, in the following chapter, attempting to break new ground in exploring the baroque elements in his epic, perhaps we should remind ourselves what an unprecedented work it is in the history of English literature, even in theme alone.²⁸ Just as the baroque itself was responding artistically to the enlarged cosmos, so here the poem is devoted, not as epic convention had demanded, to the odyssey of a hero or the progress of an ancient war, but to the creation of the entire universe. Where the new churches had discarded the modest, man-centred chapels of the Renaissance in favour of interiors opening up to the infinite and echoing the spatial dynamism of the new heavens, Milton's poem chooses as its subject the task of describing the purpose of that creation, its divine justification, and the moral implications it bore for all mankind. The theme is vast, the setting infinite, the time eternal. He could truly declare that he was pursuing '. . . Things unattempted yet in Prose or Rhyme'.

Most baroque artists have, as we have seen, a yearning to achieve the impossible, to burst the shackles of the finite, but Milton went even beyond that ambition. For a human to attempt a defence of God's cosmic plan verged on the presumptuous, and only one precedent could in any sense justify such a venture—the tradition of the biblical prophet who, though mortal like Milton himself, had been chosen to speak by inspiration, authoritatively in the name of God. Accordingly, there is, in the opening lines of the poem, a plea for such inspiration. Outwardly it resembles the standard epic invocation to the muse, but in its emotional resonance and in the nature of its appeal, it reveals the commitment of the poet to his larger and more imposing task. Significantly, the prophet he selects as his model for such mortal inspiration is not, as one might have expected, one of the major visionaries, an Isaiah or Ezekiel representing the finest traditions of biblical poetry and imaginative fire.[29] Instead he by-passes them in favour of Moses, a personality not normally associated with poetry nor even with the full flowering of scriptural prophecy. For the seventeenth-century Puritan particularly, chafing as he had been under the bondage of an oppressive monarchy and contemplating emigration to a new country, Moses had become in Milton's day the often-invoked symbol of the Lawgiver, leading his people to freedom in the Promised Land.

For Milton, however, neither his leadership nor his lawgiving were of importance at this juncture. The achievement for which he chooses Moses here is of a very different kind, one of more intimate concern both to him and to the baroque at large—as being the first mortal who, by divine inspiration, had revealed to mankind how God had created the vast universe in the beginning:

> Sing Heav'nly Muse, that on the secret top
> Of *Oreb*, or of *Sinai*, didst inspire
> That Shepherd, who first taught the chosen Seed,
> In the Beginning how the Heav'ns and Earth
> Rose out of *Chaos*.

If his acknowledged theme is man's loss of Paradise, the major

task he sees before him as a poet and for which he requires divine aid
is the description of the setting to that Fall, the formation of the
cosmos. The simple wording of the biblical account—*In the beginning
God created the heaven and the earth*—is enlarged into baroque terms.
The abyss becomes 'vast', the wings of the Spirit 'mighty' in
accordance with this expanded vision. And the muse he turns to as
the source for his instruction and inspiration is the Spirit which long
ago provided the formative impulse for the universal creation:

> Thou from the first
> Wast present and with mighty wings outspread
> Dove-like satst brooding on the vast Abyss
> And madst it pregnant.

The invocation is more than a statement of the theme he proposes to
recount. Indirectly he is pleading, like all baroque artists that some
share of that divine creativity—the intellectual meditation and
birth-giving power compressed within the ambivalent term
brooding—be passed on to him in order vicariously to energise and
make pregnant his own aesthetic endeavours. Only then, within this
universal context, can he attempt the formidable task of justifying
God's ways to men.

At the very beginning of the poem, therefore, the traditional
limits of the epic are transcended and the theme opens out into the
infinitude of the cosmos. Yet at this point an objection is bound to be
felt, one which must be answered before we begin the detailed
examination of the baroque elements in the epic. Of which cosmos,
we should ask, is Milton writing? Is it the new Copernican universe
in its expanded form, where the solar system has become one small
unit within countless constellations and galaxies; is it the Ptolemaic
universe inherited from earlier traditions; or is it some conflation of
the two such as Tycho Brahe had suggested? Early in this century,
E. N. S. Thompson argued convincingly that Milton was, at the
time of writing *Paradise Lost*, a confirmed Copernican,[30] and there
are sufficient indications in the text to substantiate this view. As
A. O. Lovejoy noted, in the dialogue on astronomy between Raphael
and Adam, Milton gives the last word to Copernicanism, and places
that word in the mouth of an archangelic authority.[31] Yet it is also
apparent that the world of the poem does not conform in all points
to the new universe. A boundless cosmos cannot be confined within
a ball suspended from a golden chain, nor is there place in the

universe revealed by Galileo for the crystalline sphere mentioned in III, 482. Milton, as has been pointed out by many scholars, was writing for a public familiar with the older conventions and continuing to visualise the universe according to Peter Apian's *Cosmographia*, with the planets and stars revolving concentrically about the earth while the earth itself remained immobile. Within such a system God's domain was conceived as being stationary in the heavens, far above the circling spheres, and maintaining a fixed relationship with the earth. One could thus still speak in terms of upward and downward movements despite the relativism implicit in the new cosmology; and such in general is the setting for Milton's mythic titanomachy, in which Satan is flung down out of heaven, falling through space for nine days and nights to sprawl headlong in the fiery gulf of hell below, from which he must then struggle laboriously to wing his way up to the new habitation of man. This is far from being the Copernican universe which had inspired the baroque artist. On the contrary, it is the more familiar, traditional world as conceived by preceding generations.

Such is the spell cast by literature that, had it suited his purpose, Milton could with ease have retained that traditional setting throughout the epic, untroubled by any conflicts with scientific cosmology. Donne, for example, although profoundly disturbed by the threatening implications of Kepler and Galileo, whose conclusions he reluctantly acknowledged as true, could, when he wished, imaginatively reduce that physical reality to a mere bagatelle as he soared beyond it to the visionary world of the Day of Judgement. He invokes '. . . the round earth's *imagined* corners', where in the traditional and unscientific setting of a four-cornered earth the angels trumpet forth the resurrection of numberless infinities of souls; and the reader, caught up in the vision, discards any potential objections based on scientific grounds as irrelevant to this inner vision. For Milton, however, the reverse process is at work. So far from wishing to escape from the scientific reality, he is powerfully drawn towards the actual cosmos as perceived through Galileo's optic glass, and is elated by the splendid pageant it reveals. Instinctively he wishes to incorporate it into his epic as a means of glorifying the divine and enlarging the immensity of creation; but at the same time he is uncomfortably aware of a troublesome obstacle that, on the most literal level, the heliocentric theory did contradict the biblical text itself.

The scriptures had stated unequivocally that the earth was four-cornered and not a revolving sphere. Calvin, for example, representing the orthodox Christian viewpoint, had dismissed the Copernican view out of hand on the basis of the Psalmist's dictum 'The earth also is established and cannot be moved' (Ps. 93, 1). In Milton's day it was too early to make those adjustments in Christian thinking which would eventually allow such passages to be interpreted metaphorically, rather than as literally binding on the true believer. Consequently, his instinctive welcoming of the New Philosophy was tempered by a fear lest, at the moment of his profoundest admiration and awe, he should, like Giordano Bruno, overstep the limits of orthodox belief, and thus disqualify himself as the spokesman of God. He had paid a visit to the ageing Galileo while the latter was under house arrest in his home at Fiesole, and in his *Areopagitica* had quoted him as an example of the restrictions on liberty imposed by a tyrannous church.[32] However, if he demanded freedom of thought and speech from the authorities, he was at the same time fully aware of the boundaries to that liberty which Holy Writ itself placed before the believing Christian. Hence that peculiar blend of conservatism and innovation in *Paradise Lost* which in effect adopts the new vastness of the Copernican universe without ever explicitly acknowledging its validity.

This ambivalence in Milton's attitude is felt at various points in the epic. In a well-known passage in Book X, for example, he employs the repeated phrase 'Some say . . .' as a means of saving himself from making any final commitment for or against the heliocentric theory, while yet allowing him to introduce it in a semi-mythological form:

> Some say he bid his Angels turn askance
> The Poles of Earth twice ten degrees and more
> From the Sun's Axle; they with labor push'd
> Oblique the Centric Globe: Some say the Sun
> Was bid . . . .
>
> (X, 668–72)

There the allusion is incidental, and a more central passage occurs during the colloquy between Raphael and Adam concerning the creation of the universe. Adam has heard with wonder and delight how God originally measured out the heavens with his golden compasses and marked the bounds of the earth's circumference. Nevertheless, impressed as he is, '. . . something yet of doubt

remains'. He, like so many of Milton's contemporaries, is troubled
at the strange disproportion between the awesome magnitude of the
newly revealed heavens and '. . . this punctual spot', the earth
which, in view of its importance in the divine plan, might have been
expected to occupy a greater place. It has rightly been noted that
the question itself, at least as Adam poses it, was not particularly
new. Ptolemy, Roger Bacon, and others had long before remarked
that the earth was a mere dot compared with the heavens, and had
discussed the implications of that disproportion for man. On the
other hand, in the days of Ptolemy or of Roger Bacon, no-one had
yet suggested that man's domain in fact spun subserviently as a
minor satellite about a vastly superior sun, and if Adam's query is
deliberately phrased in conventional terms, there is tucked away
into the reply of the Archangel (whose orthodoxy cannot be
impugned) an admission of the questioner's real intent, the conflict
between traditionalism and the findings of the Renaissance
cosmologists:

> What if the Sun
> Be Centre to the World, and other Stars
> By his attractive virtue and their own
> Incited, dance about him various rounds?
>
> (VIII, 122–5)

The answer Raphael offers paradoxically relies on the magnitude
of the universe itself, created, he suggests, in order to impress man
with a proper sense of humility. By the inversion of argument, man
has subtly been returned to his central position, since it is ultimately
for his benefit that the spaciousness of heaven has been designed.
Moreover, in the course of Raphael's reply, that very magnitude of
the universe which might at first sight have appeared to weaken
religious belief, becomes, in typically baroque fashion, the testimony to God himself:

> And for the Heav'n's wide Circuit, let it speak
> The Maker's high magnificence, who built
> So spacious, and his Line stretcht out so far;
> That Man may know he dwells not in his own;
> An Edifice too large for him to fill,
> Lodg'd in a small partition, and the rest
> Ordain'd for uses to his Lord best known.
> The swiftness of those Circles attribute,

Though numberless, to his Omnipotence,
That to corporeal substances could add
Speed almost Spiritual.

(VIII, 100–10)

With all Milton's caution, what emerges from this answer is clearly
no Ptolemaic view of the universe; for in that older world-view, the
Earth, however diminutive, still lay unquestionably at the centre of
creation. Here it has become no more than '. . . a small partition' in
which man is lodged, watching the incomprehensible workings of
the heavens, whose revolutions seem to have so little relevance to his
own needs.

Milton—not merely in these specific passages, but throughout
the epic—is treading the narrow path between an outmoded
traditionalism and an unorthodox modernism. The choice was not
only between the Ptolemaic and the Copernican systems, for there
were at least five widely accepted theories of the universe before
Copernicus appeared on the scene, and Milton remains for the most
part within one or other of those old-fashioned systems which placed
the Earth in the centre of the circling spheres.[33] What has
transformed his view so radically from all previous conceptions is
the vastness of his cosmos, and that aspect he clearly owes to
Copernicus and Galileo.

The theological commitment which prevented Milton from
formally subscribing to the new universal system inevitably produced a dangerous 'wavering' in the poem, an inconsistency which
at times troubles the reader. The hesitancy on the part of narrator or
discoursing archangel as he approaches a controversial point, and
then carefully side-steps it, is bound to weaken confidence in the
supposedly divine authority of the epic. On the other hand, such
prevarication did carry with it a valuable advantage for the poem
and for the development of its central theme, an advantage which
Milton exploited to the full. It allowed him to accommodate within
the framework of his epic the infinity of the new cosmos (with all
that it implied for his concept of the Creator), while at the same time
preserving and, indeed, reaffirming the biblical centrality of man.
We are never allowed to forget as we range imaginatively through
the spacious regions of his heaven that the celestial titanomachy
between the forces of good and evil is to be fought out finally on the
battleground of the human soul. Man's disobedience, his dire
punishment, and the eventual salvation offered him by a merciful

God, these are the themes of the epic, however immense and impressive the setting.

(iii)

In any study such as this, concentrating upon a single artistic or poetic mode, there is a danger that the originality of that mode may become dulled through familiarity. From time to time it may be useful, therefore, to move outside it in order to compare its forms and assumptions with those of other eras, and by contrast to refresh our awareness of its own individual features. It has, for example, long been customary to describe Milton as a basically Renaissance poet. Although chronologically his writings appeared a little later than those usually included in that tradition, his love of music and masque, his affection for the classical heritage, and his admiration of Spenser have strengthened the view that his roots lay in that earlier era. Perhaps, however, insufficient attention has been paid to the transformation of style and theme which took place between the writing of *Comus* and of *Paradise Lost*. For in the same way as the baroque, growing out of the Renaissance and extending many of its concepts and aesthetic forms, moulded them during that process into an essentially different mode, so Milton's poetic style and imaginative genius underwent a profound change in this period while yet preserving traces of the earlier forms.

In the realm of architecture, for example, the graceful classical porticos, the Doric, Corinthian, or Ionic columns which came into vogue during the humanism of the Renaissance, were not discarded by the baroque but incorporated into a changed setting. They are clustered together to produce a weightier effect, lavishly ornamented, multicoloured, and reduplicated by being echoed in every niche and doorway to create a form of architectonic counterpoint. The Renaissance elements remain, discernible as individual units but absorbed into a more dynamic whole.

Spenser was, like his admirer Milton, a religious poet no less concerned with the supremacy of God, but his depiction of the divine relies upon the High Renaissance tradition. The poem which comes closest to *Paradise Lost* in theme is his 'Hymne of Heavenly Love', which includes an account of the rebellion and fall of the mutinous angels, and its companion piece the 'Hymne of Heavenly Beautie'. The description there of God seated upon his throne in the heavens has, in accordance with Neoplatonic concepts, the more static quality of a securely established hierarchy. God's potential for action is acknowledged, but we see him only in heraldic form, presiding ceremoniously over all and consummating the harmony of the universe. He holds a sceptre ' . . . With which he bruseth all his foes to dust', but the sceptre is not seen at the moment of action. It is an iconographical device within an emblemmatic scene, the whole being reminiscent of some allegorical painting by Botticelli, far removed from the exuberant frescoes of Milton's day:

> His throne is built upon Eternity,
> More firm and durable than steele or brasse,
> Or the hard diamond, which them both doth passe.
> His scepter is the rod of Righteousnesse,
> With which he bruseth all his foes to dust,
> And the great Dragon strongly doth represse,
> Under the rigour of his iudgement iust;
> His seat is Truth, to which the faithfull trust;
> From whence proceed her beames so pure and bright,
> That all about him sheddeth glorious light.
>
> (lines 152–61)

In contrast, the baroque infuses the scene with extraordinary energy, expanding the dimensions of the setting into spacious heavenly vistas, yet at the same time crowding that space with numberless angels gathering about the dazzling throne of the Almighty. In *Paradise Lost*, when Milton's God summons his ministering angels, they throng about him in their ten thousand thousands, gathering from the ends of the heavens, and glittering with emblazoned splendour. It is a remarkable vision:

> . . . th' Empyreal Host
> Of Angels by Imperial summons call'd,
> Innumerable before th' Almighty's Throne
> Forthwith from all the ends of Heav'n appear'd
> Under thir Hierarchs in orders bright;
> Ten thousand thousand Ensigns high advanc'd,
> Standards and Gonfalons, twixt Van and Rear
> Stream in the Air, and for distinction serve
> Of Hierarchies, of Orders and Degrees;
> Or in thir glittering Tissues bear imblaz'd
> Holy Memorials, acts of Zeal and Love

Recorded Eminent. Thus when in Orbs
Of circuit inexpressible they stood,
Orb within Orb, the Father infinite
By whom in bliss imbosom'd sat the Son,
Amidst as from a flaming Mount, whose top
Brightness had made invisible, thus spake . . . .

(V, 583–99)

There is an excitement, a vigour, a sense of irresistible might here, entirely absent from Spenser's description because it formed no part of his conception of the universe. Wölfflin, in his seminal study *Renaissance and Baroque*, pointed out many years ago that one of the basic distinctions between the art of those two eras is to be found precisely here. The Renaissance artist, however turbulent his scene may be in subject-matter, aims in his artistic presentation at attaining a harmonious proportion suggestive of the 'calm and beauty' which he believed governed the higher elements of the universe. The Platonic theory of ideas, each of which consummates in its ideal form the shadowy and fallible instances below it and is itself subsumed in the next higher ideal, implied an increasing degree of perfection as one moved upwards towards the divine. Perfection is by definition the absence of any fault or blemish disturbing the whole, and in Platonic philosophy that freedom from disturbance was emphasised by its association with the harmony of music. Plato had learned from Pythagoras of the mathematical laws governing music, the fixed ratios between the lengths of various strings held in equal tension, which determined the harmony of the chords they produced. From this mathematical relationship was deduced the existence of universal laws of nature, producing at the highest level, as in the music of the spheres, a perfect and undisturbed concord.

Within the Renaissance, the renowned humanist and architect, Leon Battista Alberti, was among the first to introduce that concept into art. His researches into classical sources had uncovered the fact that Roman architects had incorporated those very Pythagorean ratios into their designs, making the walls, columns, and doorways of their buildings conform to the same 'universal' proportions as dominated music. From there it was but one step for Alberti to declare in a famous passage in his *De re aedificatoria* (1452) that all art must strive towards a unity in which '. . . the harmony and concord of all the parts is achieved in such a manner that nothing can be added, taken away, or altered except for the worse'.[34]

Wölfflin, in discussing this aspect of Renaissance art, noted how, in the façades of buildings by Alberti and his followers as well as in the interiors, every niche, window, and door was with scrupulous care made to conform to the fixed ratios established for the whole, both in its own dimensions and in its relative placing within the façade. As a result, the image of the whole is harmoniously echoed by the inner units to produce an undisturbed integrity. In contrast, he continues, baroque architects deliberately introduced discord into their buildings—a cramped doorway, an overhanging portico, a depressed arch—which violate such proportion, creating a visual dissatisfaction and thereby the need for a movement towards resolution. From that change, he argues, is derived the dynamism and emotional disturbance of the baroque in contrast to the more settled harmonies of Renaissance architecture.[35] In painting, too, artists from Alberti's period onwards turned to geometry as the new handmaid to art, sketching out the circles, squares, and parabolas which should form the harmonious substructures for their canvases and frescoes. Da Vinci illustrated the perfect circle formed by the human body in motion, with arms and legs outstretched; numerous preparatory drawings have been preserved from that era in which measured lines are superimposed on the drawing of a face to determine the relationship between the various features and to ensure that proportion shall be preserved even there. Pictorial themes were chosen which should be evocative of such concord. There was a surge of interest in paintings of the Madonna with Child; but no longer, as in a Cimabue or Duccio, does the Madonna clutch the child protectively to her breast in haunting premonition of the crucifixion. Instead, we are offered pastoral scenes of maternal benevolence, in which the mother gazes fondly at the children playing before her; and the triangular composition which Raphael introduced into his own versions of the Madonna and Child enhanced the aura of peace and tranquillity.

Paintings of rape, drunkenness, and high drama continued to occupy Renaissance artists side-by-side with these more serene subjects, and Wölfflin was not unaware of them when he wrote of the 'calm and beauty' of Renaissance art. For, as he and so many other historians have seen, the artist's choice of the specific moment to be portrayed, his method of presentation, and the blending of colour he introduced continued to ensure that even potentially disturbing subjects should conform to the new ideal of beauty.

Titian's *The Rape of Danae* may sound violent in its title, but it is representative of rape scenes from that era in offering an allegorisation of the incident whereby the naked soul surrenders to the divine spirit. Although at one side of the painting an aged female reaches out eagerly to catch the falling stream of gold, symbolising the greed of lesser mortals, Danae herself reclines gracefully on her couch, relaxed and undisturbed, creating the dominant restfulness of the scene.[36] Michelangelo's *The Drunkenness of Noah* depicts no wild debauch. Instead it chooses to portray the conclusion of the incident, the act of filial piety as Shem and Japhet enter with heads averted to cover the nakedness of their sleeping father; and even the bacchanalian orgies by Titian and others are carefully poised and balanced, with only hints of the supposed wildness.

In the later years of the Renaissance, writers and artists began to desert this concept of harmony and serenity. Michelangelo moved away from it in his anguished *Last Judgement* above the altar of the Sistine Chapel, Raphael in his last years pointed forward to mannerist forms, and in literature Shakespeare's Jacobean plays offer Hamlet brooding on corruption, Lear raging in the storm, and a much darker interpretation of heavenly interference in human affairs. Our comparison here, however, is with Spenser, whom Milton acknowledged as the model for much of his own verse; and Spenser was a poet writing from within the earlier and markedly Neoplatonic traditions of the Renaissance. The title of the poem from which the above passage was quoted, 'A Hymne of Heavenly Beautie', equates God with the apex of the Platonic system of ideas, the 'Beautiful-and-Good'. Within that Platonic view of heavenly beauty there was little room for the vigorous God of the biblical world. The solution Spenser offers, therefore, is to combine the two contradictory elements in a heraldic presentation, whereby the 'rod of Righteousness' can at the same time symbolise the active power of divine retribution, while yet remaining visually static, in conformity with the needs of the Neoplatonic idea.

In depicting the scene of the heavenly host attending God, Spenser employs the rhymed, end-stopped form of the verse to create an undisturbed picture of harmonious order. Unlike the powerful archangels and angels of *Paradise Lost* who, with mighty 'sail-broad' wings persevere through the immensities of space to reach their goal, Spenser's angels 'wait' about God, ready (like the rod) to move if called upon. Only then, but not while we see them, will they use their 'nimble' wings to deliver messages from place to place, or, if summoned, will carol hymns of praise:

> There they in their trinall triplicities
> About him wait, and on his will depend,
> Either with nimble wings to cut the skies,
> When he them on his messages doth send,
> Or on his owne dread presence to attend,
> Where they behold the glorie of his light,
> And caroll Hymnes of loue both day and night.[37]

In contrast, *Paradise Lost* presents the angels at the moment of action, either, as in the previous passage, streaming in their thousands to answer the divine summons or, as in the passage below, actually engaged in hymning God's praise. The scene, moreover, is like that of a Gaulli or Pozzo ceiling fresco, a soaring view of brilliance above brilliance, an *O altitudo!* where the imagination is spurred to ascend ever higher into the infinite. As the Fountain of all Light, the Almighty becomes invisible within his own radiance, so that even when he veils his skirts the Seraphim (themselves angels of fiery light) are compelled to shield their eyes before him. Here is height extended above height, splendour above splendour, until such titles as 'Immutable', 'Immortal', 'Infinite' become transformed from abstract theological terms into imaginatively forceful images. Ultimately they must remain beyond mortal grasp, but the baroque artist takes us as close as is humanly possible to their physical realisation, overwhelming us with the vision, and suggesting by extension the energised brilliance that lies beyond:

> Thee Father, first they sung Omnipotent,
> Immutable, Immortal, Infinite,
> Eternal King: thee Author of all being,
> Fountain of Light, thyself invisible
> Amidst the glorious brightness where thou sit'st
> Thron'd inaccessible, but when thou shad'st
> The full blaze of thy beams, and through a cloud
> Drawn round about thee like a radiant Shrine,
> Dark with excessive bright thy skirts appear,
> Yet dazzle Heav'n, that brightest Seraphim
> Approach not, but with both wings veil thir eyes.
>
> (III, 372–82)

If Milton admired Spenser for his Christian faith and for the purity of his Renaissance forms, in his own major work he adopted those qualities only after the same kind of change as Bernini introduced into the classicism of Palladio. The verse is energised into epic magniloquence, and the vision of heaven transformed into a turbulent conflict of infinite forces.

The change can be perceived within Milton's own verse, as he developed from his original Renaissance affinities to his later epic style. His *Comus*, performed at Ludlow Castle in 1634, was thoroughly Renaissance in theme, imagery and timbre. Within the established genre of the court masque, but with a mingling of allegorical Christian moralising reminiscent of Spenser, it celebrated the virtue of chastity; but in accordance with the Renaissance penchant for interweaving religious and pagan philosophy, the virtue it advocated had strong overtones of Ficino rather than Augustine. Sears Jayne has rightly shown how heavily the ideas of this masque lean on Neoplatonism.[38] In the concluding admonition, for example, which points the moral of the whole masque, the soul is encouraged to ascend the Platonic ladder beyond the 'chime' of the music of the spheres:

> Mortals that would follow me,
> Love virtue, she alone is free,
> She can teach ye how to climb
> Higher than the Sphery chime;
> Or if Virtue feeble were,
> Heav'n itself would stoop to her.

The pervasive harmony is discernible in the plot too. One never feels that the Lady's purity is genuinely imperilled. An Attendant Spirit, evocative of Ariel, appears in various guises to ensure that no harm should befall her, magic potions add the fairy touch, and the would-be seducer Comus (who, as Robert Adams has pointed out, makes remarkably few and feeble attempts at seduction[39]) speaks, when he has the Lady in his power, not with the gloating of a villain from Jacobean revenge tragedy, but rather with the grace and scholarship of a Renaissance sonneteer, responsive to the freshness and beauty of nature:

> *Comus*: Why are you vext, Lady? Why do you frown?
> Here dwell no frowns, nor anger, from these gates

Sorrow flies far: See, here be all the pleasures
That fancy can beget on youthful thoughts
When the fresh blood grows lively, and returns
Brisk as the April buds in Primrose-season.
And first behold this cordial Julep here,
That flames and dances in his crystal bounds
With spirits of balm and fragrant Syrups mixt.

(666–74)

There is no trace here of Milton's weightier Grand Style, but rather the courtly humanism of Renaissance poetry. Similarly, Milton himself acknowledges the classical timbre of *Lycidas*, published in 1638, in which the poet '. . . touch't with tender stops of various Quills/With eager thought warbling his Doric lay.' Some have seen in the digressions on the duty of the church pastors and on Milton's own poetic aspirations a tendency to mannerist indirection, a doubling back on theme in which the identity of the speaker is made deliberately ambiguous.[40] Nevertheless, in the overall treatment of theme, with the 'Bells and Flowrets' of the vernal scene, the shepherd-poet playing on his pipe, and the mythological appeal to Neptune and the muses to justify their supposed dereliction of duty, the poem remains firmly within the tradition of the pastoral elegy of classical times.[41]

It was at this point that an important break occurred in the pattern of Milton's life. In 1638, the same year as saw the publication of *Lycidas*, he left England on a journey to Italy which was to last for fifteen months. We have little information about that lengthy continental visit other than the very general account written by his nephew Edward Phillips, and scholars have had difficulty in identifying what connection exists between that visit and the obvious change it produced in his verse-writing. F. T. Prince, in his excellent study of the Italian element in Milton's poetry, acknowledges the decisive change which occurred and agrees that it must be attributed to the Italian visit; but by restricting his search to the literary models Milton may have found there, he can come up with no effective suggestion. At that time, he points out, '. . . no undeniably great work had yet been written' in blank verse, and, basing his comparisons on the sixteenth-century Renaissance tradition in Italy, he is compelled to admit that it is a far cry from Tasso's knights and enchantresses to the solemnities of *Paradise Lost*.[42] Even in the realm of art, the suggestion that he may have benefited from the paintings he saw there has proved abortive, since in this area too attention has been directed only towards the Renaissance. J. H. Hanford is disappointed to discover that Milton nowhere alludes to the great painters such as confronted him everywhere in Italy and concludes that the fusion of Christian and pagan imagery, of biblical legend and classical mythology in his verse '. . . are probably more indebted than Milton himself realised to what his eyes took in on the ceiling of the Sistine Chapel or the walls of the Doge's Palace'.[43] But Milton had been merging Christian and classical before his Italian visit (as Dr. Johnson complained in connection with *Lycidas*) and it is not there that the change in his style was to be felt.

If, however, we turn our attention away from the Renaissance tradition in Italy to the newer trends there, the answer becomes clearer. His visit to Italy in 1638 coincided exactly with that astonishing surge of activity which marked the crescendo of the baroque. Urban VIII, the Barberini pope who reigned from 1624 to 1644, was by nature very different from his immediate predecessors. Although he worked closely with the Jesuits and in general upheld the principles of the Counter-Reformation, he marked the end of a period of austerity and asceticism, and returned to the previous tradition of Julius II. It was he who discovered the young Bernini, and under his rule a series of lavish commissions began to change the face of Rome. The pagan ruins were plundered for marble to build the new churches and to adorn their interiors. The ancient Roman Pantheon was stripped of its bronze roof to provide the material for the famed baldachino in St. Peter's bearing his family crest, and the incident gave rise to the justified adage that *Quod non fecerunt barbari, fecerunt Barberini*.

Such was the artistic atmosphere when Milton arrived in Rome. As has been mentioned, we have no detailed account of his visit, but Phillips, the most reliable of his contemporary biographers, makes repeated reference to his uncle's responsiveness to the art and architecture of the country. He was impressed by 'the nobleness of the structures' in Florence, by the stateliness of Venice, and by the rarities and antiquities 'of that most glorious and renowned city', Rome. Even if, as was likely, Milton refrained for sectarian reasons from entering such churches as Il Gesù, whose construction had already been completed by that date, he could not have been unaware of the many baroque buildings about him whose façades alone, like that of Maderno's S. Susanna, completed in 1603, proclaimed the tenets of the new artistic code and offered so sharp a contrast to the Renaissance orders with which he was familiar. Quite apart from them, there were also the secular buildings to carry the message of the changing tastes and architectural aspirations of the period. We know, interestingly enough, from graceful letters of thanks which he wrote to his host and to the scholar through whom he obtained the introduction, that Milton accepted a personal invitation from the Pope's brother, Cardinal Francesco, to attend a musical evening held at the family home, the Palazzo Barberini, where, in the main salon, Cortona was just putting the finishing touches to his important ceiling fresco, executed in the most sumptuous baroque style.[44] In the theatre of the Barberini palace he saw one of the first Italian comic operas, with a lavish stage design by Bernini himself, which his biographer described as being something of which 'the fame will endure forever in the world'. Unfortunately, stage designs are less durable than marble buildings, and we can only guess today at the brilliance of the theatre setting by a man who had already achieved fame as a baroque stage designer.

There is, however, no need to search for evidence of specific contacts Milton may have had with the baroque during the course of his Italian visit, for the vigorous architectural and artistic activity about him at that time would have been impossible for any visitor to miss. We know, for example, that during his stay he was received with great civility and respect by Italian intellectuals and writers. They wrote canzonets in his honour, and took him on tours of their cities. In those circles, such immediately topical matters as Bernini's transformation of the interior of St. Peter's or Borromini's construction of the innovative S. Carlo alle Quattro Fontane would certainly have formed part of the conversation of the day. In brief, if we recall that his visit to Italy lasted many months and coincided with so dynamic a period in the development of the High Baroque, it would be surprising indeed if he had not been affected by the new trends. Yet the importance of this visit for an understanding of the change which took place in his own poetic style during that period has received little attention in Milton criticism. It will be the task of the following chapters to explore what light a knowledge of his growing identification with those baroque trends can throw on our understanding of his major work.

2 The Arch Antagonist

The recognition that Milton in his maturer phase belongs within a baroque context is, as was noted earlier, of only academic interest unless it can offer some deeper insights into the literary quality of his epic. Indeed, for those readers who remain suspicious of attempts to relate literature to contemporary changes in the visual arts, there is often a feeling that the very establishing of such cultural affinities detracts in some way from the achievement of the individual writer. It is as though he has been relegated from the status of an independent and original creator to that of a mere purveyor of current fashion.[1] As so often, perhaps here too Shakespeare can prove illuminating. In a well-known passage defining the function of drama—a definition which should be extended to include all creative art—Hamlet informs the players that its purpose is not only universal ('. . . to hold as 'twere the mirror up to nature') but also of immediate contemporary relevance (to show '. . . the very age and body of the time his form and pressure'). It is the task of the writer or artist, in addition to speaking to all generations, to present to his contemporaries, by means of his greater insight and sensitivity, the true image of his own era, often before they are aware of it. His duty in that respect is to crystallise, as Shakespeare did so superbly for the Renaissance, the philosophical concepts, the moral norms, and the spiritual aspirations of his age, while yet preserving the individual stamp of his own genius. So far, then, from merely purveying a current fashion, the writer shares with the other artists of his epoch the creative challenge of interpreting the contemporary condition of man. That shared task will inevitably impose some degree of unity on their responses in aesthetic terms, even though the individual still retains his personal set of beliefs or values, and his personal idiom. It is in that sense that Milton offered in *Paradise Lost* the poetic reaction of a deeply committed Puritan to the major impulses of his age, moving beyond the sectarian bounds of his own party to a more universal vision of man's place in a world so radically altered by the new cosmology.

On the other hand, the recognition of a writer's historical or artistic context can never be a substitute for objective critical evaluation, even if this substitution has sometimes been silently implied. Horace Walpole's *Castle of Otranto* may prove interesting to the literary historian when it is seen as part of the Gothic revival, preparing the way for the romantic suspension of disbelief and the fascination with incest and 'sublime horror'; but that does not make it a better novel. Obviously, each work must stand or fall on its own merits, and it is pointless to expect a modern reader to react more positively to a work merely on the grounds of its relevance to the needs of an earlier generation.

There is, however, one area in which such historical enquiry can make a significant contribution, and that is in removing modern misconceptions which may obstruct or inhibit the otherwise spontaneous admiration aroused by a work of art. This aspect has a peculiar relevance to *Paradise Lost*; for in much modern discussion of Milton there has been a noticeable discrepancy between the critic's intellectual disqualification of the epic on the grounds, say, of theological inconsistency or moral indefensibility, and on the other hand, that same critic's admission of the emotional impact the work has upon him. It is a discrepancy which leads one to suspect that the criterion for disparagement may itself be faulty, and that Milton is often being condemned for failing to conform to a specifically twentieth-century need rather than for any fundamental weakness as an artist. One critic, for example, who provided the most incisive and certainly the most persuasive of modern attacks on the epic, carefully analysing the literary defects and blemishes of the work which would appear to add up to its total negation, concluded, nevertheless, with the admission: 'We shall go on reading the poem for ever, I presume, for the glory of the writing, and for the spirit of Milton that so lives in whatever he wrote.'[2] His basic objection— and one shared by many modern critics—is that *Paradise Lost* does not turn out to be the epic which Milton *meant* to write. And herein lies the crucial point. An awareness of the cultural context in which the epic was written may or may not help the twentieth-century reader to respond more positively to the work itself; but it is likely at the very least to affect our understanding of what Milton was *attempting* to achieve by establishing the basic motivation shared by the artists closest both to his time and to his aesthetic mode. If the term 'baroque' has any meaning at all, if Rubens, Da Cortona, and Bernini do exhibit some shared concepts of activised space, of profusion, of massivity, and of animated might which, for all personal differences, distinguish them stylistically from artists of other modes, then there is at least *prima facie* evidence for assuming that Milton's epic may share, together with these stylistic features, the larger aims of the baroque mode. Only the text can be the final arbiter, but an awareness of the dominant impulses in seventeenth-century art can add a valuable dimension to our responsiveness to that text. Moreover, since that motivation, namely Milton's ultimate purpose in writing the epic, has become a focal point in Miltonic criticism, its relevance is by no means negligible.

One major criticism levelled at the epic as a whole, perhaps the most prominent of all adverse criticism, has, of course, been directed at the figure of Satan, as symbolising above all the rift between Milton's intention and his achievement. On the assumption that Milton's aim as the defender of God's ways must be to denigrate Satan (a reasonable enough assumption if one has no contrary evidence drawn from his era), the heroic elements in his initial presentation form a serious blemish in the poem, working against Milton's declared purpose. It is noteworthy, incidentally, that the first critic to single out Satan as the real hero of the poem was Dryden; for although a younger contemporary of Milton, he belonged culturally, as we know, to the following era, to the rationalist age which he helped to usher in. Accordingly, he was less responsive to the baroque features of Milton's work, to the imaginative and visionary qualities of his epic. More specifically, his view of Satan needs to be seen in the context of those changes taking place on the English stage. The new insistence upon clear distinctions between good and evil characters had made it difficult to tolerate the more complex tragic schemes of Shakespeare's plays. *Antony and Cleopatra* had to be rewritten as *All for Love* with the central characters suffering for their acknowledged sins from the very opening of the play so that the moral should be clear to all; and *King Lear* needed to be accommodated to the more simplistic demands of Thomas Rymer's 'poetic justice' in the version by Nahum Tate, which restored Lear to the throne and neatly married off Cordelia to Edgar as a reward for her constancy. It is not difficult to understand, therefore, why Dryden was disturbed by the heroic elements in the character of Satan when the latter was supposedly the villain of the piece.

In the continuation of the criticism during subsequent years the emphasis is repeatedly placed on the assumption that the heroic elements in Satan were *unintentional* on Milton's part. Blake's brief comment that Milton was '. . . of the Devil's party without knowing it', was the first to point explicitly to Milton's supposed unawareness of his own Satanic sympathies, and Shelley, for reasons obvious enough, both as a declared atheist and as an admirer of revolt against tyranny, delighted in the energy and magnificence of the arch-rebel who, he argued, 'as a moral being is . . . far superior to his God'.[3] He, too, assumes that Milton has unintentionally inverted the theological message of his poem. In the modern era, this supposed flaw began to occupy a more central place in Milton criticism, still on the assumption that Milton had not meant to make his villain heroic. E. M. W. Tillyard felt compelled to admit that Milton, by allying himself in part with Satan, was 'unwittingly . . . led away by the creature of his own imagination'; and R. J. Z. Werblowsky began his Jungian analysis of this phenomenon from the firm assumption that Lucifer here is a Promethean figure whose powerful appeal to the reader '. . . defeats his Satanic function in the poem'.[4] We may summarise the general attack by turning to Waldock who, on this point as on so many others, presents the most formidable case against Milton. Since by his very nature, he maintains, Milton inevitably sided with Satan in the fortitude, endurance and leadership which reflected so much of his own character, he found himself depicting the rebel in a more positive light than the story could bear. Villainy in any case exerts a certain fascination upon us, and Satan accordingly slips out of Milton's control, becoming far more impressive than he had intended. The technique he adopted to correct this warping of the epic theme was, according to Waldock, aesthetically invalid, a form of 'literary cheating' which seriously damages the poem. After Satan has delivered a particularly noble and inspiring speech, Milton, in his authorial voice, introduces a derogatory comment, such as the reminder that Satan's words bear only 'Semblance of worth, not substance', in order to deflate the impression of splendour unintentionally created, and to restore him to his role of villain. A character, as we know, must develop from within and if, like Macbeth, he is to degenerate, that degeneration must be embryonically visible in earlier scenes and develop recognisably within his thought and speech. It cannot be imposed extraneously by the asides of an omniscient author. Here, Waldock feels, lies the central weakness of the entire epic.[5]

It is now some twenty to thirty years since the attack on Milton reached its climax, and so many replies and counter-replies have appeared since then that one might feel a need to apologise for returning to it again, were it not for one important point. Although the fervour of the participants has to some extent subsided—largely because, after a certain point, the arguments became repetitive— the Satanist aspect of the debate never reached any clear or decisive end. The other prong of the twofold attack did eventually become blunted. The furore over the quality of Milton's verse, instigated primarily by T. S. Eliot's attack, led in due course to a public modification of his earlier position, and today the overwhelming view is that Milton has been fully reinstated as a poet. The same does not hold true, however, for Satan's role in the epic. In 1961, William Empson fired off a new and powerful salvo in his *Milton's God* to remind us that the battle was still far from over, and produced in 1965 a revised edition of the book in which he answered the criticisms that had been levelled at his arguments. The appearance since then of important works such as those by Dame Helen Gardner, Stanley E. Fish, Wayne Shumaker and many others leaves no doubt that the controversy is still very much with us.

Waldock's premises have been questioned on grounds which do not concern us directly here, such as whether authorial comment is not in itself a perfectly legitimate literary technique. Fielding often pauses to discuss with his reader the moral implications of Tom's escapades, and in drama there is the accepted tradition of a choric figure, who comments on the actions of the protagonists to sway the sympathies of the audience and to move them in the direction desired by the author.[6] There have, however, been two main attempts to answer the more specific charge that Milton's uncon- scious admiration of Satan badly flaws the poem. C. S. Lewis, in a witty defence of Milton's Christian stand (which preceded Waldock's book but was aimed more generally against the growing attack on Milton) begins by reminding us that in the seventeenth century people believed in Satan's existence as an actual being, and knew him to be by nature an inveterate liar. Such knowledge would have protected the reader at the time of the poem's publication from slipping into the mistakes of later eras and imagining that his vaunting was in any sense justified. The most specious aspects of Satan, he argues, are thus deliberately placed at the beginning of the epic, with all their 'rants and melodrama', in order that we should perceive the depths to which such self-intoxication will eventually lead.[7] The trouble with this answer is that it assumes on

1. Andrea Pozzo: *The Glory of St. Ignatius*. Ceiling fresco, S. Ignazio, Rome.

2.   G. B. Gaulli: *The Worship of the Holy Name*. Ceiling fresco, Il Gesù, Rome.

3.   Vignola: Interior of Il Gesù.

4. Bernini: Ceiling of S. Andrea al Quirinale, Rome.

5. Maderno: S. Susanna, Rome.

6. Pietro da Cortona: Frescoes in the dome and apse of S. Maria in Vallicella, Rome.

7. Wren: St. Paul's Cathedral, London.

8. Rubens: *Hercules Slaying Envy*. Banqueting Hall, Whitehall, London.

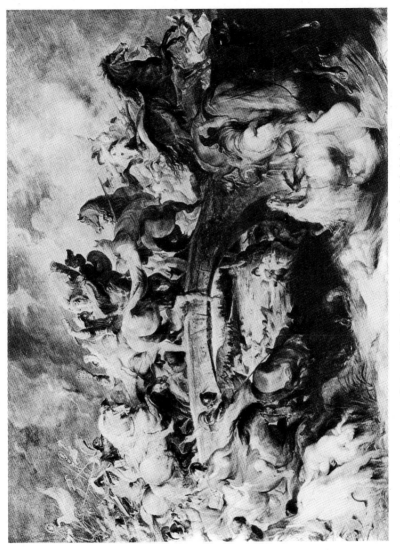

9. Rubens: *The Battle of the Amazons.* Alte Pinakothek, Munich.

10.   Hieronymus Bosch: *The Fall of the Damned*. Detail from the left panel of *The Haywain* triptych. The Prado, Madrid.

11. Rubens: *The Fall of the Damned*. Alte Pinakothek, Munich.

12. Pietro da Cortona: Stucco decoration in the Sala di Giove, Palazzo Pitti, Florence.

the part of the reader a simplistic response, free from any gradations or subtlety. Satan is evil; therefore we will reject anything he says as an untruth. If he sounds glorious, it is only a deception, and any good Christian will immediately discount his speech as insidious. In brief, he answers the charge by a denial of Satan's attractiveness and such a rebuttal will not satisfy a reader sensitive to the spell which he does exert in these early books.

More recently, Stanley Fish has offered an ingenious extension of the theory, particularly attractive for our own age, with its increased awareness of the ambiguities of literature and a writer's ability to manipulate the response of the reader. He agrees with C. S. Lewis that Milton is exploiting the contemporary reader's knowledge of Satan's mendacity, but he takes the argument an important stage further by perceiving in the poem a repeated process of delayed reaction. On reading Satan's more splendid speeches, he argues, we are lulled momentarily into a genuine admiration of his prowess. Only when we reach the authorial comment a little later with its reminder of his villainy do we realise with a guilty start that we ourselves have been seduced by Satan's wiles. Like Adam and Eve, we too have been 'surprised by Sin', experiencing within our own consciousness the process of temptation and fall; and, having fallen, are able to respond with greater empathy to the enmeshment of our Grand Parents in the subtle net of Satan's rhetoric. By a repeated series of lapses and recognitions, the reader eventually becomes educated to his position and responsibilities as a fallen man removed from innocence, and this lesson, Fish suggests, is the ultimate purpose of the poem. In such a reading, those omniscient interventions by the author to which Waldock objects are no longer lame attempts to rectify an error on the author's part, but are instead the author's taunting accusation of the reader for having himself become temporarily fascinated by Satan's charms.[8]

This is a fine insight into one of the techniques used in the poem, notably in such scenes as the description of the Fall. There, when Satan's words to Eve fall persuasively on our own ears, when God appears by his prohibition to be jealously denying man the right to wisdom and knowledge, we do receive a jolt at the authorial comment 'So glozed the Tempter . . .'. We awaken to our own disposition to slide away from our moral commitments. However, the theory does not function in the opening books as well as is suggested, and for a number of reasons. There, it is important to note, the splendour of Satan is not confined to *his own* utterances, but appears repeatedly in the descriptions of him provided by the narrator; and these can by no stretch of the imagination be attributed to the deceitfulness of Satan's rhetoric. It is Milton who keeps reminding us of the splendour of the rebel host:

> Forthwith from every Squadron and each Bank
> The Heads and Leaders thither haste where stood
> Thir great Commander; Godlike shapes and forms
> Excelling human, Princely Dignities,
> And Powers that erst in Heaven sat on Thrones.
>
> (I, 356–60)

He will modify the praise a few lines later by recalling that in subsequent years these Godlike shapes were to become the false pagan idols of mankind, but it is he, not Satan, who points to their magnificence at the time of the rebellion itself. Satan here is the 'great Commander' not by his own reckoning but by the judgement of the authorial voice of the epic. It would be self-defeating for that same authorial voice to taunt us a little later for having trusted it; for if our faith in the bardic narrator is impaired, then the persuasiveness of the entire epic will be irrevocably damaged.

Even in the speeches which Satan himself delivers, a problem arises in applying the theory. Certainly the Devil was by tradition an inveterate liar, but he was never conceived as a pathological liar. He spoke falsely only at such times as falsehood suited his purpose. When tempting a soul into hell, he would flatter and cajole in order by deceit to tempt the sinner over the slippery edge to doom. In the seduction of Eve we watch him at his most brilliant, discerning her feminine weaknesses and playing on her foolish vanity to trick her into the fatal act of disobedience. But in the opening books, particularly in the earliest scenes, his purpose is not to trick others, but to convince himself. What place is there in that setting for diabolical wiles or deception in such self-communion? He is struggling there against the 'deep despair' which racks his own soul, as he deliberates whether to submit or to resume the fight. Only when his decision is reached does he begin to rouse his shattered host to battle, and then he is the military commander *par excellence*, exhorting his troops to war, raising their flagging spirits, and inspiring them with visions of victory. It would be the height of absurdity to deceive his own troops for the mere sake of deception, when the failure of the enterprise would rebound ultimately upon himself. It is difficult to see, therefore, how the reader is supposed in that section to condemn the duplicity of his words even retrospectively, and thus to disqualify his potential attractiveness.

Moreover, there is a distinction to be preserved here, and to ignore it is to oversimplify the complexity of our moral response. As anyone will acknowledge who has participated in a battle or has at least read first-hand accounts by combatants, there is no contradiction between a loathing for one's enemy's aims, and a soldierly admiration for the courage or professional skill with which he carries them out. A Japanese *kamikaze* pilot hurling his plane as a living bomb into an American destroyer may appear to us to be on the wrong side of morality, allied with the despicable cause of Nazism, but this does not deter us from acknowledging his personal and selfless dedication to what he considers his patriotic duty. So it is with Satan. His desire to corrupt mankind as a means of revenging himself on God deserves our fullest condemnation; but the qualities he displays in achieving that goal—his magnificent resourcefulness, his refusal to be intimidated, and his contempt for craven submission—these may, and do, arouse our legitimate admiration which is not cancelled out retrospectively. In a speech such as the following, we are of course expected to deplore the simmering envy, the boastfulness, and the desire for vengeance, but are we, as has been suggested, to feel subsequently guilty for having recognised the nobility of his bearing in defeat, and the courage of his resistance to despair?

> What though the field be lost?
> All is not lost; the unconquerable Will
> And study of revenge, immortal hate,
> And courage never to submit or yield:
> And what is else not to be overcome?
> That Glory never shall his wrath or might
> Extort from me. To bow and sue for grace
> With suppliant knee, and deify his power
> Who from the terror of this Arm so late
> Doubted his Empir, that were low indeed,
> That were an ignominy and shame beneath
> This downfall.

(I, 105–16)

If, then, Satan's heroic qualities are not nullified by the authorial comments but remain positive attributes of the rebel leader, we must return to examine once again the major critical attack upon the epic, the view that they are a blemish arising from Milton's unconscious sympathy with his defiance of tyranny, and hence militate against the author's declared purpose. To quote Waldock:

> . . . it is evident that portraiture so sympathetic, drawing such strength from Milton's own life and nature, could be very dangerous for Milton's scheme. Of course it was dangerous; and nothing is more interesting, technically, in the opening books than to note the nervousness that creeps on Milton as he becomes aware of what is threatening. It is an instructive and in some ways an amusing study. If one observes what is happening one sees that there is hardly a great speech of Satan's that Milton is not at pains to correct, to damp down and neutralize. He will put some glorious thing in Satan's mouth, then, anxious about the effect of it, will pull us gently by the sleeve, saying (for this is what it amounts to): 'Do not be carried away by this fellow: he *sounds* splendid, but take my word for it . . .'. We have in fact, once again, two levels: the level of demonstration or exhibition, and the level of allegation or commentary; and again there is disagreement.[9]

A question, however, needs to be asked at this point, the logical extension of everything implied in this attack on the epic. If, as is claimed, the attractiveness of Satan in the opening books is a literary flaw weakening the structural and thematic unity of the work, the removal of that flaw ought to improve the work as a whole. Yet would any reader who is even mildly responsive to *Paradise Lost* genuinely wish Satan to be diminished in stature in those earlier books, whatever the supposed structural or theological advantages? These opening scenes, including the battle in heaven, have a range, a splendour, and an audacity of conception of which Satan's Promethean qualities form an essential part, and to surrender the charismatic aspects of his character would be to enfeeble the epic itself. One need only imagine for a moment a cringing, Fagin-like figure in his place to recognise the damage it would cause to the timbre of the work; and yet such is the implication of the charge that Milton was seduced *away* from his true conception into an unintentional enlargement of Satan's stature.

Once it is acknowledged that the heroic Satan occupies an integral and indispensable place within the epic, we might be well advised to begin the enquiry from the other end of the scale. Instead of disqualifying Satan's depiction on the grounds of its conflict with the supposed purpose of the epic, perhaps we should use Milton's portrayal of the devil as a criterion for determining more accurately what that purpose really was, and the techniques he adopted for its achievement. It is here that a knowledge of the baroque both as an art form and as the expression of a religio-philosophical viewpoint may assist us in understanding the poet's larger aim, although here too the text of the poem itself must provide the final evidence.

The previous chapter, it will be recalled, argued that the mainspring of the Christian baroque was the desire to accommodate artistically an enormously augmented concept of God as the supreme power in a universe incomparably more impressive than that imagined by immediately previous generations. We are no longer dealing with God as the venerable old gentleman creating Eve on Ghiberti's doors in Florence, nor even with the more powerful but still man-size God on the ceiling of the Sistine Chapel, indistinguishable in form from the bearded prophet Jeremiah. We are dealing instead with a God of infinite proportions who hurls the planets into their orbits, restrains and directs their courses, and, in return to Old Testament tradition, brings out each of the myriad stars by name '. . . by the greatness of his might, for that he is mighty in power' (Is. 40, 26). When depicted visually in the baroque, he appears there either symbolically as a dazzling light too bright for human gaze, or surrounded by a numberless host of angels to suggest his boundless majesty.

The task of the religious artist in this period was to depict the immensity of that newly conceived power, no longer as an abstract attribute of the divine but in physically realisable terms. His problem was how to do so. If, for the purpose of illustration, we descend from the sublime to the banal, the nature of that problem and its solution may become more readily apparent. Car manufacturers often speak for convenience of the cubic capacity of an engine, but in fact the only effective method of gauging, or even of conveying conceptually, the actual power generated by a new motor is by measuring the resistance which can be built up against it. Brake-horsepower measures the force needed to restrain the engine in its stationary position when running at full throttle. An alternative system calculates what force would be required to halt the vehicle, if it were hurled full-speed against a solid buffer; but the principle is the same in either instance. The power can only be measured by a counter-force or resistance. If the power is generated in a vacuum, there is nothing against which it can thrust, and the force fails to materialise in any perceptible or tangible form. The baroque artist, fascinated by the new physical forces revealed in the universe, and attempting to convey them visually, instinctively resorted to scenes where the impact or resistance of contrary forces could suggest the enormous energy generated on either side.

One aspect of this innovation can be seen in the change which began to affect pictorial and sculptural representations of heroic scenes. In an earlier period, before this concern with physical force had made itself felt, the Renaissance artist had preferred to impress the spectator with the calm potential and self-confidence of his heroic figures. Accordingly, he portrayed them either before the fight was joined, or after victory had been safely achieved. We may recall Donatello's *St. George* standing quietly with his shield at rest before him, Verrochio's equestrian statue of *Colleone* boldly setting out to engage in war, Cellini's *Perseus* displaying the already severed head of the Medusa, and, of course, Michelangelo's *David* gazing thoughtfully before him as he awaits the arrival of Goliath. The baroque artist, on the other hand, changes his focus to the climax of the conflict itself, the struggle between two mighty forces at the moment before victory has been finally achieved. There is Giambologna's statue of *Hercules Wrestling with the Centaur*, pitting all his muscular strength against a formidable adversary who refuses to submit; there is Rubens' painting of the same Hercules forcing down Envy's head with a powerful thrust of his leg as he is about to bring his thick club crashing down for the death-blow (Plate 8). The tremendous thigh muscle bulging in exertion illustrates clearly enough the desire here to demonstrate enormous strength in action.[10] A new phenomenon too is to be found in the many battle scenes painted in this era (a subject rare indeed in the Renaissance[11]) where the clash of two massed cavalry charges creates a dynamic vortex of violent movement as in *The Conquest of Tunis by Charles V* or *The Battle of the Amazons* (Plate 9), again by Rubens.

The latter painting offers a classic instance of the change suggested here. Rubens' *Battle of the Amazons* is based on one of the very few battle scenes painted during the Renaissance, *The Battle of Cadore* by Titian. This mural was destroyed by fire in 1577, but sufficient contemporary copies and engravings of it survive for us to have an accurate picture of the original; and a comparison with Rubens' canvas is instructive. The narrow curved bridge in the centre of the two pictures is identical, but Titian catches the battle scene at the moment when the enemy has already been vanquished. To the left we see the enemy troops already fleeing from pursuit, while a victorious figure on horseback has just galloped across the empty bridge to finalise his triumph. In contrast, Rubens moves the battle back in time to the high-point of the combat. The two opposing forces have met in tremendous collision at the very centre of the bridge, with horses rearing on their muscular haunches, as warriors struggle vigorously around them. The narrowness of the bridge constricts and thereby intensifies the main impact, and as a result, the pressures created force themselves outwards in the form of bodies flung turbulently to either side. In all such paintings, then, it is the resistance of the hostile force which elicits and thereby displays to the viewer the strength of the hero's flexed and straining biceps, or reveals the enormous energy created by the collision of two onrushing armies, whose participants, evocative of the new infinity of forces, are made to appear countless in number as they crowd upon one another.

For the same reason, the baroque rejects that easy margin of victory which had previously marked the assured superiority of the legendary hero. In Raphael's *St. George and the Dragon*, for example, the knight, seated astride a white charger, is unperturbedly about to slice off the head of some wretched dragon which obviously stands not the slightest chance against its noble opponent, while a grateful maiden admires her rescuer from afar. Now, however, it is the narrowness of the victory over an otherwise invincible enemy which arouses respect; for the strength and fury of the foe demonstrates *a minori* the greater might required from the hero in order to overcome him. In this respect, the baroque ideal might be described as an attempt to come as close as humanly possible to depicting that hypothetical moment when an Irresistible Force meets an Immovable Object, and the viewer can gaze in awe at the magnitude of the struggle.

In architecture there is a similar concern with the pressures created by contrary stresses and tensions. Inside the building as well as without, the crushing weight of heavy masonry is held up by massive pillars clustered together to convey with full visual effect the strain of supporting the downward gravitational pressures. Within the baroque setting, the pillars are always far in excess of the structural requirements of the building, frequently performing only an illusory function as pilasters protruding from the flat wall. They are placed there not only as ornamentation but to create the impression of a dynamic interplay between the weight exerted from above and the support required from below. Where previous eras had used spacious stained-glass windows, slender columns, and graceful fan-tracery to produce an atmosphere of airiness and light, the baroque interior usually creates a sense of oppressive solidity, and in contrast to the tall arcades of Brunelleschi, the baroque church lowers and thickens the side arches set into the walls until they appear squat, as though with difficulty supporting the countless courses of stucco and marble which themselves bear the stone cornice above. On the façades of these churches, inner stone porticos seem, as we have seen, to struggle against the constriction of the outer frames by which they are enclosed, again suggesting the resistance of opposing forces; entire buildings are, as it were, placed ponderously one upon the other; and the massive domes, unlike the delicate spires or pinnacles of the Gothic, now press downward on the solid supporting structure below.

Even paintings devoid of struggles between protagonists catch something of this concern with resistant forces. In Rubens' *Descent from the Cross*, particularly the fuller version in Antwerp Cathedral, the burden of the lifeless body is wonderfully conveyed by the mourners bracing themselves as they strain to support it from below while another figure, holding fast to the upper section of the cross, grasps the corner of the taut shroud in his clenched teeth to help relieve the heavy downward pull of the corpse. One need only compare with this the insubstantial body in Rogier Van der Weyden's earlier version of the scene to perceive how this new interest in gravitational stresses had begun to dominate art. Each force here is matched by a counter-force, not to create the proportioned balance admired by the Renaissance, but to depict, particularly in the battle scenes, the enormous energy exerted and hence the prodigious strength required from the victor in order for him to prevail.

This baroque impulse to display mighty forces in combat has, I believe, a very special relevance to the problem of Satan in *Paradise Lost*. It has long been assumed that Milton's main purpose in the epic was to argue for the rightness of the divine cause and thereby to win the reader over to God's side. Accordingly, the poet was expected, rather like the Renaissance artist in depicting his hero's victory, to display the clear triumph of God over the forces of evil. Judged by such expectations, the positive elements in Satan's character—his vigour, fortitude, and resourcefulness—were seen as a failing on Milton's part, the result of his unconscious empathy with the rebel which serves to swing our own sympathies away from God towards the wrong side. Blake saw the epic in terms of this need for alliance with one or other side. There are two factions at war; Milton ought to have stood together with God, but, without knowing it, he was, as Blake put it, '. . . of the Devil's party'.

That assumption concerning Milton's purpose needs to be questioned. From our knowledge of the baroque mode, as indeed from the text itself once we are made aware of the connection, it seems more likely that in the early books Milton was less interested in taking sides, in offering the reader an unequivocal choice between good and evil, than in creating a vision. His aim initially was rather to impress the reader with the immensity of the conflict between two awesomely powerful forces. Only after that immensity had been visualised and the reader had seen invincible might set against apparently irresistible power, could the magnitude of the eventual victory for God's forces be appreciated.

That change in the conception of Milton's purpose may not provide a final answer to the question of Milton's success or failure with the figure of Satan, but it does at the very least suggest a different set of criteria. For in that baroque setting, the elevation of Satan to heroic dignity ceases to be in itself a literary failing. On the contrary, it becomes an essential ingredient in the overall design, a positive factor in creating the dynamic grandeur of the epic theme. Without such enlargement of his strength, leadership, and valour, Satan could not fulfil his role as the redoubtable challenger of God whose defiance will call forth the panoply of heavenly might before he can be subdued. God the Creator had always been formally recognised in Christian theology as omnipotent. The baroque artist, however, wanted to conceive this abstract heraldic attribute in terms of a physical demonstration of divine power which he could depict in visual or epic form. It could only be so conceived by the device of placing in opposition to God a formidable antagonist whom the forces of heaven would need to resist and eventually crush. The greater the courage, strength, and tenacity of the rebel challenger, the more impressive would be the final victory.

Such a view has implications for Milton's choice of theme; for it is significant that after long deliberation, and after considering numerous alternative subjects, he eventually selected the only theme in all Christian history which would allow him to present a celestial conflict of such vast dimensions—a battle between the martial host of heaven and the rebel forces drawn from within their own ranks whose strength could feasibly equal their own. In the course of presenting that conflict, Milton elevates Satan from his traditional role as the gloating, crafty, and often comic dragger of souls to hell familiar from medieval and Renaissance art and literature into the dignified figure of—as he now calls him—the 'Arch Adversary'. Satan's new titles, unprecedented in previous literature, such as the Arch Rebel, the Grand Foe, the Arch Antagonist (titles conferred upon him not by his followers but by the authorial voice of the epic) suggest an enemy worthy of God's concern who, while we are under the spell of the more heroic passages, seems indeed to threaten the security of the divine throne. In this Miltonic setting, he becomes imaginatively that powerful counter-force of the baroque who *durst defy the Omnipotent to arms*.

However impossible it may be within the bounds of logical thought for any creature to overthrow the Supreme Creator, Satan is never presented in the early books as a petty or trivial challenger to be brushed aside like a troublesome insect, but rather as one who 'trusted to have equalled the Most High'. He is, as we are so often reminded in the epic, the erstwhile Archangel, clothed until recently in transcendent light, whose form has not yet lost its original brightness, nor all its splendour. If we know he is doomed to fail in his major enterprise of usurping the divine throne, a full-scale battle will be required in order to prevent him, and even then he will succeed in snatching out of his defeat that partial victory which is to have such dire consequences for mankind. Throughout the early books, it is the *seeming* threat to heaven that holds us enthralled, and that illusion is created in no small part by the impressive stature of Satan himself and of the army he leads. There is a ring of truth in the awed description of him by Beelzebub:

> Leader of those Armies bright
> Which but th'Omnipotent none could have foil'd.
>
> (I, 272–3)

Militarily they are the mightiest force that could ever have been assembled to hurl themselves in defiance against God. Even after their defeat, as the scattered troops reassemble in Hell under the 'experienc't eye' of their Commander, they present a stirring image of martial splendour, a force to be reckoned with, even as adversaries to the celestial host:

> . . . forthwith from the glittering Staff unfurl'd
> Th' Imperial Ensign, which full high advanc't
> Shone like a Meteor streaming to the Wind
> With Gems and Golden lustre rich imblaz'd
> Seraphic arms and Trophies: all the while
> Sonorous metal blowing Martial sounds:
> At which the universal Host upsent
> A shout that tore Hell's Concave, and beyond
> Frighted the Reign of Chaos and old Night.
> All in a moment through the gloom were seen
> Ten thousand Banners rise into the Air
> With Orient Colors waving: with them rose
> A Forest huge of Spears: and thronging Helms
> Appear'd, and serried Shields in thick array
> Of depth immeasurable. Anon they move
> In perfect Phalanx to the Dorian mood
> Of flutes and soft Recorders: such as rais'd
> To highth of noblest tempers Heroes old
> Arming to Battle . . . .
>
> (I, 535–53)

Those who, like Blake, have regarded Satan's heroic qualities as militating against Milton's purpose, may have been too far removed from the seventeenth century to recognise in Satan that vital baroque counter-force required to demonstrate God's might. On the other hand, such critics did have evidence in the text to support their assumption that Milton's intent in the poem was primarily theodical. He did, after all, declare it as his aim to *justify the ways of God to men,* and for such a purpose the Promethean attractiveness of Satan does seem inappropriate. If, however, in the context of this baroque reading we turn back to the passage in the invocation on which that assumption was based, the evidence to be found there is by no means so conclusive. For there the attempt to offer divine justification is only the second of two declared purposes. The first, Milton states, is to *assert Eternal Providence,* an aim identical with the main baroque impulse—to demonstrate that even the vast, newly revealed cosmos is under the supervision of a Supreme Power who, from the beginnings of creation until eternity, controls and watches over all. And within Milton's statement can be perceived the further desire of the artist, to achieve in the course of that demonstration an enlargement of our vision both of the heavens and of the moral issues involved:

> What in me is dark
> Illumine, what is low, raise and support;
> That to the highth of this great Argument
> I may assert Eternal Providence,
> And justify the ways of God to men.
>
> (I, 22–6)

The two aims are not identical, as has so long been assumed, but in a broader sense sequential. It is only after he has proved or 'asserted' against the growing concept of a mechanistic and self-governing heaven the idea of a Creator infinite in power, authority, and wisdom, that Milton can proceed to the implications of that divinely controlled universe for mankind in his justification of God's role in the Fall and Expulsion of man from Eden.[12]

In a different connection it was pointed out some years ago that in the last line of this quotation the words 'to men' are ambiguously placed. The phrase does not necessarily mean, as has normally been thought, that Milton will offer to men a justification of God's ways but rather that he will justify *the ways of God to men*, that is, God's treatment of mankind.[13] This view is greatly strengthened by its repetition later by Raphael (this time, unambiguously) when he remarks that the angels always '. . . inquire/Gladly into the ways of God with Man' (VIII, 225–6). Although the latter reading is not essential to this present interpretation, it certainly lends a greater sharpness to the phrase, and strengthens the impression that Milton had two distinct purposes in mind. First comes the assertion of Eternal Providence as he recounts the challenge of Satan, the demonstration of God's heavenly might, and the divine supervision of the cosmos at large. Then, with that established, we turn to the second theme, the ways of God *to men*, focussing down from the heavens and the angelic hosts to Adam and Eve in the Garden, their fall, their punishment, and the act of divine mercy offering them future redemption.

The significance of all this for the problem of Satan is considerable. By the previous looser reading of the text which saw the two aims as being one, the theme of divine justification has generally been read back into the opening books too, as though there Milton was concerned with persuading us of the justice of Satan's punishment. If that were indeed his main aim, then clearly any sympathy aroused for the rebel would enfeeble the author's defence of God, and the more villainous Satan appeared the more convincing would be God's justification. We should recall, however, that Milton defines the main subject of the epic as being *Man's* disobedience, not the devil's; and the early books are concerned not with God's treatment of Satan but with the baroque display of cosmic might in which Satan's heroic qualities increase enormously the range and vigour of the scene.

So far this suggestion of a dual theme in the epic has concentrated on the wording of the invocation, and that alone might appear finally to be a matter of individual interpretation; but as the epic proceeds, the text confirms time after time that the purpose of the early books is, as has been suggested, to elicit a demonstration of divine power by means of a challenge. In his opening speech, Satan ruefully admits that his abortive rebellion has achieved the very reverse of its desired aim. Instead of dislodging God as he had hoped, their insurrection has provided proof of what they most had feared, the supremacy of the Creator. His own defeat is the strongest evidence of divine might:

> . . . into what Pit thou seest
> From what highth fall'n, *so much the stronger prov'd*
> *He with his Thunder: and till then who knew*
> *The force of those dire Arms?*
>
> (I, 91–4)

Until their attempt, he points out, no-one knew the strength of God except by hearsay but now, after this demonstration, there can be no doubt of God's power.

His lieutenant Beelzebub offers the same testimony from a contrary viewpoint. While agreeing with Satan that the result of their mutiny has been perversely to glorify God, he finds cause for comfort even in that fact. The rebel forces may not have evicted the Creator from his throne, but in Beelzebub's eyes it was enough of an achievement to have compelled God to come forth and answer their

challenge, and thus put his great powers to the test. In recognition of
that accomplishment, he can still address his commander with awe
even after their defeat, for having put God to the proof:

> O Prince, O Chief of many Throned Powers,
> That led th' imbattl'd Seraphim to War,
> Under thy conduct, and in dreadful deeds
> Fearless, endanger'd Heav'n's perpetual King:
> *And put to proof his high Supremacy* . . . .
>
> (I, 128–32)

In this first book which, like the invocation, sets the stage for the
events which are to follow (and, in a sense, even for those which
have already occurred, since the War in Heaven is to be recounted
to the reader retrospectively in Book VI), we return repeatedly to
this central theme, the enormous power of the apparently unconquerable rebel forces, and the even greater power which God had
till then held in abeyance, having never been called upon to utilise
it. Our realisation in the accounts of the battle scenes that in fact
God scarcely stirs in crushing the revolt, employing only a fraction
of his strength and that through emissaries, augments yet further
our sense of his immeasurable force. Thus Satan, gazing at his
own vast army, impressive even after their defeat, expresses his
amazement that such martial strength could ever have been conquered:

> O Myriads of immortal Spirits, O Powers
> Matchless but with th' Almighty . . .
>   . . . what power of mind
> Foreseeing or presaging, from the Depth
> Of knowledge past or present, could have fear'd
> How such united force of Gods, how such
> As stood like these, could ever know repulse?
>
> (I, 622–30)

Again he reminds himself that the Creator's strength had never
previously been tested and who, he asks, could have assessed his
might merely on repute? The Arch Rebel had insisted on seeing that
force in action, on calling God, as it were, forth from his hidden
place, and it is his very insistence on testing God's 'concealed' power
which fascinates Milton as a baroque artist, longing himself to

witness the display imaginatively and to share his wonder with the reader:

> But he who reigns
> Monarch in Heav'n, till then as one secure
> Sat on his Throne, upheld by old repute,
> Consent or custom, and his Regal State
> Put forth at full, *but still his strength conceal'd,*
> *Which tempted our attempt, and wrought our fall,*
> *Henceforth his might we know.*

(I, 637–43)

Such references can be multiplied many times over from the poem. Their combined effect is to suggest that Milton's purpose in the early books is not simply to teach the lesson that the wicked are punished in heaven as well as on earth. For that he could have managed very well with a traditional Satan, jealous, malignant, and corrupt. As he repeatedly informs us, however, his aim is rather to provide a physical demonstration of God's supremacy in terms of a cosmic clash of forces. In such a setting, Satan's stature in the poem as the formidable challenger needs no apology, nor psychological explanation on the grounds of Milton's personal or political predilections. It has, for example, been rightly shown by C. S. Lewis that Milton made a clear and very logical distinction between the Republicanism he advocated on earth where all men are created equal, and the unquestioned kingship in heaven of God whose supremacy is of right.[14] The attempt to project Milton's dislike of human autocracy into the celestial sphere and hence to assume an unwitting identification with Satan's 'Promethean' revolt is to attach to Milton a confusion of mortal and divine prerogatives of which he was never guilty.

There does, indeed, seem a touch of perversity in the way scholars have spoken of Milton's supposedly *unconscious* sympathy with the rebels, as though so experienced a poet would have been quite unaware of the positive responses evoked by his more stirring images. Here, for example, as the scattered rebels form their serried ranks once again in preparation for resuming the war, he describes how

> Anon they move
> In perfect *Phalanx* to the *Dorian* mood

Of flutes and soft Recorders: such as rais'd
To highth of noblest temper Heroes old
Arming to Battle . . . .

(I, 549–53)

Can one seriously argue that Milton was unaware of the effect
produced by these lines, that he did not know of the admiration he
was evoking by associating the rebels with the noblest heroes of old,
marching in perfect phalanx, and breathing 'deliberate valor'? Any
theory that maintains such associations are unintentional must
assume an extraordinary obtuseness on Milton's part. And the same
applies to Waldock's argument that the authorial comments in the
epic were attempts by the poet to rectify the excessive attractiveness
of Satan's speeches by dampening them down for the reader. If a
writer discovers that he has overwritten a speech, and glorified the
speaker in a way he has not intended, what is to prevent him from
rewriting the speech? No author in his senses, having recognised
that he had made such an error, would have left the badly written
passage untouched and appended a corrective; yet that is ultimately
what Waldock's argument implies.

When, however, we have perceived that the more positive
qualities in Satan's depiction are deliberate, and form an integral
part of the epic's structural form, they can then be acknowledged in
their own right without suspicion on our part that they militate
against Milton's purpose or against our moral code. A condemnation of the Arch Antagonist for his diabolical plan to corrupt
mankind can exist side-by-side with an admiration for his sense of
the responsibilities inherent in his assumption of leadership and his
courage in fulfilling them—for these are precisely the qualities
highlighted in Milton's description of the event. After outlining his
plan, Satan waits for a volunteer to stand up and declare himself
from among the 'Heav'n-warring Champions', as being willing to

      . . . undertake
The perilous attempt; but all sat mute,
Pondering the danger with deep thoughts; and each
In other's count'nance read his own dismay
Astonisht: none among the choice and prime
Of those Heav'n-warring Champions could be found
So hardy as to proffer or accept
Alone the dreadful voyage; till at last

> *Satan*, whom now transcendent glory rais'd
> Above his fellows, with Monarchal pride
> Conscious of highest worth, unmov'd thus spake . . . .
>
> (II, 419–29)

His reason for undertaking the intimidating task, at least as Milton presents the picture, has no hint of selfishness or duplicity about it, such as might have been expected from the Prince of Darkness, but rather a consciousness of the duties which belong to office, and a willingness to accept the dangers involved together with the honours:

> Wherefore do I assume
> These Royalties, and not refuse to Reign,
> Refusing to accept as great a share
> Of hazard as of honor, due alike
> To him who Reigns, and so much to him due
> Of hazard more, as he above the rest
> High honor'd sits?
>
> (II, 450–6)

Satan's charisma is, of course, only one aspect of his portrayal, and in drawing attention to his more admirable traits there is no intention here of minimising the real evils present in his complex character from the very beginning of the poem. His vain boasting, his envy of superior worth, his implacable hatred, these are the qualities which prepare the way for our later and total rejection of him. They are the filaments leading from the early characterisation to his degradation in the form of a hissing serpent at the conclusion of the epic. But the process of degradation is a long one, reaching its consummation only after Satan has accomplished his daring mission. In the earlier books when the reader is introduced, partly in retrospect and partly at the moment of action, to the celestial conflict between the forces of good and evil, this seventeenth-century concern with the powerful counter-force in art demanded a Satan of stature and martial eminence.

What has been left open is the function of the authorial asides within the context of this reading of the poem. If they are not there as lame and tardy attempts to rectify an unfortunate overwriting of the scene, why are they there at all? Milton, in fact, has a subtle balance to maintain. On the one hand, as a baroque artist he must

convey the impression that the two contrary forces are approximately equal in might and each still struggling to attain mastery,
yet at the same time he must endeavour to align our sympathies with
the eventual victor lest, through that near-equality, they move in
the wrong direction. Within such a context, the grandeur of Satan's
presentation elevates him to the level of the formidable opponent,
while the 'asides' serve as reminders in the course of our watching
the celestial conflict that Satan, for all his vigour, remains the
subordinate counter-force whose ultimate defeat we are to anticipate.
Both the ennoblement of Satan and his subordination must
therefore be carefully co-ordinated to produce a unified and not a
self-contradictory effect.

This process can be seen at work in one of the passages most
frequently quoted by those arguing for the 'Satanist fallacy'. In the
following lines Satan is first depicted in full splendour, associated
with the vigour of cosmic exploration, his spear compared to the
mast of some great warship:

> . . . the superior Fiend
> Was moving toward the shore; his ponderous shield
> Ethereal temper, massy, large and round
> Behind him cast; the broad circumference
> Hung on his shoulders like the Moon, whose Orb
> Through Optic Glass the *Tuscan* Artist views
> At evening from the top of *Fesole*,
> Or in *Valdarno*, to descry new Lands,
> Rivers or Mountains in her spotty Globe.
> His Spear, to equal which the tallest Pine
> Hewn on *Norwegian* hills, to be the Mast
> Of some great Ammiral, were but a wand . . . .
>
> (I, 283–94)

The initial phrase 'superior Fiend' already contains a hint of the
duality, but it is his superiority, not his fiendishness, which absorbs
our attention as the description becomes charged with grandeur.
Then at the height of his exaltation comes the reminder that he is
the defeated combatant. It comes, though, not as a humiliating
deflation, nor as nullifying completely the majestic quality of his
movement towards the shore. There is instead a quiet shift of focus
down towards his feet as they step painfully over the scorching
surface of hell, the symbol of his ultimate inferiority to God:

> . . . a wand
> He walkt with to support uneasy steps
> Over the burning Marl, not like those steps
> On Heaven's Azure, and the torrid Clime
> Smote on him sore besides, vaulted with Fire . . . .

The overall perspective of the conflict has been restored. With Satan's secondary position established, the elevating description can be resumed at once, now emphasising the courage of his endurance, and his determination to resist, which make him the only fit rival to stand against God:

> Nathless he so endur'd, till on the Beach
> Of that inflamed Sea, he stood and call'd
> His legions, Angel Forms . . . .

Here the balance is achieved internally, within the same descriptive passage, but it provides a valuable pointer to the famed 'authorial' comments too. Waldock had argued that whenever Satan delivers one of his 'glorious' speeches, it is always followed by a snub, jab, or growl from Milton as the poet realises that he has gone too far. In fact, we find not a nervous jab as he suggests, but a restoration of the controlling viewpoint as Satan's claim to eventual victory over God is seen to be baseless. Satan's heroic speech is followed by the comment:

> So spake th' Apostate Angel, though in pain,
> Vaunting aloud, but rackt with deep despair:
> And him thus answer'd soon his bold Compeer.
> O Prince, O Chief of many Throned Powers . . . .
>
> (I, 125–8)

Even within this authorial comment, the dignity of Satan is maintained; for his inferiority to God is presented in a manner which evokes almost as much admiration for him as disdain. Waldock asks here: 'Has there been much despair in what we have just been listening to? The speech would almost seem to be incompatible with that.' But surely that is Milton's point. This is not literary inconsistency but dramatic insight. Although inwardly racked with doubts, Satan has allowed no hint of his own fears to escape his lips as he exhorts his followers to resistance. This is the fortitude of Satan, as Beelzebub later recalls, which has always inspired his troops when their situation had seemed most bleak. His voice has at all times been 'thir liveliest pledge/Of hope in fears and dangers.' Now too, vanquished as they are, at the very nadir of their hopes in the gulf of Hell, they flock to his banner, relieved '. . . to have found thir chief/Not in despair'. His high words may, as the narrator remarks, have only a semblance of worth, but they achieve their purpose to the full in having '. . . gently rais'd/Thir fainting courage and dispell'd thir fears'. What has been seen as a discrepancy between soaring speech and authorial jab is a perfectly integrated depiction of a military leader daunted within, yet determined to rally his troops for a bold counter-attack, and succeeding even in overcoming his own doubts.[15]

In the larger view, then, there is little cause for the reader to feel guilty at his instinctive admiration of certain nobler traits in Satan, nor to blame Milton for having unintentionally aroused our sympathies for the wrong character; for it is that very admiration which, in the cosmic conflict projected by the baroque artist, succeeds in elevating Satan to the status of a worthy challenger of God—worthy, if not in the moral, then at least in the martial sense of the term, where such qualities as strength, resourcefulness, leadership, and personal courage have their rightful place.

One last point in this connection. In a famous comment, Dryden remarked that *Paradise Lost* violates the tradition of the epic; Milton, he says, would have had a better claim for membership in the genre '. . . if the giant had not foiled the knight and driven him out of his stronghold'.[16] According to this view, then, the rightful hero of the poem was Adam, and his succumbing to Satan damaged the literary form Milton had adopted. John Steadman, in a wide-ranging study, has provided a full picture of the ideal Renaissance hero as he was conceived in the period prior to the composition of *Paradise Lost*, and he examines the way Milton needed to adapt that tradition to the requirements of his biblical theme.[17] Sidney had stated that the hero in such works '. . . doth not only teach and move to a truth, but teacheth and moveth to the most high and excellent truth; who maketh magnanimity and justice shine through all misty fearfulness and foggy desires'.[18] The problem is that such enquiry into the nature of the adaptation to a biblical theme assumes Milton to have been essentially a Renaissance humanist and, as I suggested previously, there is every indication that when he wrote *Paradise Lost*, and certainly by the time he had concluded it, he had already transferred his allegiance from that Renaissance tradition to the newer baroque mode. In the latter setting, the calm moral dignity of the central character was of far less interest than the demonstration of might by means of a clash of forces, where Satan's depiction gains a justifiable prominence at the expense of Adam's. In other words, Satan's vigour is a literary blemish in the poem only if the work is judged by the standards of the tradition Milton had discarded.

A close examination of the changes which Milton gradually introduced into his plans for the poem between the late 1630s and the time of its completion thirty years later suggests that each decision on his part marked a further stage in his progression away from that High Renaissance tradition and towards the newer art form. When Milton began plans for this major poem he was, of course, as yet unsure whether it should take the form of tragedy or epic. About one point, however, he was at that early period quite certain—that he must decide '. . . what king or knight before the conquest might be chosen in whom to lay the pattern of a Christian hero'.[19] On his own testimony, therefore, he was at this stage still thinking in terms of a work conforming to the Renaissance pattern, something after the style of Spenser or Tasso, with a hero embodying moral, Christian ideals. The Trinity College manuscript, assigned by most scholars to the period just after his return from Italy, 1639–41, is particularly helpful for gauging the direction of his thought at this time. Of some hundred or so topics listed there, drawn mainly from the Bible or English history, prominence is already given to the biblical themes, with detailed drafts of plot for *Adam Unparadiz'd* and the stories of Abraham and Lot.

The choice of these subjects and their treatment in the outlines indicate that the new trends with which he had come into contact in Italy had not yet been assimilated; and it is even possible that the list was compiled before the visit took place. The plots here are basically humanistic in their concern, focussing attention upon man and his activities on earth. *Adam Unparadiz'd* is set entirely within the confines of Eden, where Gabriel and Lucifer visit Adam in order respectively to protect and corrupt him, and the expulsion of Lucifer from heaven is merely recounted as a past event. After eating the fruit:

Adam then and Eve returne accuse one another but especially Adam layes the blame to his wife, is stubborn in his offence Justice

appeares reason with him convinces him the chorus admonisheth
Adam, and bids him beware by Lucifers example of
impenitence . . . at last appeares Mercy comforts him promises
him the Messiah, then calls in faith, hope and charity, instructs
him he repents gives God the glory, submitts to his penalty the
chorus briefly concludes.[20]

There is no hint here of a battle in heaven, of the prominence of
Satan in the poem, nor of the spatial dimensions whereby Milton
was eventually to expand the epic form. Only a few years later does
Satan begin to rise to the fore in Milton's mind. Edward Phillips
records that some fifteen or sixteen years before Milton began
serious work on *Paradise Lost* (its composition being postponed by his
political obligations) he showed his nephew some lines he had
written for the proposed tragedy. Intended as an opening speech, it
was later incorporated into the epic as Satan's envious address to the
Sun:

> O thou that with surpassing Glory crown'd,
> Look'st from thy sole Dominion like the God
> Of this new World: at whose sight all the Stars
> Hide their diminisht heads; to thee I call,
> But with no friendly voice, and add thy name
> O Sun, to tell thee how I hate thy beams . . . .
>
> (IV, 32-7)

Compared with the vitality, the range, and the poetic vigour of the
epic as a whole in its final form, these lines were with justice singled
out long ago by critics as being relatively tame, lacking the
complexities and pressures of feeling which distinguish the epic
elsewhere.[21] After the 'immortal hate' with which Satan is associated in the rest of the epic, and the defiant pride which drives
him to revenge, it comes as an anticlimax to find him calling to the
Sun' . . . But with no friendly voice'. The theme of rebellion has
emerged, but the language as yet lacks the imaginative vigour and
sense of resisted might which mark Milton's High Baroque phase.
    These lines show, however, that Milton was leaving behind the
allegorical world which had formed the setting for his *Comus*. In the
original draft outline quoted above, he had sketched out in the
Spenserian tradition visits by the personified figures of Justice and
Mercy, who come to admonish and comfort Adam, leading to the

climax as Faith, Hope, and Charity enter to lend their assistance. It is all a little reminiscent of *Everyman* and *The Faerie Queene*. But now there is a growing interest in the cosmic possibilities of the theme as Satan addresses the Sun, crowned with surpassing glory. Those cosmic possibilities become increasingly exploited until Adam, although still the nominally central figure of the poem, is eventually dwarfed by the immense struggle taking place in the heavens, a conflict whose outcome would determine his own fate.

In fact, Milton's final choice of the epic in preference to tragedy may well have been dictated by this very gravitation towards the baroque ethos. Originally his instincts were all for drama. Apart from the list of projected tragedies which make it clear which way his thoughts had then been tending,[22] it has been pointed out that even in its final form *Paradise Lost* is 'an epic built out of dramas', remaining close to Milton's earlier inclinations.[23] What, then, prompted him finally to transfer to the epic form despite his natural proclivity for drama? Sir Arthur Quiller Couch many years ago explained the change with a bold rhetorical flourish: 'I give you the answer to that in a dozen words. *In 1642 Parliament closed the Theatres; which remained closed until the Restoration.*'[24] We should recall, however, that the Puritan opposition to the theatre did not prevent Milton from writing *Samson Agonistes* as a closet drama, and if this opposition may have acted as a contributory factor, it certainly does not alone explain Milton's decision.

There is, I think, another and more cogent reason. Tragedy by definition depicts the fall of a man through some blemish in his own character, and it is the pathos of his fall from high estate which is of absorbing interest. For such a genre, the story of Adam was ideally suited, as long as Milton conceived of Adam as occupying the centre of the stage, and as long as he regarded as the main purpose of the play the arousing within the audience of a sense of horror at his act. The classical epic, however, possessed a quality which must have appealed increasingly to Milton as his baroque interests drew him towards a more cosmic vision. For however independent and self-determining the hero of that genre may appear to be, he is in all forms of the classical epic a pawn in the hands of the gods, an instrument through whom one deity can wreak his spite or vengeance upon another. Odysseus is plunged into the seas by an angry Poseidon to be rescued by means of a magically buoyant scarf obligingly provided by the kindly Ino. The entire Trojan War began because Paris, giving the golden apple to Aphrodite, offended the other divine candidates who were in a position to make their anger felt. Accordingly the domestic conflicts and intrigues of the gods on Olympus occupy a major place in the subsequent unfolding of the story. It was a tradition adopted by the Roman epic too, where Aeneas, befriended by Neptune, is saved by him at the last moment from a watery death designed by an implacable Juno. It is this conflict between the gods above which lends the epic its larger dimensions, with the hero elevated above the level of normal human-beings by the protection or animosity of the various deities fighting each other over his fate. Such a setting was ideal for Milton's purpose as his focus moved beyond Adam's personal tragedy to his new conception of Eden as a testing-ground for the celestial battle above. His own epic, unlike that of Greece or Rome, would of course adopt the overall moral framework of the biblical tradition, ensuring that Adam should not be the entirely innocent victim of Satan's revenge upon God, but by his own disobedience should contribute to his fall. However, the cosmic possibilities of the epic lay ready to hand as the changes in Milton's artistic conceptions moved from a humanistic concern towards the conflict taking place in the infinite regions of heaven. There are strong grounds, therefore, for suspecting that his hitherto unexplained shift from the tragic genre to the epic may have reflected the change in his aesthetic affiliation, and his need for a literary form more closely suited to his new baroque aims.

At all events, the final version of the poem marks the culmination of Milton's gradual development away from the Renaissance ideal dominating his early writings. If, as is now generally believed, the two first books were in fact written last,[25] then the chronological progression is complete. Originally the work is conceived as a humanist tragedy, focussing on Adam's experiences in the Garden of Eden. It slowly becomes enlarged into a cosmic battle between heaven and hell as related in Book VI, to which the Fall is now a sequel. Then in the final stages of composition, the opening two books are added, where Satan's stature rises to that of the powerful baroque counter-force, challenging God to reveal his hidden strength and to display the immensity and infinitude of his power. In its completed form it now provides the most brilliant consummation of the baroque vision in English literature, and perhaps in literature at large. Even if those two opening books which have caused so much disturbance to critics were not written last, one may still perceive the overall change which took place between the composition of *Comus* and of *Paradise Lost*. That progression offers sufficient confirmation that Milton was not, as it were, born into the Grand Style and the cosmic setting, but developed these gradually as his own originally Renaissance sensibilities responded to the new mode spreading across Europe.

3 Corporal Forms

One characteristic aspect of the baroque has, until now, received here only passing mention, that aspect which has proved least attractive to our own era. As one moves from High to Late Baroque, there appear with increasing frequency sculpted or painted scenes of ecstasies and ascensions in which sacred figures from the Gospels or recently canonised leaders of the church are caught at the moment of visionary experience, or float heavenward on clouds, surrounded in their glory by admiring cherubs. Such subject-matter could at times be handled with real artistry, as in the finest of the ceiling frescoes examined in an earlier chapter, or in Bernini's famed Cornaro Chapel; but for others the theme of spiritual exaltation proved only too often an invitation to melodramatic overstatement. The extravagant gestures and theatrical emotionalism of such lesser works reflect a loosening of artistic control, and an appeal to stock response. Melchiorre Caffà's *The Ecstasy of St. Catherine* (1667) is typical of this type, a work of florid sentimentality, with the saint dramatically gathering her robes about her as though enamoured of her own purity and afraid of contamination by the mundane, as she floats upwards on a billowing cloud.[1]

The less palatable vein within the baroque has been ignored here not through personal selectivity on my part, but because it occupies no place in Milton's writings; and for a very good reason. The cosmic vision which attracted him to the baroque, although it had been artistically developed within the Counter-Reformation movement, was, as we have seen, not in itself a specifically Catholic view, and therefore remained accessible to Milton. On the other hand, the cult of sainthood and the apotheosis of mortals had always been a point of bitter theological controversy between the Catholic and the Reformed churches since the time of Luther's original protest in Wittenberg against the veneration of saints' relics. Martyrdom, as the supreme Christian act of *imitatio dei*, remained a noble act in Protestant theology, but opposition to the sanctification of saints' shrines became a prominent and recurrent theme in Protestant polemic. Joseph Mede, for example, castigated it as a pagan practice and a 'doctrine of daemons'.[2] For a Puritan such as Milton, the worship of saints or martyrs was anathema.

Even within the confines of the Catholic church, the accusations of the early Protestants had, during the sixteenth century, created an uncomfortable sensitivity on this point. As with many other charges of abuse, formal and public denial by the church was accompanied by a quiet attempt at rectification from within. While the sanctity of reliquaries and the use of saints' images were officially confirmed as valid parts of church ritual, at the same time efforts were made to reduce the element of pagan idolatry which, it was now recognised, had often entered into such worship. The Council of Trent reminded Christians that the honour shown to images when they genuflected before them '. . . should be directed to the prototypes which the images represent', and not to the images themselves. There was even a marked iconoclastic tendency among some of the new leaders. St. John of the Cross discouraged the use of images altogether, Loyola's meditative exercises laid a new stress on an *imaginative* visualising of the holy figures in place of their physical representation, and, as has been noted, Philip Neri forbade entirely the introduction of statues or frescoes into the newly built church of the Oratorians. Where images of saints were permitted, the Council laid down new restrictions, forbidding nudity as being a pagan importation, and above all requiring that religious art should be under strict disciplinary surveillance. It was to aim solely at moral instruction, providing an emotional stimulus to Christian piety.

Only when the fervour of the Counter-Reformation had subsided in the mid-seventeenth century did the artistic depiction of martyrs and saints come into its own again, and then, ironically, often in celebration of those very leaders who had been most vigorously opposed to it. They in their turn had now been canonised by the church, and formed the central figures in lavish sculptural representations of their apotheoses, executed in solid silver, lapis lazuli, onyx, and porphyry.[3] The lesson had, however, been learnt in one respect. No longer a vehicle for classical nudity nor a sop to semipagan superstition, the baroque epiphanies were now consciously aimed at arousing in the spectator a devotional mood. This marked a more positive religious purpose. On the other hand, such overt didacticism had its own disadvantages, often introducing a degree of mawkishness into the works. It has been rightly said in defence of the didactic intent that there existed in that era an unwritten code whereby such scenes were intended not to convert an antagonistic viewer, but rather to set off in an already sympathetic Catholic the mood of elevated devotion which he was himself anxious to experience. For that reason, such statuary deliberately exploited the stock or shared response which could most easily trigger off the desired emotion.[4] Whether in the final analysis that historical justification absolves the artist on aesthetic grounds is a question which need not concern us here, but it does at least offer some explanation of the motive behind that over-dramatisation and sentimentality, which were to become hallmarks of the later baroque.

In English poetry Crashaw is the most faithful exponent of the continental Catholic tradition, with his visions of disembodied saints rising from this earth to begin their spiritual existence in the skies. His 'Hymn to St. Teresa' describes in glowing images how she will be 'exhaled' heavenward as a vapour-like spirit, to be absorbed into the ranks of the other incandescent souls above:

> So fast
> Shalt thou exhale to heaven at last,
> In a dissolving sigh, and then
> O what! ask not the tongues of men,
> Angels cannot tell, suffice,
> Thyself shalt feel thine own full joys.
> And hold them fast forever. There,
> So soon as thou shalt first appear,
> The moon of maiden stars; thy white
> Mistress attended by such bright
> Souls as thy shining self, shall come,
> And in her first ranks make thee room.
> Where 'mongst her snowy family,
> Immortal welcomes wait on thee.[5]

Milton will have none of this. His heaven does not consist of vapour-like spirits floating on billowing clouds in dream-like ecstasy. On the contrary, the solidity of his heavenly scene is established from the beginning of the poem. Every part of his cosmos, infinite though it may be, is located precisely in space, and his angels have nothing in common with the baroque *putti* flitting adoringly about the feet of the rising saint. They are, instead, creatures of heroic stature and, indeed, of epic quality. From a

strictly theological point of view, Milton must of necessity acknowledge the insubstantiality of the angels, noting, for example, the
gradual decrease in physical solidity as one ascends the hierarchical
rungs of creation. The closer one draws to the divine throne, the
more refined, spiritous, and pure God's creatures become; and in
Book V he draws a graceful analogy to a flower whose lower section
is rooted in the soil, whose stalk and leaf spring lighter and more
airy, and whose topmost blossom breathes out intangible 'spirits
odorous' representing the angels themselves. However, within the
epic narrative his depiction of those angels remains closer to the
belief he enunciated in his prose tracts, that all creation (and angels
too are God's creatures) is imperishable, since matter itself is of
divine origin; '. . . if all things are not only from God, but of God,
no created thing can be finally annihilated'.[6] Whatever his
theological stand may have been, the angels as he presents them
imaginatively in *Paradise Lost* are far from being flimsy creatures
who, as medieval scholars had visualised them, could cluster by
their thousands on a pin's head. They are stalwart warriors of
muscle and vigour, guarding the outposts of heaven, patrolling the
approaches to earth, and in times of danger forming solid phalanxes
to resist hostile infiltration. On their missions, they do not appear
effortlessly at their destination, as diaphanous creatures lightly
imprinted upon the air in the normal Renaissance tradition,[7] but
must struggle laboriously through the immense regions of space,
surmount battlements, and obtain entrance through gates blocking
their way in order to pass from place to place.

Here too Milton was not fabricating a new idea, but selecting
from older traditions the version which suited his own needs
and preferences. The *putti* had been a late and essentially pagan
introduction into Christianity, serving in the Renaissance as a
means of sanctioning in religious paintings the cupids of Greek and
Roman mythology. The belief that the biblical cherub possessed the
face of an innocent child had helped to authorise that merger, but
conveniently ignored were the other physical characteristics implied by the biblical account. The stationing of a cherub with a
flaming sword at the entrance to Eden in order to prevent man's
return is a picture which scarcely accords with their portrayal in
painting and sculpture as harmless infant *amorini*. It was in that
former biblical tradition, conceiving of them as heavenly warriors,
that Milton refers to Satan as the 'Fallen Cherub', ignoring the
artistic changes that had intervened in the use of that term.

Behind Milton's preference for the tangible lies a change which goes beyond his Reformation opposition to saints' relics and apotheoses to a broader post-Renaissance theme of which that opposition was itself a symptom. Max Weber may have exaggerated in attributing to Protestantism the origins of the entire capitalist system, as though capitalism could not have arisen without it. It is now recognised that many of the early indications of new banking interests and the move away from the medieval suspicion of monetary profit as being a form of usury had appeared well before the rise of Protestantism.[8] It is nevertheless true that the Reformation coincided with and to no small extent sanctioned the surge of mercantile activity in the sixteenth century; and there was an interesting historical background to that sanctioning.

The Protestant, in an attempt to create a theological basis for his break-away from the Catholic church and his rejection of the supposedly divine authority of the Pope, had found in the early stories of the Old Testament the sources he required, and those stories began to take on a new importance in his eyes. There he discovered anew the doctrine of the Covenant, that God had originally made his contractual promise not with the body of the Church but with successively chosen individuals, each of whom had to deserve the right of election. Initially established with Abraham, the divine covenant had been renewed with Isaac and not with Ishmael, and in the next generation with Jacob and not with Esau, each time in contravention of the natural right of the firstborn. Here was proof that man's salvation depended ultimately on his individual relationship with his God, and not on the inalienable right of a priest or Pope through whom he must seek intercession.

However, in his reading of these Old Testament stories, a change occurred. They ceased to be merely shadowy prefigurations of New Testament events as the medieval world had regarded them, but came suddenly alive as the account of real people, men and women of flesh and blood with whom the Protestant, as the direct heir of that tradition, experienced a new and profound sense of identity. Gradually there came the realisation that, in contrast to the ascetic renunciation of wordly wealth advocated by the Gospels, the Old Testament (whose sanctity had never been abrogated), offered as a reward for the righteous the tangible gifts of this world. Abraham had been blessed for his faith '. . . with flocks, with herds, and with many servants'. Accordingly, the Protestant began to look into the material aspects of his own life for evidence of divine blessing, and hence of personal election to grace. As part of this affinity to the Hebrew tradition, he now welcomed the command to be fruitful and multiply which, as it now appeared, had never been specifically revoked by the New Testament; and in general he saw his Christian task as demanding not a meditative withdrawal from the world but rather an industrious application to honest labour which, favoured by heaven, should lead to legitimate material as well as spiritual recompense.

Here, then was a further meeting-point between Milton and the Catholic baroque, whatever else might divide them. His Puritanism led him towards a celebration of the created world, of the powerful physical forces operating within it, and of the bounty which God had bestowed on nature. The Catholic baroque too had chosen to convey a major part of its message through a validation of the actual, in its massive architraves and marble plinths, its exploitation of spatial stress, and its pictorial display of muscular conflict. To these more vigorous elements within the baroque Milton could respond unhesitatingly, while remaining impervious to the beatific epiphanies and other-worldliness which existed side-by-side with them. The Italian baroque, for all its glorification of the rich texture of God's universe, remained inevitably committed to the central Catholic doctrine that the flesh is corrupt and the soul alone pure. It was that doctrine which lay behind the ecstasies and apotheoses of the Counter-Reformation, where the soul rises in purity having discarded the encumbrance of the flesh. Here Milton parted ways. As a confirmed 'mortalist', he had argued in his *Christian Doctrine* that matter was not separable from the soul but an integral part of it: 'For the original matter of which we speak is not to be looked upon as an evil or trivial thing, but as intrinsically good, and the chief productive stock of every subsequent good.'[9]

At first sight there may appear a touch of absurdity in suggesting Milton's preference for physical materiality when so much of his epic is devoted to the discourse of heavenly angels and to the radiant assembly gathered about the divine throne. Such a response, however, can only occur away from the text; for among the most powerful achievements of *Paradise Lost* is its ability to convey the ethereal infinity of heaven in fully realised corporeal terms. From the very opening of the poem, as we move from the invocation into the narrative itself, that spatial security of the setting is firmly established. As Satan plummets down from heaven, he falls, we are told, 'Nine times the Space that measures Day and Night/To mortal men'. On the one hand, a fall of such magnitude suggests to the imagination the vast vacuity separating heaven from hell, and yet on the other hand that supposedly infinite distance is presented in measurable terms, a precise number of days and nights conveying the sense of a beginning and an end, with a clearly defined area between. Moreover, as Donald Davie has wisely observed, the syntactical inversion which places *Him* at the beginning of this passage:

> Him the Almighty Power
> Hurl'd headlong flaming from th' Ethereal Sky . . . .

creates an almost physical sensation of topsy-turviness, of Satan's falling head-over-heels in his plunging descent through the skies.[10]

Yet how, we may ask, could such a scene be described any differently, since the expulsion and fall from heaven down to hell form, after all, an integral part of the story and imply necessarily a physical movement through space with a beginning, a middle, and an end? Once again, it is the way the artist depicts the scene that counts even more than the subject-matter itself, and we need only compare earlier versions of the same story to perceive the qualitative difference in imaginative presentation and in the timbre of the verse. In that earlier tradition, particularly in the Renaissance with its desire to emphasise the ease of victory for the hero, the rebel angels are simply blown off the edge of heaven with an effortless puff. There is no sense of muscular conflict, no panic-stricken somersaulting through measurable space, no vivid actualisation to draw the reader into the terrifying scene as though he were experiencing that fall himself. Spenser, for example, leaves the heavens virtually undisturbed by the foolish attempt of the rebel angels:

> The brightest Angell, euen the Child of Light,
> Drew millions more against their God to fight.

> Th' Almighty seeing their so bold assay,
> Kindled the flame of his consuming yre,
> And with his onely breath them blew away
> From heauens hight, to which they did aspyre
> To deepest hell, and lake of damned fyre.[11]

In Milton's version, reader participation is well-nigh irresistible because of the tangibility of the description, and also because the verse contains a quality additional to that noted by Davie. For apart from the syntactical inversion to suggest headlong flight, the texture of the poetry compels us as we read it to descend the voice scale from the high opening of *Him* to the deep notes of *bottomless perdition* which mark the end of the grim journey, accompanying him vocally, as it were, as he plummets down:

> Him the Almighty Power
> Hurl'd headlong flaming from th'Ethereal Sky
> With hideous ruin and combustion down
> To bottomless perdition, there to dwell
> In Adamantine Chains and penal Fire . . . .

(I, 44–8)

Pictorial presentations of this scene by contemporary artists confirm that the difference between the passages by Spenser and Milton is not a matter of personal preferences distinguishing the two poets but of their instinctive response to the changing concepts of their respective eras. In the early sixteenth century, Hieronymus Bosch created his great triptych *The Haywain*. At the top of the left-hand panel, which depicts the story of man's expulsion from Eden, appears the Fall of the Angels (Plate 10) as the first step towards that expulsion. There a heavenly host of minute, winged creatures surrounds God in the form of a nimbus, while below them the rebel angels, looking for all the world like a cloud of gnats, float weightlessly downwards on their transparent wings. They constitute no threat to God, other than as a minor irritant, and their only significance lies in the damage they will do to man, whose Fall is depicted in the foreground of the panel. In contrast, Rubens' *Fall of the Damned*, painted in 1616 (Plate 11), captures the full dynamic impact of the baroque. In a blaze of light, an angel swoops from above holding a gleaming shield before him and driving myriads of fleshy, naked bodies tumbling in twisting and terrified flight down to the hell awaiting them below. By crowding the sprawling figures into a steep diagonal slope across the canvas, and by the chiaroscuro use of light and shade, he creates in the comparatively small area of his painting the effect of innumerable solid figures falling heavily through infinite space. And below, as in Milton, the unquenchable flames of hell burn unnaturally, producing 'No light, but rather darkness visible.'

There can be no precise counterpart for poetry in painting. They are separate media, each employing its own techniques and needing to overcome the limitations specific to its art-form, but it is instructive to explore how each uses its own resources to achieve the desired effects. In this instance, poetry had an initial advantage. Any visual presentation has no choice but to make darkness visible—without an overlay of darker paint the murkier hues cannot be conveyed. In poetry, however, the phrase 'darkness visible' is already a forceful paradox, presenting the mere absence of light as if it were a concrete entity which strikes the eye. The sense of its palpability is already achieved, and Milton reinforces it syntactically by then making darkness the active subject of the sentence. It usurps the function of light, and itself strangely 'discovers' the sights of hell and the shades within it:

> . . . one great Furnace flam'd, yet from those flames
> No light, but rather darkness visible
> Serv'd only to discover sights of woe,
> Regions of sorrow, doleful shades . . . .

> (I, 62–5)

The chiaroscuro effect of his scene, moreover, arises from a verbal device familiar in poetry, whereby a word such as *flam'd* can function in two opposite directions simultaneously. At the surface level, the literal meaning, we are informed that the flames emit only darkness, and their light is therefore negated; yet the very phrase *one great Furnace flam'd* has already conjured up a vision of brilliance before it is nullified, and that brilliance remains in the mind, intensifying by antithesis the blackness of the scene, and thereby creating verbally that energised contrast of opposites so central to the baroque.

Rubens, on the other hand, has no such verbal contrasts at his disposal, but he has other means no less effective. The lower section of his painting, the scene of hell, could have been presented by means of an evenly spread gloom, as in Michelangelo's *Last Judgement*, with its dark cavern just visible through the mists. Instead, Rubens' gloom comes alive and turbulent. Nightmarish shapes, suggestive of black monsters, surge up from below to overwhelm the bright falling figures by means of their huge bat-like wings or snaking tentacles. The monsters are not clearly delineated, only hinted at in the murky scene, so that the darkness itself seems to be rising hideously to suck the flesh into its depths. To the left burns the furnace of hell—but Rubens makes sure that it is not seen. The jagged rock-like rim of the crater obscures it, and set against its after-glow the blackness of that rim strikes the eye more forcibly than the brightness behind it. That contrast, together with the turbulent dark shapes below, again creates, although by different means, a palpable, dynamic blackness intensified by the incandescence.

Milton's technique of describing the immeasurable in finite terms might be thought to be no more than a natural extension of biblical anthropomorphism necessary for human understanding; and so it has generally been regarded. The Scriptures, while insisting doctrinally on divine incorporeality and ubiquity, nevertheless described God as stretching out his 'right hand' or as 'seated' upon his throne in order to accommodate the incomprehensible to the limited mental grasp of man. In the same way, it is argued, Milton was compelled to speak of the impalpable and the infinite as though they were bounded and solid. He does, indeed, openly acknowledge the need for such modification when Raphael, in relating to Adam the story of Creation, assures him that whatever surmounts the reach of human sense he will delineate by '. . . lik'ning spiritual to corporal forms' (V, 578). Since the reader shares Adam's human limitations and requires the concessions no less than Adam himself, Raphael's assurance in fact constitutes Milton's broader apology for the adjustments necessarily made throughout the epic.

Milton, however, goes far beyond the traditions sanctioned by biblical usage, and at the same time far beyond the modifications necessary for adapting the celestial to mortal comprehension. When, for example, the Bible relates in Genesis that God sent three angels to visit Abraham, it does not trouble to explain where precisely those angels were before their mission began, how long it took them to descend from heaven to earth, or what wing-span was needed to bear the weight of their bodies. They simply appear from nowhere, perform their tasks, and disappear as the story requires. In *Paradise Lost*, however, the mechanical, spatial, and dimensional elements of the celestial scene take on a prominence unprecedented in earlier accounts. The heavens are now endowed with powerful gravitational forces, with measurable distances, with massive colliding planets, and with marble, adamant, and brass familiar from the terrestrial sphere. It is as though that love of textured surface and of heavy, multicoloured stone which characterises the baroque had been projected on to the celestial scene; but, in contrast to the porphyry and onyx which seem visually to dissolve in the Catholic scenes of heavenly epiphanies, in Milton's depiction they retain, even in heaven, all the hardness and durability of their earthly form, multiplied many times over.

One reason for the change is an aspect of the new seventeenth-century cosmology which has not yet been mentioned here, although it forms an integral part of the changed concept of the universe. For a Renaissance poet such as Wyatt, Sidney, or Shakespeare, the moon in its fullness was still regarded as a perfect heavenly sphere, circling smoothly and harmoniously in the sky and, metaphorically at least, sympathising with the sonneteer's unrequited love. Part of the impact created throughout the civilised world when Galileo announced his discoveries was the revelation of the rough, corrugated surface of the moon which his telescope now afforded for the first time. The moon, he stated in his *Sidereus Nuncius*, '. . . certainly does not possess a smooth and polished surface, but one rough and uneven, and just like the face of the Earth itself, is everywhere full of vast protuberances, deep chasms, and sinuosities'. The British ambassador in Venice, Sir Henry Wotton, wrote excitedly to the Earl of Salisbury on the very day that the *Sidereus Nuncius* was published informing him that it had overthrown all former astronomy and astrology, and singling out for especial mention the discovery that '. . . the moon is not spherical, but endued with many prominences'.[12] Milton, like so many of his contemporaries, must himself have seen through such a telescope the deeply pitted surface of that moon, the craters, valleys, and hill ranges which showed it to be not a perfect 'celestial orb' in any Neoplatonic sense, but a craggy, physical mass moulded out of material substances, for he describes it in his poem as a 'spotty Globe' on which could be descried ' . . . new Lands/Rivers or Mountains'. (I, 290–1) The early telescope was not yet capable of providing detailed close-ups for the surfaces of all the more distant planets and satellites, but with the moon as evidence a similar consistency could be assumed for the other heavenly bodies too.[13]

The effect of this knowledge on poetry is apparent throughout Milton's epic. In the scene, for example, when Satan lands upon the sun, Milton, whimsically imagines him becoming visible from earth as a 'spot' unlike any normally seen by astronomers (the discovery of sun-spots had been amongst the most sensational events of the century), and with that reminder of the new science he proceeds to describe the surface of the sun in terms of the hard rocks, metals, and precious stones embedded in the soil of our own earth. In the same way as Galileo had revealed the moon to be 'just like the face of the Earth itself', so other heavenly bodies were now being viewed in those terms.

> There lands the Fiend, a spot like which perhaps
> Astronomer in the Sun's lucent Orb
> Through his glaz'd Optic Tube yet never saw.
> The place he found beyond expression bright,
> Compar'd with aught on Earth, Metal or Stone . . .
> If metal, part seem'd Gold, part Silver clear;
> If stone, Carbuncle most or Chrysolite,
> Ruby or Topaz . . . .
>
> (III, 588–97)

Similarly the Hell he envisages is, as so often in the poem, a reverse image of heaven, corrupt and horrid, yet constituted of basically the same elements, so that Mammon who (as his name suggests) is interested primarily in hoarding wealth, argues that hell offers the same resources as heaven above:

> This Desert soil
> Wants not her hidden lustre, Gems and Gold;
> Nor want we skill or art, from whence to raise
> Magnificence; and what can Heav'n show more?
>
> (II, 270–3)

One cannot miss in such descriptions, whether of heaven or hell, Milton's delight in the tactile quality and mineral wealth of the created world, projected imaginatively on to the distant celestial scenes, and it marks the convergence in his writings of two closely related impulses. By expressing infinity in measurable terms, and the heavenly scene as composed of firm, corporeal objects, he succeeds in celebrating at one and the same time the newly discovered physical cosmos, together with his own Protestant validation of the material world about him. For him they formed twin facets of the same divine creation. Where the Catholic baroque

continued in the main to spurn this world as transitory, offering up
its basalt, silver, and quartz as tributes to the ethereal beatification
of saints and martyrs, Milton moves in the opposite direction, so
authenticating the temporal that he informs the heavens themselves, even in their supposedly visionary form, with those material
properties and riches with which the earth is endowed.

The late Walter Curry, in a study of the physical laws and
cosmological processes operating in *Paradise Lost*, took a different
view. He was disturbed, for example, by the scene in which Sin and
Death build a Mole or causeway to link earth with hell. The
account, he felt, contains an unfortunate mingling of allegory and
literalism which creates 'artistic and logical difficulties' bordering
on the absurd.[14] Behind his criticism lies the assumption that, if
Milton was writing allegory, he ought to have restricted himself,
rather as Bunyan did, to abstract symbols, such as the Slough of
Despond (or, in this instance, we may say, the Mole of Backsliding)
only tenuously related to actuality, instead of cluttering up his
image with the mundane physical details of its construction.
However, what may have suited Bunyan's purpose would not suit
Milton's, where these details form an essential ingredient of the
sharply realised scene, without which we would be floating in an
insubstantial dream-like heaven such as Murillo's. Here the
incident is vividly conceived as Sin and Death, in ironic parody of
the dove-like Spirit of Creation, hover like birds of prey over the
watery chaos separating earth from hell. They drive together the
slimy flotsam tossed up by the waves, propelling it towards the
mouth of hell, where with Death's 'petrific Mace' they hammer it
into a firm and solid substance to form a massive, sloping bridge
down which man can more easily slither to the nether world:

> Deep to the Roots of Hell the gather'd beach
> They fasten'd, and the Mole immense wrought on
> Over the foaming deep high Archt, a Bridge
> Of length prodigious joining to the Wall
> Immovable of this now fenceless World
> Forfeit to Death; from hence a passage broad
> Smooth, easy, inoffensive down to Hell.

(X, 299–305)

The new 'de-fencelessness' of earth is expressed here not as an
abstract idea, but as a fact, mythic perhaps, but within the epic

setting presented in tactile terms in a universe where everything has its place, weight, and concrete reality.

Even such intangibles as light and dark are, as we have seen, treated in *Paradise Lost* as though they were substances to be felt and touched. Satan speaks of the '*palpable* obscure' through which the challenger must find his way, the word lending a murky solidity even to the emptiness and waste of Chaos:

> . . . who shall tempt with wandering feet
> The dark unbottom'd infinite Abyss
> And through the palpable obscure find out
> His uncouth way . . . ?

> (II, 404–7)

For many years it was taken for granted that the images of light and darkness predominating in the poem were a natural corollary of Milton's blindness, but in the context of the contemporary changes in the visual and plastic arts, they may be seen as deriving primarily from a baroque source. Certainly there are times when he makes that imagery touchingly applicable to his own affliction, when he complains, for example, that the piercing rays of God's sovereign lamp no longer visit his eyes. On the other hand, the dazzling brilliance of his heavens and the contrasts he draws with the darkness visible below are too intimately a part of the artistic scene in his day to be attributed to his personal disability alone. The evenly-spread light suffused through High Renaissance painting from a calm sky (the so-called 'Italian sky' imitated by so many painters) had been replaced in his era by an entirely new conception of light as a blazing, energised force, overpowering in its splendour. There is nothing in any earlier period comparable to the radiant sun symbol placed by Bernini above the Cathedra in St. Peter's, where from the bright yellow window surrounded by clustering cherubs solid bronze rods radiate to catch and reflect the light, making that light too appear tangible and solid. In painting, contrasting shafts of light now illumine faces or objects otherwise shrouded in darkness. In Caravaggio's *Death of the Virgin*, as in so many of his canvases, the hand of a weeping disciple, the bent head of a female mourner are picked out dramatically as islands of light in the sea of gloom. Or we may turn again to the Gaulli and Pozzo ceilings, where the refulgent blaze in the centre, although only painted on a flat ceiling, seems against the surrounding patches of shadow and cloud to pain the eye with its dazzling energy. Milton too describes God in his heaven as a blaze of light too bright for an angel's eye to look upon, even when God shades himself as with a cloud:

> Fountain of Light, thyself invisible
> Amidst the glorious brightness where thou sit'st
> Thron'd inaccessible, but when thou shad'st
> The full blaze of thy beams, and through a cloud
> Drawn round about thee like a radiant Shrine,
> Dark with excessive bright thy skirts appear
> Yet dazzle Heav'n, that brightest Seraphim
> Approach not, but with both wings veil thir eyes.
>
> (III, 375–82)

The image here is drawn *a minori* from the sun hiding its brilliance behind a cloud and suggests once more how profoundly the new view of the universe had changed the religious conception of the heavens. God had, of course, been identified with light since biblical times. Its appearance in the universe was the first act of creation, and the Psalmist had declared 'The Lord is my light'; but not in terms of a blinding radiance. One might imagine that Isaiah's description of the seraphim hiding their faces in the presence of God was close to this baroque view, particularly after the allusion in the passage above. In fact, Milton had adapted that passage to suit his own needs, and the change he introduced offers a further instance of the different paths which poetry and painting must take to achieve their effects.

In Pozzo's fresco, the sharp brightness is there to be seen. Even in that visual form, however, the lightness of the colours is insufficient to produce the blazing intensity he requires, and he employs various optical devices to create it. In the soaring infinity of the painting, the clearly defined figures of the angels nearest to us give place to mistier forms as they approach the source of the light. At the highest point, the angels are difficult to discern among the bright rays, just as they would be were an incandescence actually half-blinding our eyes; and the head of the cross held aloft there disappears completely in the blaze. In brief, the artist transfers to his fresco the light distortions which such blinding would create in the human eye. Milton can achieve part of that effect by description. He can speak of God as invisible in his glory, and intensify the brightness by verbal contrast ('Dark with excessive bright'); but he cannot make the reader himself experience physically the painful, dazzling brilliance which forces one to close one's eyes. He resorts therefore to a vicarious experience, inserting into his description the angels who, although themselves 'brightest Seraphim', the flaming angels of light, need to veil their eyes with both wings in order to protect them from the glare. It sounds biblical in origin, but in fact all we are told in the Isaiah passage is that: 'Above stood the seraphim; each had six wings, with twain he covered his face, with twain he covered his feet, and with twain did he fly.' With the first pair of wings, we should note, he covered not his eyes, but his face. He did so not to protect it from the light but, as ancient commentary pointed out and as the continuation of the verse makes clear, in order not to offend by exposing his face and feet in God's presence. The change which Milton introduced is the poet's method of allowing us to experience by transference the intense brightness which Pozzo effects by visual means.[15]

Here in Milton's poem, divine light is, like the sun, physical in its impact, blinding the rash viewer, and like it also in conveying warmth and life-giving properties:

> . . . and to each inward part
> With gentle penetration, though unseen,
> Shoots invisible virtue even to the deep.
> So wondrously was set his Station bright.

> (III, 584–7)

Once again, a comparison of Milton's usage with that of his immediate predecessors reveals the change. For Du Bartas too, God is

> Incomprehensible, all spirit, all light,
> All Majestie, all self-Omnipotent,
> Invisible . . .

but the light here is a static property of God, not the blazing force of creativity for which the newly placed sun had become the physical representative within man's own planetary system. As part of this changed view, the mystical and messianic movements of the seventeenth century, including the revitalised Kabbalism of the era, no longer spoke of inspiration in traditional terms as the breath of God's spirit, but as an inner illumination by the *Zohar* or

Incandescent Splendour of divine truth. When Milton himself pleads for heavenly assistance in the opening of Book III, he turns for it to the holy Light, 'Bright effluence of bright essence increate' which, as he recalls, existed even before the sun was formed. He prays there that it will 'shine inward', and irradiate his own poetic creativity.[16]

Was it chance, one may wonder, that the two major discoveries which marked the close of the baroque and the beginning of a rationalist era were Newton's explanations of mass and light? As the energised forces of the cosmos, they had come to represent for his age the awesome, mystical powers of creation. Accordingly, as a scientist exploring the workings of the universe, it was to them that he instinctively turned in enquiry, eventually establishing his two monumental theories of gravity and of the light spectrum. Once reduced to its prosaic components, light seemed to lose its mystical force for the following generation, and the gap between God and rational man to have been significantly lessened. There is a subtle realignment of relationships implicit in Pope's wry comment:

> Nature and Nature's laws lay hid in night.
> God said, Let Newton be and all was light.

All this, however, was still to come, and within the world of Milton the blaze of divine light still shines undimmed, together with the awe inspired by the material cosmos. We must now move back, then, two eras, to the time prior to Milton when the dominant view of the heavens was of an insubstantial region, a translucent world inhabited by vaporous angels. In order to transform that traditional vision into the cosmos of rugged masses whirling dynamically about each other under the forceful control of the Creator, Milton knew that he must proceed with caution. So unconventional a picture could not be thrust at the seventeenth-century reader without preparation. In literary criticism of the last half-century, we have become increasingly aware of the way a literary work imposes its standards upon the reader, indirectly manipulating his responses in order to deflect potential antagonism and to lull him into a receptive frame of mind. If Coleridge's *Ancient Mariner* had plunged us at its very opening into the weird tale of a ghostly crew working the rigging and spectres dicing over the soul of a mariner, its effect would have been no greater than that of some 'Gothic' tale. The brilliance of the poem lies to no small extent in the gradual mesmerising of an initially sceptical reader, vicariously through the Wedding Guest, who is slowly compelled by the Mariner's glittering eye to submit and listen like a three-year child. By the end, we seem, like that Guest, to have been singled out for the rare privilege of learning the spiritual message of the Mariner's experience, and treasure that privilege accordingly. So here, we are not propelled at the opening of Milton's epic into the vastness of the cosmos, nor into the celestial battle, but are introduced step by step into a growing acceptance of the specifically Miltonic heaven, so markedly at variance with that of established convention. It is fascinating to watch the gradual process whereby this progression is achieved.

The principle on which Milton works can perhaps be best conveyed by means of an analogy. A child cannot easily conceive of the number one hundred, except as something vaguely large. The only effective way of leading him towards a more valid grasp of that figure is by beginning with something tangible. He can be asked to visualise clearly ten individual building blocks, and then encouraged to multiply them in his imagination into ten such groups of ten. The picture he creates in his mind at the first attempt may not be exactly one hundred, but it will certainly be closer, as well as more vividly conceived, than the original cloudy idea. The same formula may be applied to an adult at a more sophisticated level. The universe, we are told, is infinite, and the human mind shudders away from the thought. Yet by visualising, perhaps in model form, the earth on which we stand circling with its fellow planets about the sun, and then attempting to multiply that scene first into ten solar systems and then into a hundred, we can, at least in embryonic form, approach some more valid concept of the innumerable galaxies of the skies. That is basically the technique which Milton uses here.

Hence it is that *Paradise Lost* begins its story not in the vast range of heaven where the rebellion and, in fact, the entire story began, but within the lower, more limited context of Hell which, for all its horror and gloom, is a setting not very different from that of our own earth in its more arid areas. If Marjorie Nicolson is correct, Milton's Hell was actually modelled on the volcanic Phlegraean fields near Naples which he, like most tourists of his day, must have visited during his sojourn in Italy, not least because of its rich literary associations. Regarded by tradition as the entrance to Hades through which Aeneas and others had descended to the nether regions, it too possessed a lake of 'frightening blackness' (as Milton's contemporary Athanasius Kircher described it). It is still today an area barren of vegetation, with acrid fumes of 'ever-burning Sulphur unconsum'd', rising through the earth to create a scaldingly hot surface like the burning marl over which Satan must painfully make his way.[17] In the same way, the gulf of hell into which Satan falls in Milton's poem is not, as so often in earlier accounts, some insubstantial fiery inferno placed in a vague, misty locale below, but is situated within clearly defined territory and bounded by a towering wall. The exit itself is barred by a series of massive gates, whose description leaves no doubt of their solidity and durability:

> . . . thrice threefold the Gates, three folds were Brass,
> Three Iron, three of Adamantine Rock,
> Impenetrable . . . .
>
> (II, 645–7)

Similarly, the landscape surrounding Hell is depicted in topographical detail in order to convey the fixity of its location. Four rivers—Styx, Acheron, Cocytus, and Phlegeton—pour their baleful streams into the burning lake, while a fifth, the famed Lethe, marks the border separating this infernal world from a 'frozen Continent' lashed by storms, whirlwinds, and hail, an area subject to the fiercest extremes of heat and cold. This is the continent which Satan must later cross on his way to the newly created Earth, and as a result of this carefully charted description, his eventual journey towards Eden is one the reader feels able to follow as on a map, with a sense of the distances to be traversed and the obstacles to be overcome before the attainment of his goal.

The description of the fallen angels within Hell is also surprisingly terrestrial and everyday, in contrast to such traditional depictions as that of Dante's *Inferno*, with its unremitting agonies and tortures. Once they have reached the shore, they busy themselves with mundane occupations, digging trenches and ramparts, mining gold from the hillside, and building their citadel. With these main tasks accomplished, they are free to wander about exploring their new abode, and to relax like human beings in sports and races while others 'more mild' retire into a silent valley (perhaps as Milton himself would have done) to sing to harp accompaniment of their heroic deeds and lamentable defeat. The scenes are comfortable in their familiarity, a familiarity enhanced by the recurrent allusions to the Homeric or Vergilian episodes on which they are based. This is the locale from which the epic begins, not the ethereal dimensions of the celestial battle which chronologically begins the tale, but a more solid, limited setting, human in scale.

The reason for beginning the account in Hell has generally been attributed to the tradition of the classical epic, since that also began *in medias res* and not in chronological order. In the *Odyssey* we are plunged into the dramatic present as Ulysses is about to return home and rescue Penelope from her suitors, and only in Book VII will he be asked to relate his past adventures and the events which have led up to that point in his travels. A greater immediacy is gained by focussing on the climactic episode first, and then using a flashback narration to record the earlier history in more leisurely fashion. Even more significantly, Achilles' anger is the announced theme of the *Iliad* and that central theme is the starting-point for the epic, with the causes of the Trojan War described much later. Within Milton's poem, Raphael's retrospective description of the rebellion in heaven and of the creation of the universe from Book VI onwards clearly accords with that epic technique. Nevertheless, the tradition of beginning *in medias res* does not explain Milton's decision to open the poem in hell. The declared theme here is man's disobedience and fall. That is the central episode. Hence the most natural opening scene in this classical tradition ought to have been, as it was for so many of Milton's predecessors, the Garden of Eden, where the temptation of Adam is about to be enacted. Du Bartas' *La Seconde Semaine*, Grotius' *Adamus Exul*, and Andreini's *L'Adamo* had all begun within the Garden, recounting much later in the work the events responsible for Satan's malevolence. There is, indeed, an echo of this tradition in Book VI of *Paradise Lost*, when Raphael warns Adam to beware of Satan's wiles and explains the source of the devil's motives:

> . . . he who envies now thy state,
> Who now is plotting how he may seduce
> Thee also from obedience, that with him
> Bereav'd of happiness thou mayst partake
> His punishment, Eternal misery;
> Which would be all his solace and revenge,
> As a despite done against the most High . . . .

> (VI, 900–6)

That was the natural place for the retrospective account if Milton was following the *in medias res* tradition. His decision, therefore, to split off the scene of Satan in hell and to place it at the very opening of the poem cannot be simply attributed to the epic form. It should be seen rather as a structural device for obtaining a firm visual actuality upon which the reader could mentally be transported by stages to the ultimate vision of a vast, yet physically realised heaven and the battle that took place there.

The first two books, as we have already noted, are believed to have been written later than the main body of the epic, and not to have formed part of the original design. If that is so—and it seems most likely from the evidence available—it would point even more strongly to Milton's realisation that he needed the scene in hell as a stepping-stone to the celestial vision. One has only to read the opening lines of Book III, which would otherwise have constituted the opening scene of the epic, to recognise how necessary it was for him to add the first two books if a sense of concrete physicality was to be conveyed. There, in a blaze of ethereal light, we find ourselves imaginatively projected into some vague, amorphous vastness, unplaced in time or space, floating, as it were, in an infinite eternity, with no possibility of taking our bearings or establishing any measure for comparison:

> Hail, holy Light, offspring of Heav'n first-born,
> Or of th' Eternal Coeternal beam
> May I express thee unblam'd? since God is Light,
> And never but in unapproached Light
> Dwelt from Eternity, dwelt then in thee,
> Bright effluence of bright essence increate.

It was a *tour de force* to open instead with the more lowly invocation 'Of Man's First Disobedience . . . Sing Heav'nly Muse', which places us here on earth, together with the author of the poem as he asks for aid in relating the story of man, then to move to a terrestrial-type hell, and only gradually to rise from that more familiar setting to the bolder vision of 'Things unattempted yet in Prose or Rhyme'. The movement within this invocation foreshadows in miniature the structural progression of the epic narrative itself, moving from below, upwards to the cosmic splendour of the heavens.

This process of elevation is closely connected with the change which Milton introduced into the figure of Satan. The distinctly corporeal quality of his Satan has become so firmly embedded in our minds that it requires an effort to recall the long-established tradition which it supplanted, stretching back to the Middle Ages and continuing through with rare exceptions to Milton's own era. Thomas Heywood, for example, in his 'Hierarchie of the Blessed Angells' published in 1635 (when Milton was already contemplating his new work), summarised the tradition with no thought of any possible alternative. For him Lucifer and the Rebellious Angels are by common agreement disembodied spectres flitting about the world to trouble man's thoughts:

> A Spirit is but a mere Intellect,
> Not burden'd with a body, of agilite
> Nimble and quicke . . .
> They waking trouble us, molest our sleepe;
> And if upon our selves no watch we keepe,
> Our bodies enter, then distract our braine,
> They crampe our members, make us to complaine
> Of sicknesse or disease . . . .

There is no hint here of the muscular warrior, the burly Arch Antagonist of *Paradise Lost*, which was to replace the disembodied wraiths of previous tradition.

True art conceals art, and a new viewpoint should be so dextrously imposed that we are unaware of the change wrought upon us until it has been accomplished. Only the critic analysing the mechanics of the work discerns the apparently insignificant details, the unnoticed connotations which cumulatively produce the shift in allegiance. If we examine the opening books of *Paradise Lost* with that criterion in mind, it becomes apparent how conscious Milton was of the difficulties he faced in divesting the contemporary reader of his traditional assumptions about the devil, and supplying in their place an essentially new figure of Satan as the stalwart baroque challenger of God, and, by extension, introducing a new conception of the heavens as an infinitude composed of solid masses in motion.

Our initial introduction to Satan in the poem is a case in point. As the bardic invocation ends, with its brief restrospective account of the rebels' headlong fall from heaven, the story itself begins, and we turn for the first time to focus on the fallen angels in their present condition in hell, just awakening to the full realisation of their defeat. Yet we do not see them. Milton understood that at this early stage he must avoid any jarring confrontation between the reader's preconception of the angels as insubstantial apparitions and the firm brawn which he plans to present. He therefore employs a remarkably tactful transitional device. A blanket of darkness descends to prevent that visual confrontation. The flames of hell, we are now told, emit not light but darkness visible. Accordingly, we are forced back into an exclusively aural response to the scene, listening to the voices of the fallen angels as they call to each other mournfully through the gloom, but seeing nothing through the eyes of the narrator. Satan, still retaining some remnant of his former angelic sight, peers through the darkness and dimly discerns the form of his lieutenant Beelzebub, so changed from the glorious figure he had been in heaven; but we are given no glimpse of him for ourselves. The darkness temporarily neutralises our responses, directing us instead to the speeches alone, which by their majestic tone begin to create in our minds a sense of the epic stature of the protagonists as they move from near-despair to warlike resolution. Only then, with their stature and martial force established, are we permitted to see Satan himself, and the contrast between his conventional presentation and his depiction here is less sharply felt by the reader, as the speeches have already laid the groundwork.

Traditionally, Satan, once fallen, had been presented as a horrendous figure, rather like the ghastly Sin or Death of Milton's own poem. Tasso's account in his *Gerusalemme Liberata* is perfectly conventional in portraying him as spitting forth brimstone:

> And as Mount Etna vomits sulphur out,
> With clifts of burning crags, and fire and smoke,
> So from his mouth flew kindled coales about,
> Hot sparks and smels, that man and beast would choke . . . .[18]

Similarly Erasmo di Valvasone describes him in his *L'Angeleida* of 1590:

> The seven caverns of his mouths exhaled
> A cruel stench, from slimy slaver reeking;
> In fourteen eyes a deadly anger flailed,
> Beneath his bristling eyebrows fiercely speaking;
> Across his livid cheeks stray flushes trailed
> And scornful shadows, all his visage streaking,
> Within whose midst dark Sorrow had her house;
> While locks of writhing snakes enwreathed his brows.[19]

Mephistopheles from Marlowe's play we remember as a more human figure, but we should recall that there too he is so horrific on his first appearance that he elicts the cry:

> *Dr. Faustus*: I charge thee to return and change thy shape;
> Thou art too ugly to attend on me.
> Go and return an old Franciscan friar;
> That holy shape becomes a devil best.

and for the rest of the play Mephistopheles appears not in his natural form as a devil, but in the guise of a human being. In Milton's portrayal of Satan, then, a certain nobility of bearing and dignity have already been established aurally before we see him in the poem, and in the description itself when it does come there is nothing hideous or terrifying. Attention is drawn instead to his physical bulk as he lies stretched out on the water like some huge sea-beast, so large that mariners might mistake him for an island or promontory beside which to moor their vessels. His head is uplifted above the waves, and

> . . . his other Parts besides
> Prone on the Flood, extended long and large
> Lay floating many a rood, in bulk as huge
> As whom the Fables name of monstrous size,
> *Titanian*, or *Earth-born*, that warr'd on *Jove*,
> *Briareos* or *Typhon*, whom the Den
> By ancient *Tarsus* held, or that Sea-beast
> *Leviathan*, which God of all his works
> Created hugest that swim th' Ocean stream . . . .
> (I, 194–202)

In accordance with the principle of the child and the building blocks, we may note how this initial description insists on finite dimensions, measurable by human standards although already suggestive of the vast. Satan stretches 'many a rood' on the surface of the water, and if the references to the Titan and the Leviathan have a touch of the fable about them, we are reminded at once that the Titan was 'Earth-born' and that the biblical Leviathan was an actual creature, to be found in the ocean (as was then believed). In brief, impressive as Satan may be in his gigantic size, there is at this stage nothing cosmic or limitless about him to make the mind shudder away and lose its sense of firm physicality.

With his 'mighty stature' physically established, the first hints of celestial proportions are cautiously introduced, proportions more suited to the later wide-ranging universe of the baroque vision. Such hints appear in a manner designed to lessen their impact, and to leave a certain ambiguity in the degree of literalcy implied. Milton knew that his seventeenth-century reader, familiar with Homeric metaphor, expected to find within an epic that type of imagery which, with pardonable exaggeration, might compare the hero to a raging storm, or his gleaming armour to 'the lightning that Zeus seizes in his hand and brandishes from radiant Olympus'. These were the normal tools of classical poetry, enhancing the status of the warrior without actually removing him from the more limited setting of human battle. In the first hesitant applications of such imagery to Satan, then, their effect is tempered by this tradition, as when we learn that his shield of broad circumference

> Hung on his shoulders like the Moon, whose Orb
> Through Optic Glass the *Tuscan* Artist views
> At Ev'ning from the top of *Fesole* . . . .

The metaphorical form, despite its astronomical range, prevents the reader from being swept too swiftly into unfamiliar areas, and Milton, as though concerned that even such cautious metaphor has moved his reader on too quickly, at once modifies the image, returning us to a terrestrial setting, with Satan's spear dwarfing the tallest pine tree hewn on Norwegian hills. The lunar simile has nevertheless left its imprint on the reader's mind, preparing the way for those subsequent scenes in which Satan will in fact soar through the heavens, visiting the sun and other celestial spheres on his journey towards Eden, and becoming visible through optic glass like a newly discovered sun-spot.

The gathering of the fallen angels and the Council of War which occupy the remainder of Book I and part of Book II, remain both literally and metaphorically within a setting evocative of the terrestrial.[20] In a passage encrusted with rich detail like some stucco frieze, the assembled rebels are identified as the dark idolatries of biblical and pagan times, with Astoreth, Thammuz, Dagon, Belial, Isis and Osiris, and the vicious or wanton human rites which they inspired here on earth in earlier times. Again the cosmic is replaced by the local and familiar:

In Courts and Palaces he also Reigns
And in luxurious Cities, where the noise
Of riot ascends above thir loftiest Tow'rs,
And injury and outrage: And when Night
Darkens the Streets, then wander forth the Sons
Of *Belial*, flown with insolence and wine.
Witness the Streets of *Sodom*, and that night
In *Gibeah*, when the hospitable door
Expos'd a Matron to avoid worse rape.

(I, 497–505)

Then follows the council itself, clearly reminiscent of the kind of human debate in which Milton, as the Latin Secretary to Cromwell, must himself have participated. It is a scene depending for its dramatic effect on the realism with which human sophistry and political self-seeking are expressed through the rhetoric of the various speakers. Only when the debate is over and they begin to contemplate the enormity of the task ahead does the setting open out as they wonder which of them will dare to attempt the crossing of that 'dark, unbottom'd infinite Abyss' which separates them from their objective. As Satan volunteers for that task and sets out on his journey, the intimidating vastness of space begins to make itself felt, with Milton carefully retaining the concreteness of the earlier scenes and extending it to the cosmos, lest the reader slip back into the inherited tradition of celestial insubstantiality. Satan soars aloft, sometimes scouring the right coast, sometimes the left, until the high-reaching bounds of Hell appear before him, the exit barred by massive ninefold gates of brass, iron, and adamantine rock. There Death, his hideous, unrecognised offspring, threateningly blocks his way, and Satan, angered but unafraid, opposes him

> . . . and like a Comet burn'd,
> That fires the length of *Ophiucus* huge
> In th' Artic Sky . . . .

From this point on, the process of cosmic expansion moves from metaphor to actuality. With Satan's paternity established, the bolts are opened, the infernal doors grate thunderously on their hinges, and beyond them is revealed the Chaos that must be crossed. In earlier versions, that Chaos is an ugly, confused region, but with no suggestion of infinitude or vastness. For Du Bartas it is

A confused heap, a chaos most deform,
A gulf of gulfs, a body ill-compacked,
An ugly medley, which all difference lacked;
Where the elements lay jumbled all together,
Where hot and cold were jarring each with either . . . .[21]

In Milton there is an enormous difference. If his hell has, as a stepping-stone to the cosmic, been evocative of the terrestrial in its compactness and human familiarity, the opening of its gates introduces us at last to the immensity of the universe beyond. To Satan is now revealed

> . . . a dark
> Illimitable Ocean without bound,
> Without dimension, where length, breadth, and highth,
> And time and place are lost . . . .
>
> (II, 891-4)

Even the Arch Antagonist is momentarily daunted and, hesitating at the brink, ponders the magnitude of his cosmic undertaking. Then, gathering his courage, he begins the fateful journey.

The description here of Satan's ascent into the higher realm serves as the culmination of the change which Milton was introducing into the traditional view of angels as bodiless apparitions 'imprinted' on the air or, at the very most, spirits tenuously connected to bodies of fire which, as we have seen, continued to predominate in Milton's era. In 1660, for example, when Milton was probably putting the finishing touches to the work, Henry More, relying on a wide range of sources from Neoplatonic to Protestant, had declared categorically that there were three main opinions current on the subject: 'Concerning angels, some affirm them to be *fiery* or *airy* Bodies; some pure spirits, some Spirits in airy or fiery bodies . . .'[22] None of these definitions could possibly be applied to Satan as he is presented in this poem. he is no feathery creature floating on a breath of wind, nor an insubstantial flame flickering in the breeze, but a solid, muscular, heavy being who cannot hope to rise from the ground without the aid of enormous 'sail-broad' wings with a span huge enough to lift his great weight into the air. Even then, to soar aloft he needs to harness the upward thrust of surging smoke, which he catches within the spread of those broad wings. When he meets a vast vacuity a little later, the wings, just as in our own world, having nothing to beat against, and he plummets down helplessly, until a chance meeting with a tumultuous storm cloud, pregnant with fire and nitre, provides the physical impetus which drives him upward once again:

> At last his Sail-broad Vans
> He spreads for flight, and in the surging smoke
> Uplifted spurns the ground, thence many a League
> As in a cloudy Chair ascending rides
> Audacious, but that seat soon failing, meets
> A vast vacuity: all unawares
> Flutt'ring his pennons vain plumb down he drops
> Ten thousand fadom deep, and to this hour
> Down had been falling, had not by ill chance
> The strong rebuff of some tumultuous cloud
> Instinct with Fire and Nitre hurried him
> As many miles aloft . . . .
>
> (II, 927–38)

Milton has, in effect projected into the heavenly scene the same physical conditions as operate in the terrestrial sphere, where thrust is met by counter-thrust, where the same gravitational pulls need to be resisted for upward flight, and where objects, awesomely larger and more powerful than on earth, still possess a solidity and weight comparable, in due proportion, to their equivalents below.[23]

Satan's corporeality and his need to struggle against contrary forces are not, as might be thought, the result of his fall from grace and the loss of angelic spirituality which it entailed. In Milton's poetic world, even the purest of angels is subject to these same limitations of time and space. The faithful Abdiel, hastening towards the divine throne to report the news of Satan's imminent attack, cannot magically dispense with, nor even shorten the distance separating him from his destination however urgent his task, but must fly steadily on through many weary hours to traverse the intervening space:

> All night the dreadless Angel unpursu'd
> Through Heav'n's wide Champaign held his way, till Morn . . . .
>
> (VI, 1–2)

For all his efforts, by the time he arrives his mission has proved pointless, for the news has been learnt from another source.[24] Even the archangel Uriel who (as his name 'Divine Light' implies) is privileged to glide swiftly along the sunbeams, can, amusingly enough, only slide *down* them, and Milton is careful to record which way the sunbeam slopes in order to preserve the gravitational implications of the entire scene:

> So promis'd hee, and *Uriel* to his charge
> Return'd on that bright beam, whose point now rais'd
> Bore him slope downward to the Sun now fall'n
> Beneath th' Azores . . . .

>   (IV, 589–92)

The sun's setting has conveniently reversed the beam's slope to allow him a downward return journey. The point may sound trivial, even a little absurd, but such trifles, presented with due seriousness in the poem, contribute to that sense of spatial realism which Milton felt was so essential to the epic at large.

It was probably this desire on Milton's part to stress the physicality of his angels which led him into those notoriously awkward discussions of the angels' digestive tracts and sexual activities—matters which would have been best left discreetly unmentioned as being more likely to arouse amusement than awe. Their presence in the epic does, however, suggest how strongly he wanted imaginatively to counter the tradition of their incorporeality.

Satan, then, is not in this respect specifically penalised by his fall, and the laws of fixed weight and distance apply to all the celestial host. On the other hand, the very nature of Satan's journey, as an escape out of the imprisonment of the Dungeon below up to the higher reaches of Heaven from which he is at least nominally barred, inevitably involves a more intense struggle against resistant forces. We are reminded that '. . . long is the way/And hard, that out of Hell leads up to light'. The obstacles placed in his path demand a supreme effort of will and stamina for them to be overcome, and in the course of the struggle the pitting of his strength and ingenuity against them creates that sense of physical dynamism in the poem which is uniquely Milton's. In Marlowe's *Dr. Faustus*, for example, Mephistopheles always appears instantly, like a genie at the rub of a lamp, whenever Faustus pronounces the magic words. He is simply there, conveying no impression of a journey travelled. Andreini's Lucifer does much the same, complaining as he enters the stage:

> Who calls me from my dark abyss to see
> Excess of light? What further miracles
> Dost thou reveal to me today, O God?[25]

But here we are made to witness Milton's Satan in the lengthy process of the journey itself, wading on through marsh and bog, mile after mile, and exemplifying in his progress the conflicting forces of will and matter which function so powerfully throughout the poem:

> Quencht in a Boggy *Syrtis*, neither Sea
> Nor good dry Land, nigh founder'd on he fares,
> Treading the crude consistence, half on foot,
> Half flying . . .
>> So eagerly the fiend
> O'er bog or steep, through strait, rough, dense, or rare,
> With head, hands, wings, or feet pursues his way,
> And swims or sinks, or wades or creeps, or flies . . . .
> > > > (II, 939–50)

The struggle continues through the lower regions until he reaches the border separating the dark kingdom of Chaos from the light-filled realm of Nature. Until this point, Milton has concentrated on conveying the physicality and tangibility of the smaller unit, with only an occasional hint of the immensity beyond. Now, with that sense of concreteness fully established, he moves on to the next stage, the infinite multiplication of that solid unit to create a more valid conception of the vast created world; and he does so by viewing it from the opposite angle, from the vision of immensity. As Satan reaches the border of Chaos, the celestial panorama at last opens out before him in all its splendour. He pauses

> . . . at leisure to behold
> Far off th' Empyreal Heav'n, extended wide
> In circuit, undetermin'd square or round
> With Opal Tow'rs and Battlements adorn'd
> Of living Sapphire, once his native Seat;
> And fast by hanging in a golden Chain

> This pendant world, in bigness as a Star
> Of smallest Magnitude close by the Moon.
>
> (II, 1046–53)

The 'pendant world' here is not, of course, the earth, but the entire cosmos of planets orbiting beneath the divine throne, yet seen from so far away that the whole universe appears in size no more than a tiny star in the boundlessness of heaven. This is the kind of scene which could never have been visualised in quite the same way before the advent of the new relativist cosmology, with Giordano Bruno and others mentally projecting themselves on to distant vantage-points in the heavens in order to conjecture how the universe would appear to the inhabitants of other stars.

The literary device which Milton now employs to combine this awareness of the solidity of the smaller unit with the infinitude of the heavens is basically similar to the use of a zoom lens in modern cinematography. Repeatedly from this point onwards we are shown through Satan's eyes how some minute dot of light twinkling in the sky among myriads like it grows, as he approaches, into an entire world in its own right, replete with mountains, valleys, and oceans. Until Galileo's day, we should recall, there had been numerous theories concerning the nature of such galaxies as the Milky Way, most commonly the belief that it was an immense heavenly stream. It was only when the telescope focused upon it that the galaxy was seen incontestably to consist of myriads of individual stars. As Galileo pointed out, '. . . all the disputes which have tormented philosophers through so many ages are exploded at once by the irrefragable evidence of our eyes, and we are freed from wordy disputes upon this subject, for the Galaxy is nothing else but a mass of innumerable stars planted together in clusters. Upon whatever part of it you direct the telescope straightway a vast crowd of stars presents itself to view; many of them are tolerably large and extremely bright, but the number of the small ones is quite beyond determination.'[26] So in Satan's journey through the universe of Nature, galaxies appear within the cosmos, constellations within the galaxies, planetary systems within the constellations, and the tiny dots of light forming these constellations are, as he draws close, revealed as independent worlds in themselves, comparable to the entire earth or even larger.

The age of Galileo had no zoom lenses at its disposal such as afford us today this effect of swooping from a wide panoramic view to a detailed close-up; but the telescope did offer for the first time in history the opportunity of moving from a distant view with the naked eye to the sudden enlargement visible through the optic instrument, which multiplied the scene one-thousandfold to demonstrate the immensity of what had appeared so small. In the literary setting, however, Milton could provide that enlarging and shrinking zoom effect of which contemporary instruments were then incapable. So it is that the 'pendant world' which constitutes the totality of the created cosmos is first described within the spaciousness of the heavens as being 'in bigness as a star/Of smallest Magnitude close by the Moon'. The alternating series *bigness, smallest, magnitude* and the final dwarfing of the star beside the moon creates a pulsating effect of expansion and contraction. It suggests by verbal means what then was so new, the sensation of gazing at a tiny dot of light, yet knowing that through the telescope it had been revealed as an enormous world in its own right. So Satan, winging his way across the distances separating him from that small ball, is astonished as he approaches by the infinite size of what had appeared so puny:

> . . . a Globe far off
> It seem'd, now seems a boundless Continent
> Stark, waste, and wild.
>
> (III, 422–4)

On he flies from the outer crust of the pendant globe to the point from which it is suspended from the golden chain, and from there he obtains his first prospect of all the created universe.

> Round he surveys, and well might, where he stood
> So high above the circling Canopy
> Of Night's extended shade; from Eastern Point
> Of *Libra* to the fleecy Star that bears
> *Andromeda* far off *Atlantic* Seas
> Beyond th' Horizon; then from Pole to Pole
> He views in breadth.
>
> (III, 555–61)

The amplitude of the scene is impressive enough, but as he proceeds on his journey each of the countless stars by which he passes takes on its own immensity. They

> . . . shone
> Stars distant, but nigh hand seem'd other Worlds,
> Like those *Hesperian* Gardens fam'd of old,
> Fortunate Fields, and Groves and flow'ry Vales,
> Thrice happy Isles, but who dwelt happy there
> He stay'd not to enquire.

Fortunately for Milton, Satan has no time to stop, and although the poet is clearly sympathetic to the 'plenitudinous' view that the planets and stars are inhabited, he is able to leave his commitment open.

We have now been led almost to the end of the journey—a journey making this account so different from all previous versions of the Fall. Instead of beginning in the Garden of Eden, it takes us from the uttermost limits of the heavens, swinging through the actuality of interstellar space among the countless galaxies of solid stars to land at last on that tiny spot on earth where Adam and Eve tend their plants.

One would expect, perhaps, that having reached the Sun, Satan will now swoop directly down to Paradise to commence the task of corrupting mankind. Milton, however, has not forgotten the main purpose of these opening books in presenting the baroque vision of Eternal Providence supervising a vast phsyical cosmos which testifies to the splendour of its Creator. Before the story of the Temptation and Fall begins, therefore, he inserts a timely reminder, first of the act of creation itself, and then of the relationship between that universal creation and man. Although Satan had until now experienced little difficulty in finding his way through the wide range of the skies, he is here made to need guidance in finding Earth, and hence provides Uriel with the opportunity of supplying that reminder. Uriel, as one of the loyal angels forever hymning God's praises, recalls the impressive moment when the material shape of the universe was formed out of the infinite waste, and order was imposed on the orbiting planets:

> . . . at his Word the formless Mass,
> This world's material mould, came to a heap:
> Confusion heard his voice, and wild uproar
> Stood rul'd, stood vast infinitude confin'd;
> Till at his second bidding darkness fled,
> Light shone, and order from disorder sprung:

Swift to thir several Quarters hasted then
The cumbrous Elements, Earth, Flood, Air, Fire,
And this Ethereal quintessence of Heav'n
Flew upward, spirited with various forms,
That roll'd orbicular, and turn'd to Stars
Numberless, as thou seest, and how they move;
Each had his place appointed, each his course . . . .

(III, 708–20)

For the last time in this section the epic focuses down from the immense to the minute; but this time the purpose of that movement is not to reveal the physical largeness of the smaller unit seen close-up, but rather to assert its *spiritual* primacy. We move here from the immensity of universal creation to that small creature for whom all the universe was ultimately intended, and who is soon due to become the central figure of the narrative:

Look downward on that Globe whose hither side
With light from hence, though but reflected, shines:
That place is Earth, the seat of Man . . .
That spot to which I point is *Paradise*,
Adam's abode . . . .

In a stimulating essay published many years ago, Marjorie Nicolson pointed out for the first time that the wide-ranging perspectives of Milton's epic could not have come into being without the discovery of the telescope, in much the same way as, a little later, Gulliver's visit to the Lilliputans could not have been conceived without the invention of the microscope. The purpose of this chapter has not been to argue that same point over again, but to suggest that the relationship between Milton's poem and the new astronomy was far more profound than the technicality of an expanded imagery or an enlarged perspective to which Professor Nicolson pointed. She rightly noted the originality of *Paradise Lost* as being '. . . the first modern cosmic poem in which a drama is played out against a background of interstellar space'.[27] There are the sudden views of distant prospects as God, Satan, or Uriel gaze down on the cosmic scenes laid out before them, and throughout the epic can be sensed a fresh awareness of the infinity of the heavens. Yet for all her perceptiveness, her comments point only to the novelty which the telescopic view offered to Milton in presenting his poem poetically. I have tried to suggest here that the relationship goes far deeper, that his response to the new astronomy is not a casual backdrop to his epic but forms one of the central and most intimately religious concerns of the work. The challenge to Christianity implicit in that astronomy had seemed, for so many of his era, to negate all further need for soulful striving on man's part, and to validate instead a confident reliance upon rational empiricism as a substitute for religious awe. The mapping out of the heavens by the cosmographers, and their ability to predict the courses of the stars, seemed to deprive the heavens of their mystery, as John Donne had bitterly complained:

> For of Meridians and Parallels
> Man hath weav'd out a net, and this net throwne
> Upon the Heavens, and now they are his owne.
> Loth to goe up the hill, or labour thus
> To goe to heaven, we make heaven come to us.[28]

Milton, on the other hand, in fulfilment of the ideal dominating so much of the baroque, inverted the process by absorbing the mechanistic universe into the framework of Christian belief, and endowing the material realities of contemporary astronomy with the archetypal resonance and ethical imperatives of biblical myth. The vastness of space is seen by him not as a negation of man's significance but, in accordance with the central concept of that mode, as testifying to the splendour of the Creator and hence restoring to man, created in that image, the spiritual importance in the universe which he appeared to have lost. He was in a sense translating into literary terms the cry of Bruno on discovering the new cosmos:

> Thus is the excellence of God magnified, and the greatness of his kingdom made manifest; he is glorified not in one, but in countless suns; not in a single earth, but in a thousand, I say in an infinity of worlds.[29]

The effect on Milton's universe is thus two-directional; the orbiting stars are endowed once again with the lambent quality of a heaven created and controlled by an Eternal Providence, while the concourse of angels hymning God's praises becomes enlarged to the innumerability of the newly discovered galaxies of stars. In such a setting, the insubstantial heaven of medieval or Neoplatonic Christianity, with translucent angels gathering on a pin's head, seemed a denial of the physical actualities revealed through Galileo's optic tube—the pitted surface of the moon, the dark spots on the sun, and the realisation that the comets were huge masses hurtling through space. What I have attempted to trace here, then, is the way Milton gradually substituted in the reader's mind, in place of the older tradition, a conception of the heavens more suited to the new cosmos, infinite in size and yet operating, like that cosmos, according to the laws of weight, mass, and measured space. It was a prerequisite for a further and major aspect of the baroque which we shall examine in the following chapter.

4 The War in Heaven

During the earlier part of this century, when Milton's reputation was at a low ebb, the War in Heaven became, like the problem of the Satanic hero, a favoured target for censure, with comments ranging from mild admissions of embarrassment to outright condemnation, the latter being more frequent. No reader, it was argued, could be expected to take seriously the ludicrous picture of rarefied spirits buckling on swords and breastplates to engage in bodily warfare when the reader knew that none of the participants could be killed, or even more than momentarily injured. Although critics have more recently taken a very different view, that dismissal of the battle-scenes as a serious blemish on the work still has its adherents. J. B. Broadbent, for example, maintains that, since any attempt to depict the war seriously was hopeless from the start, Milton ought to have abandoned all effort to portray it in terrestrial terms and simply to have '. . . treated it all as science fiction'.[1]

In this instance too, the modern attack was not entirely new, but formed the culmination of a disturbance first expressed in the eighteenth-century era of rationalism, which was by nature less responsive to the religious and often to the aesthetic aspirations of the baroque. Although Dr. Johnson for the most part held Milton in high regard, he had disapproved strongly of the 'confusion of spirit and matter' in the work, the absurdity of presenting immaterial and immortal spirits as engaged in physical warfare. He scoffed at the manifest contradictions:

> When Satan walks with his lance upon the burning marle, he has a body; when, in his passage between hell and the new world, he is in danger of sinking in the vacuity, and is supported by a gust of rising vapours, he has a body; when he animates the toad, he seems to be mere spirit, that can penetrate matter at pleasure; when he starts up in his own shape, he has at least a determined form; and when he is brought before Gabriel, he has a spear and a shield, which he had the power of hiding in the toad, though the

arms of the contending angels are evidently material.[2]

This passage was quoted repeatedly by subsequent critics to underscore the weakness in Milton's description of the heavenly scene.

Before we deal with the major problem, it may be worth noting that a close examination of this comment in fact reveals Milton to be a good deal less confused than Johnson imagines. With the sole exception of Satan's transformation into a toad, every instance cited in the passage—walking on the marle, sinking in vacuity, raised by gusts, holding a spear and shield—demonstrates that Satan *has* a body and a determined form. Even the toad transformation can scarcely be regarded as a serious inconsistency. It adopts an ancient tradition whereby the Devil has the ability on earth to adopt various disguises or bodily forms in order to deceive man (witness the widespread legend of the cloven hoof which he was unable to transform, and by which he could be identified even when in disguise). The attack is thus far less damaging than might at first appear, pointing not to multiple internal contradictions in Milton, but to Johnson's dislike in principle of conceiving angels as physical beings.

In recent years critics have swung round to an entirely different view. The scene is now validated as a positive contribution to the development of the epic, but on rather strange grounds. Professor Arnold Stein, in a stimulating and influential essay first published as an article and then in his *Answerable Style*, argued that the entire battle in Book VI is a piece of deliberate comedy on Milton's part, with the combatants being ridiculed throughout. If the scene is taken literally, he maintains, we cannot escape Dr. Johnson's verdict that the confusion of spirit and matter fills the whole narrative with incongruity. How, he asks, can we imagine immortal spirits uncomplainingly confining themselves in hindering armour to fight with material weapons? The alternative he offers is to see the clash of forces as a kind of 'epic farce', a humorous account intended to provoke laughter at the literal level, and thereby to impress us with the profounder message that Satan's attempt to overthrow God is utterly vain. The dominant mood of the War, according to him, is thus 'terribly funny', reaching its full force in the scene where the rebel angels tear up whole mountains and fling them like custard-pies (the analogy is his) in the faces of their heavenly foes. The comic tone, he suggests, is established in advance by the Son's prologue-like comment before the battle begins:

> Mighty Father, thou thy foes
> Justly hast in derision, and secure
> Laugh'st at thir vain designs and tumults vain . . .
>
> (V, 735–7)

and throughout the events, in the foreground of the narrative, '. . . the great laugh, omniscient and uncircumscribed, cannot fail to be heard'.[3] Stein's view has been widely accepted, and during the past twenty years or so since its publication most critics have followed his lead in assuming that the War is, in ironic metaphor, a primarily comic scene.

Read in isolation, the essay is impressive and persuasive. The trouble arises as one turns back to the poem in order to apply this comic reading to the text; for the humour simply is not there. Indeed, there are numerous indications both in the overall setting and in the details that, so far from being humorous, it is intended as a deeply serious scene and, in fact, climactic for the first half of the epic. If, for example, Satan and his crew are supposed to appear ludicrous in their reliance as ethereal beings on clumsy swords and constricting armour, what possible purpose could Milton have in presenting Michael, Gabriel, and the loyal angels in precisely the same fashion, clothed in armour and engaging in physical strife? Custard-pie scrimmages have an awkward habit of smearing both sets of combatants. The problem, however, goes much deeper, for any theory that Milton was consciously striving after comic effect here must explain why at every turn he takes such care to underscore the solemnity of the battle and to stress that no human words can convey even faintly the magnitude of the heavenly conflict.

Stein, as we have seen, uses as his starting-point the laughter of God, which he sees as setting the comic tone for the subsequent scene. Laughter there certainly is, but not the kind associated with humour and comedy; only laughter in the biblical sense of cold mockery, the scorn poured upon one's enemy. There is an enormous difference between God confidently scorning his enemies as he assures the faithful of his eventual triumph, and the picture suggested here of hilarity in heaven at the absurd antics of angels (both good and bad) clattering about in armour and indulging in farcical slapstick. The former retains all the solemnity of the epic tradition, with the combatants taunting each other before the fight, while the second view reduces the participants to mere buffoons.

The passage upon which so much of Stein's argument rests, is an obvious echo of Psalm 2,4 which Milton's reader was expected to recall: 'He that sitteth in the heavens shall laugh: the Lord shall have his enemies in derision. Then shall he speak unto them in his wrath, and vex them in his sore displeasure.' The Bible, as has long been recognised, is a body of literature singularly devoid of humour. One has only to leaf through the listings of a biblical concordance to confirm that the word *laugh*, both in its Hebrew and its Greek forms, appears only in the caustic sense of triumph or contempt, and never as a light-hearted response to an amusing scene.[4] Sarah laughs in harsh and bitter disbelief when she hears in her old age that she will yet bear a child; the upright man is 'laughed to scorn' by the wicked of this world; and Wisdom 'will laugh at your calamity and mock when your fear cometh'. There is nothing to parallel there the good-humoured, unquenchable laughter of the gods in Homer when Mars and Venus are amusingly trapped naked in bed for all to see. So here in Milton's text, every instance that Stein quotes, including the passage cited above (which specifically stresses the 'derision'), comes clearly within the traditional category of cold scriptural mockery, untouched by humour, and hence in no way diminishing the seriousness of the battle itself. When, in the course of the fight, Satan and Belial appear in 'gamesome mood'

> So they among themselves in pleasant vein
> Stood scoffing . . .

> (VI, 628–9)

their jeering is presented as an act of pride before their own fall, and one with which the controlling viewpoint of the narrator is never identified. To interpret the entire War in Heaven as 'terribly funny' because of the impossibility of ethereal spirits engaging in armed battle is to impose a modernistic reading on the text and thereby to emasculate its imaginative force. In the following passage, for example, which focuses directly on this use in heaven of solid armour and physical weaponry, is there any hint of amused condescension on Milton's part, or is it, as I would argue, a solemnly conceived scene of immense vigour and turmoil, a baroque clash of forces such as Rubens would have delighted to paint?[5]

> . . . Arms on Armor clashing bray'd
> Horrible discord, and the madding Wheels
> Of brazen Chariots rag'd; dire was the noise
> Of conflict; over head the dismal hiss
> Of fiery Darts in flaming volleys flew,
> And flying vaulted either Host with fire.
> So under fiery Cope together rush'd
> Both Battles main, with ruinous assault
> And inextinguishable rage.
>
> (VI, 209–17)

One is led to suspect, since there is so little supporting evidence in the text, that the interpretation of the War as an amusing episode arises from the critic's own discomfort or embarrassment at the mingling of spirit and flesh it contains rather than from Milton's intent. The modern critic, in other words, perplexed by the baroque attribution of muscle and vigour to the supposedly insubstantial angels, solves the difficulty by reading into the text a humour which releases him from the need to take it seriously. At times one can even catch him in the act. A recent commentator, for example, who accepts wholeheartedly Stein's view of custard-pies and farce, remarks on the way Satan recovers after being wounded in the duel with Michael. Instead of being dragged around the battlefield in epic style behind his conqueror's chariot, he is allowed, we are told, '. . . to heal, immediately, without aid, like a puncture-sealing automobile tyre'.[6] This really is rather funny, and were it in the poem would offer sound evidence of a comic intent. But one searches in vain for any hint in the text itself. The humour is entirely of the critic's making, an amusing image quite unparalleled in the poem. On the contrary, there Milton is at pains—heavy-handedly one may add—to explain the peculiar constitution of angels which allows them to function as bodily creatures, giving and receiving blows, while yet preserving the immortality of their being. He interrupts the excitement of the battle with a discourse on the theological distinctions between death and annihilation as applied to angelic creatures:

> Yet soon he heal'd: for Spirits that live throughout
> Vital in every part, not as frail man
> In Entrails, Heart or Head, Liver or Reins,
> Cannot but by annihilating die:

Nor in thir liquid texture mortal wound
Receive, no more than can the fluid Air.

(VI, 344–9)

Such solemnity scarcely encourages the view that this is a farcical depiction of Satan as a self-sealing automobile tyre.

One further reason for the modern tendency to see humour in this scene may be the fact that, in a later era, Pope parodied it in his *Rape of the Lock*. There, one of fair Belinda's sylphs, attempting heroically to defend his mistress's curls, too fondly interposes and is sliced in two by the fatal scissors. Fortunately, Pope tells us, its 'airy substance soon unites again' and all is well—with the poet adding a footnote to recall the parallel incident of Satan's wound in *Paradise Lost*. The parody functions so successfully for the very reason that here it is *mock* epic, relying on the contrast or gap between the gravity of the original passage and the light-hearted humour and triviality of Pope's scene. It would not have succeeded if the Miltonic scene had been comic. Yet partly on the basis of Pope's parody, the humour has mistakenly been read back by modern critics into the scene of Satan too.

Nevertheless, a problem remains. If the interpretation of Milton's War in Heaven as farce has no basis in the text, and arises primarily out of the critic's embarrassment at the strange mingling of physical and spiritual elements in the depiction of the angels, that embarrassment itself could prove a damaging indictment of Milton, an indication of his lack of artistic control. It would suggest a failure on his part to persuade us of the validity of his poetic world—unless, once again, the modern response is due to the lapse in time since the period of its composition, and a change of viewpoint which a knowledge of his era and his specifically baroque aims may help to dispel.

We should, perhaps, begin by noting the new prominence which Milton assigned to the rebellion and war of the angels in comparison with earlier traditions, and hence the importance he obviously attached to it in developing his epic theme. Throughout previous literature, from the earliest sources of the legend, the rebellion of Lucifer had been recounted in only the briefest of forms and in primarily symbolic terms, with little sense of actual battle or physical conflict. The passage from Isaiah out of which the central story grew is so far removed from any clearly visualised titanomachy that, according to the Jewish commentators, it had no relevance

whatever to Satan and the rebel angels, and merely formed part of a
political diatribe aimed against the threatening power of Babylon:[7]

> How art thou fallen from heaven, O Star, son of the morning!
> how art thou cut down to the ground, which didst weaken the
> nations!
> For thou hast said in thine heart, I will ascend into heaven, I
> will exalt my throne above the stars of God: I will sit also upon the
> mount of the congregation, in the sides of the north:
> I will ascend above the heights of the clouds: I will be like the
> most High.
> Yet thou shalt be brought down to hell, to the sides of the pit.
>   (Is. 14, 12–15)

In a typical biblical metaphor, King Nebuchadnezzar is ironically equated here with one of his country's pagan deities, *Istar* the
star of the morning, and the prophet foretells the king's fall from
power as a punishment for his military arrogance. Within
Christianity this passage was linked with another enigmatic account
in Revelation 12, 4–11, where the 'Dragon' is defeated by Michael.
Perhaps under the impulse of the Gnostic and Manichean tenden-
cies of the time, these scenes were elaborated into a broader conflict
between the forces of good and evil, and the star ('Lucifer') was now
identified with Satan. Jerome seems to have been the first to
perceive how valuable this incident of a supposed abortive rebellion
in heaven could prove in providing a motive for Satan's corruption
of mankind; and from his time onwards the scene of the Fall was
understood as Satan's revenge on God for having crushed his own
earlier attempt to seize power.[8]

In the accounts of that rebellion during the Middle Ages and
Renaissance, the incident remained no more than a brief precursor
to the central story of the Fall in Eden, a momentary act of defiance
punished immediately by Satan's expulsion from heaven. In
medieval drama Lucifer arrogantly sits on the divine throne, at
which moment *Deus* appears and proclaims:

> Thu lucyfere ffor þi mekyl pryde
> I bydde þe ffalle from hefne to helle
> And all þo þat holdyn on þi syde
> in my blysse nevyr more to dwelle
> At my comawndement anoon down þou slyde . . . .[9]

Lucifer promptly falls to hell, and the scene moves on to Eden. In Du Bartas' *La Sepmaine* of 1578, the scene remains equally brief and undeveloped, the conspirators being hurled from heaven before the effect of their rebellion can even be felt. In this poem, as God showers his blessings on the angels,

> . . . some Legions of those lofty Spirits
> (Envying the glorie of their Makers merits)
> Conspir'd together, strove against the streame,
> T'usurpe his Scepter and his Diademe:
> But He, whose hands doe never Lightnings lack
> Proud sacrilegious Mutiners to wrack,
> Hurled them in th' Aire, or in some lower Cell:
> For, where God is not, everywhere is Hell . . . .

As one approaches the era of the baroque these accounts begin to display more interest in the actual conflict of forces, though even here the event is described as an isolated act rather than as a full-scale war. In Vondel's *Lucifer* (1654), which offers the fullest account of the rebellion prior to Milton's epic, the incident is embryonic in comparison to his, little more than a symbolic gesture. After a momentary meeting of forces, Lucifer raises his battleaxe to strike at God's banner, and is at once blasted by a divine thunderbolt. The war is over in a few lines:

> The axe upon the holy adamant
> Rang loudly and was shiver'd into pieces.
> Then Michael raised his hand, and with a bolt
> Of thunder, strengthen'd by Omnipotence,
> He smote the wicked one through helm and head
> So pitilessly that he toppled back,
> Hurl'd from his chariot, which overset
> And soon with Dragon, Lion, and all else
> Follow'd its falling master as he sank . . . .[10]

In Milton's *Paradise Lost* the War in Heaven occupies not a few lines but an entire book—even more if the military preparations for that battle are included. There is, moreover, a significant change; for here, as was noted earlier, the scene is pulled out of its correct chronological sequence and placed at the centre of the epic. When the poem opens, the celestial battle has already been fought and won, and Satan sprawls defeated in the gulf of Hell together with his rebel troops. The motive for Satan's revenge has therefore already been provided, and the retrospective narration of the War in Book VI adds nothing to the plot's forward movement. It is clear, then, that in its central positioning and in the greater prominence accorded to it, the account of the War fulfils some larger function in Milton's overall design.

In the earlier discussion of Satan as Arch Antagonist, challenging God's authority and evoking thereby a visible display of divine power, the reader was no doubt aware of an anomaly, which I preferred to postpone for fuller examination in this present chapter. I argued there that in seventeenth-century representations of heroic scenes, the artistic focus had shifted from the quiet self-confidence of a hero before battle to the climactic moment of combat itself when, by a supreme effort of muscle and will, he struggles to overcome a redoubtable adversary; and that this new interest accounted for the enlarged stature of Satan in the epic, as a means of enhancing the ultimate victory of God. However, in transferring this baroque concept of an immense conflict from the human battle scenes of a Rubens canvas or such pagan struggles as Hercules and the Centaur, and applying it to the biblical ethos, Milton was faced with a profound problem. While the basic theory remained true— that the greater the power of the challenger, the more impressive would be the final victory—it was obvious that any direct confrontation between Satan and God, so far from augmenting the reader's respect for divine omnipotence, would in itself defeat one of the main purposes of his epic. Any depiction of God himself as engaged in a personal struggle would inevitably detract from that awesome infinitude of the Creator which Milton was at such pains to convey to the reader, and drag God down from his great heights. Satan must never be allowed in any real sense to match even momentarily the immensity of God's power, nor even to approach such equality however impressive he appears in the challenge he poses. The conception of God as a Supreme Incorporeal Being, a blinding radiance above the heavenly chariot, left no room in this epic for anything even vaguely evocative of a hand-to-hand struggle with an Adversary. In brief, then, the anomaly which Milton faced was the task of depicting a trial of strength between God and the Arch Antagonist while at the same time ensuring that God himself must never participate.

The impossibility of such a confrontation was, in fact, not quite so axiomatic as might at first appear. It would not have arisen, for example, had Milton adopted the traditional God of the medieval or Renaissance eras. The *Pantocrator* of the Middle Ages, to which we referred before, seated upon his throne with one hand solemnly raised in blessing and an *Alpha* and *Omega* engraved on either side to symbolise his eternity and all-embracing power, could, as in the Coventry play quoted above, himself sweep aside the rebel angels without any derogation of his own dignity. Nor would it have been difficult to present some sort of celestial battle with the kind of God appearing on the ceiling of the Sistine Chapel. There, in accordance with the Renaissance view of man as a creature '. . . in action how like an angel, in apprehension how like a god', Michelangelo sees no particular daring in presenting Adam as comparable to God in size, in intelligence, and in potential strength, however remote that equality might be from formal theological doctrine. It is only when Milton presents God in the new baroque form as vast beyond human comprehension that such direct confrontation with a single challenger becomes quite impossible. It can, I think, be argued that these two elements in the epic—the enlarged concept of the divine, and the impossibility of direct conflict—are intimately related, and it was in the process of solving the problems inherent in the first of these that Milton found a method of coping with the second.

Before examining the problem of the divine duel, it may be helpful to consider a more general aspect of the battle scenes in the poem. It has long been recognised that illusionism occupies a central place in the baroque mode. Reduplicated columns and pilasters which actually support nothing are introduced to create optically an impression of massivity; yellow light is shed on golden rods to produce a dramatic sense of levitation, and *quadratura* extensions painted in false perspective on a flat ceiling seem to make the ceiling open up to the sky and carry the eye into the distant heavens. There is, however, a fundamental difference between mannerist illusionism and the illusionism of the baroque. In the former, the ultimate purpose is to weaken the viewer's sense of physical solidity. In the altar at S. Stefano in Florence, Buontalenti built two stairways which appear stable and secure from the distance, but as one approaches, they disintegrate before one's eyes, becoming shell-like ornaments impossible to climb. The house which Giulio Romano built for himself in Mantua has basement windows just peeping up above ground level, to suggest from the distance that the building is sinking into the earth; and the famous entrance to the Laurentian Library by Michelangelo contains a 'fluid' staircase which seems to be cascading downwards in widening circles. Such mannerist illusionism constituted a questioning of the spatial stability dominating Renaissance art and architecture, and in a larger sense it marked a resistance to the new rationalist empiricism with its firm reliance on objective, verifiable facts. The mannerist artist—sometimes amusingly, but often in full seriousness—aimed, then, at creating a moment of doubt as the optical impression was contradicted by reality, and the viewer began to distrust the evidence of his senses.

In the baroque, however, the purpose of the illusionism is not to weaken one's faith in the actual but, on the contrary, to convince, either permanently or as long as the viewer can be kept under the spell of the vision. The pilasters and marble slabs used to face a brick wall and thereby to make it appear built of solid stone, are permanent in the visual effect they produce, and only the repair worker or architectural expert will discover their structural redundancy. Similarly, the source of the concealed lighting or the means by which a theatrical effect is achieved are kept hidden from the viewer as far as possible. At times the nature of the deception cannot be completely or permanently concealed. In the Church of S. Ignazio, Fra Pozzo's ceiling (Plate 1) is designed with extraordinary skill to make the columns on the walls appear to project beyond into space, so that it is at first difficult to distinguish where the real columns end and the *trompe l'oeil* begins. The trouble is that such false perspective has its limitations—it only functions effectively when seen from certain angles. From the entrance to the church and, indeed, from almost anywhere in that part of the nave, the effect is superb; but as one wanders away towards the apse, the paintings on the ceiling and those on the interior of the dome become grotesquely distorted. In contrast to the Buontalenti stairs, where the moment of revelation is a source of delight (and the ultimate purpose of the illusion), here there is a feeling of regret as the beauty of the illusion is lost. The distinction is underscored by the fact that in S. Stefano one is intended to walk forward towards the altar and thereby to experience the visual disintegration, while in S. Ignazio the viewer is encouraged not to move, lest the illusion be lost. The artist has placed within the marble floor a small circle on which the spectator is invited to stand, in order to savour from the most perfect vantage-point the full effect of the illusion.

In other words, although the optical devices employed by the baroque artist are deliberately contrived (Pozzo wrote a number of treatises on the technique of artificial perspective), and both artist and viewer are fully aware that the ceiling is actually both solid and flat, the vista itself when the viewer surrenders to the illusion is richly rewarding, more than justifying the deception.[11] If the means used are patently false, the experience to which they lead is a true vision of heaven as the artist conceives it—the blaze of energy and light as Loyola is triumphantly welcomed above, and countless angels are wafted upwards into the dazzling vortex. We are invited by the artist voluntarily to submit to his directions, to stand at the spot designated, and temporarily to disregard the prosaic, struc-tural realities of wall and ceiling in order to be rewarded by a spectacle of celestial infinity and splendour otherwise beyond the perception of man.

That temporary subduing of reason occurs in literature too—what Coleridge once described as the 'willing suspension of disbelief'. It is not that the reader, on taking up a poem, makes a conscious decision to suspend his rational faculties and to believe whatever he reads. The process is more complex. In such forms of literature there is rather a gradual weaning of the reader away from his mundane setting into the world of the imagination. An aroused curiosity, the pleasure of the aesthetic experience, the feeling of being a privileged spectator initiated into a mystery, all these elements may encourage us, while under the spell of the work, eventually to accept weird, dream-like phenomena which our reason would instantly reject outside it.

The critical faculty is not discarded even during the reading, but remains watchful, ready to intervene if the delicate balance is disturbed. To return to Coleridge's own poem, the Ancient Mariner has fascinated us with the mystery of his dream-journey; but when he relates that the seamen there fell lifeless one by one to be replaced by spectres on that ghost ship, a suspicion crosses the sensitive reader's mind. Is the Mariner himself, the narrator now returned to the real world, also supposed to be only a wraith? That would be straining credulity too far. But before the thought can be ar-ticulated, the Wedding-Guest expresses it for him and is at once reassured:

> 'I fear thee and thy glittering eye,
>   And thy skinny hand so brown'—

'Fear not, fear not, thou Wedding-Guest!
            This body dropt not down.'

The poet has forestalled the danger, and the imaginative experience can now be continued. A comparable duality of response operates as we gaze at the Pozzo fresco. The knowledge that it is really a solid, opaque ceiling remains present in the mind; but as the illusion painted upon it draws the eye through the ceiling into the vista beyond and the superb spaciousness of that scene elevates and inspires, so our rational awareness that it is an illusion temporarily recedes, allowing precedence to the imaginative response.

To return to *Paradise Lost*, if the War in Heaven or the wounding of Satan are viewed from a strictly logical angle, then of course the scenes are absurd. As Milton well knew, and as he openly acknowledged more than once in the epic, no angel can suffer bodily wounds or be crushed by a cannon-ball. But to view the scene from a strictly logical angle and to condemn it because of its theological inconsistencies is like condemning Coleridge's poem because stars do not in fact appear within the moon's nether tip nor are ships driven along by the Spirit of the south pole. Such criticism takes these elements out of their context, ignoring the gradual lulling of rational disbelief as the work casts its spell upon the mind. If we submit to the imaginative ambience of the poem and within its context allow ourselves to be led by stages from the beginning of the epic into a heaven of Milton's making, where space and mass preserve their fixed qualities and angels are mighty warriors, then to complain at the climactic moment of the narrative that the scene of war contradicts the laws of reason or the technicalities of theological dogma is tantamount to pulling by the sleeve the rapt spectator in S. Ignazio church, and leading him towards the apse to prove that the perspective is really false. He knows that perfectly well—but from the apse he cannot see that marvellously soaring vision for the sake of which he has voluntarily taken his stand on the designated circle. The technical anomaly here either of muscular angels or heavenly cannon-fire is a prerequisite for the illusion. If, according to Christian belief, a war in heaven *did* occur, there is no other way for the human mind to conceive it, except in terms of devastating gunfire and the clash of arms. The rapt reader, like the rapt spectator in the church, would not for the sake of that technical infraction of logic surrender the awesome scene which Milton has imaginatively created for us:

So spake the Sovran voice, and Clouds began
To darken all the Hill, and smoke to roll
In dusky wreaths, reluctant flames, the sign
Of wrath awak't: nor with less dread the loud
Ethereal Trumpet from on high gan blow:
At which command the Powers Militant,
That stood for Heav'n, in mighty Quadrate join'd
Of Union irresistible, mov'd on
In silence thir bright Legions, to the sound
Of instrumental Harmony that breath'd
Heroic Ardor to advent'rous deeds
Under thir God-like Leaders, in the Cause
Of God and his *Messiah*.

(VI, 56–68)

In a broader sense, this illusionist technique provided Milton
with the solution to one of his central problems. Although any
personal duel between Satan and the omnipotent God of his epic
was quite out of the question, yet such a conflict was essential to his
purpose in offering a baroque demonstration of divine might. The
solution he found—and one permeating the first six books of the
epic—is to create a powerful impression of direct conflict between
God and his Adversary, while yet avoiding any actual confrontation. The illusion is cumulative in nature, the product of
numerous concealed hints and false pointers scattered through the
work and reaching its culmination in the battle scene itself.

At the opening of the poem, as though to assure the reader of
Satan's utter defeat, Milton describes him unequivocally as having
been hurled down to Hell, and the authorial voice of the epic
reminds us of the vanity of the attempted rebellion. Yet tucked
away, even within that initial account, is the stirring comment that
Satan had 'trusted to have equall'd the most High', and the phrase
implants the seed of an idea in the reader's mind. The picture is
momentarily created of two rival powers matched on high, God and
his Arch Antagonist, and though the attempt eventually failed, it
does not at that moment seem to have been so utterly hopeless a
venture as might have been thought:

           . . . aspiring
To set himself in Glory above his Peers,
He trusted to have equall'd the most High,

> If he oppos'd; and with ambitious aim
> Against the Throne and Monarchy of God
> Rais'd impious War in Heav'n and Battle proud
> With vain attempt.
>
> (I, 38–44)

His challenge, we should note, is not treated here with the ridicule or contempt usual in such accounts, and although the outcome, we know, was a crushing victory for God, there is the suggestion of a momentous prelude or 'Battle proud' before that outcome was achieved. Even in the account of his ignominious fall, he is not described as some foolish upstart, but as one who '. . . durst defy th' Omnipotent to Arms'. Within the latter phrase there can be no doubt of the sense of personal duel which Milton wishes indirectly to suggest.[12]

Since this is the opening of the epic, the reader has as yet no detailed knowledge of the events that occurred other than these allusions. For this reason, he must rely on whatever scraps of evidence are offered, and the following scene seems to supply that need. As the fallen angels begin to recover from their plunge to Hell and in the darkness mourn their defeat, it is through them that we obtain our first retrospective account of the War. Normally, their version might be viewed with reservation as being biased, but they so readily admit the totality of their defeat that they disarm our suspicions, and their other comments, in the absence of any contrary view, appear as credible to us as to them. We have no means at this stage of identifying those slight distortions or misapprehensions on their part which together produce the false perspective. Satan describes, for example, how he and his followers

> His utmost power with adverse power oppos'd
> In dubious Battle on the Plains of Heav'n,
> And shook his throne.
>
> (I, 103–5)

Here is the characteristic baroque struggle as in a Rubens battle-scene but enlarged to heavenly proportions, in which we witness the impact of two immense forces held in turbulent stasis until the 'dubious' equilibrium is broken by the final thrust of the victor. The scene is presented as being a direct conflict between God's power and Satan's. Only much later in the epic will we learn how far the defending force actually was from constituting God's 'utmost' power, but at this stage the impression is created of a dangerous rebellion beginning to topple the divine throne and crushed only just in time. Significantly, there are no authorial comments inserted here to deflate their account of the battle, as for the moment Milton wants them to be believed. When, at the end of this long speech, Satan is eventually accused of 'vaunting aloud', the phrase seems to point to his boastful claim of future vengeance, and not to his account of the past War. To lend added credence to his version, there follows at once the reply of Beelzebub who, despite their defeat, still regards his leader with awe for having (as he believes) so seriously imperilled the sovereignty of God:

> O Prince, O Chief of many Thronèd Powers,
> That led th' imbattl'd Seraphim to War
> Under thy conduct, and in dreadful deeds
> Fearless, endanger'd Heav'n's perpetual King . . . .
>
> (I, 128–31)

Time and again the power of the rebels is exalted in this way, partly in order to raise proportionally the splendour of the ultimate victory of God, but partly also to suggest a near-equality of strength. The defeated angels, for example, now recognise God as supreme because their own force was so immense that it could never have been crushed by any other power. He is

> our Conqueror (whom I now
> Of force believe Almighty, since no less
> Than such could have o'erpow'rd such force as ours) . . . .
>
> (I, 143–5)

By placing these assessments in the mouths of the fallen angels, Milton is able, without any danger of heresy, to build in the reader's mind a compelling picture of God challenged personally and forced, as it were, to defend himself with difficulty against a massive attack; and by this device he will at the same time be able to retain the reader's confidence when the truth will later be exposed.

What, then, is the truth as it later emerges? At the conclusion of the discussion in Hell, a decision is taken for war, open or understood, and as though in repetition of the earlier rebellion in heaven, a host of 'mighty Cherubim' hurl their defiance at God.

> He spake: and to confirm his words, out-flew
> Millions of flaming swords, drawn from the thighs
> Of mighty Cherubim; the sudden blaze
> Far round illumin'd Hell: highly they rag'd
> Against the Highest, and fierce with grasped Arms
> Clash'd on thir sounding shields the din of war,
> Hurling defiance toward the Vault of Heav'n.
>
> (I, 663–9)

The threat is immense. The council of strategy is held, and Satan
sets out on his task of vengeance, eventually reaching the bounds of
Heaven. Then the scene and tone of the poem suddenly undergo a
change. The epic narrator pauses, praying for celestial light to shine
inward and permit him to '. . . see and tell/Of things invisible to
mortal sight'. We are wafted far aloft, where the Almighty Father in
the pure Empyrean sits enthroned above all height, and bends his
eye down to the worlds below. Dramatically a new perspective is
offered, revealing the infinite gulf which actually separates Satan
from God. We comprehend the sheer impossibility of his ever
achieving the ambition of dislodging the Supreme Being, or even of
harming God in any way, except within that severely limited area
where free choice has graciously been extended to man by God
himself.

> Now had th'Almighty Father from above,
> From the pure Empyrean where he sits
> High Thron'd above all highth, bent down his eye,
> His own works and their works at once to view:
> About him all the Sanctities of Heaven
> Stood thick as Stars, and from his sight receiv'd
> Beatitude past utterance; on his right
> The radiant image of his Glory sat
> His only Son.
>
> (III, 56–64)

From his calm security, the Omnipotent gazes down at the violent
rage of Satan, whose revenge will only redound on his own head,
just as man's disobedience will redound on his. A different
perspective, validated by the authorial voice of the epic, has been
momentarily glimpsed, and from now on the two perspectives will
need to be carefully integrated.

We mentioned earlier the gradual weaning of the reader away from the rational world of disbelief into the imaginary, with the latter gaining predominance as the celestial vision casts its spell upon him. Now, within that envisioned world, there emerges a further duality of viewpoint. On the one hand there is the conception that the rebel forces did indeed constitute a grave threat to God's power, placing his kingship in jeopardy and being eventually overcome only by an enormous effort on the part of the defending forces; and on the other hand our knowledge of God's supreme inviolability, far beyond the reach of any of his creatures. Initially the two views appear mutually exclusive, but by a remarkable technique, an alternating limitation and expansion of perspective, Milton is able to justify each viewpoint in turn and thereby to create that genuine struggle required by the baroque as a prelude for the final thrust of victory.

One key to the artistic process whereby it is achieved can be found in an apparently minor comment, given no prominence as one reads the poem, yet creating the conditions necessary for the struggle. In the original passage in Revelations upon which this idea of a heavenly battle was based, it is stated that Satan (or 'the Dragon') drew after him one-third of the heavenly host; and Milton dutifully records the fact more than once in the poem.[13] One third of so vast a host certainly constituted a substantial army, but it left a defending force precisely double in size which, on simply logistic grounds and without the need for any miraculous intervention, could effortlessly have swept the rebels out of heaven. Such a ratio would not serve the purpose of the baroque artist at all, fascinated as he is by the meeting of two approximately equal forces, the invincible with the irresistible. It would have been too reminiscent of the easy margin of victory accorded to the traditional Renaissance hero. Instead, therefore, Milton introduces an entirely new idea, which allows him to provide that central baroque demonstration of might. He has God hold back one half of his remaining forces in order to demonstrate that even with forces *equal in number* his own troops cannot be conquered. He commands his archangels:

> Go Michael of Celestial Armies Prince,
> And thou in Military prowess next,
> Gabriel, lead forth to Battle these my Sons
> Invincible, lead forth my armed Saints
> By Thousands and by Millions rang'd for fight;

Equal in number to that Godless crew
Rebellious . . . .

(VI, 44–50)

The result is a perfect compromise between the two perspectives. It leaves God far above with his military superiority untouched, and yet offers the possibility of our witnessing, by his permission, an immense conflict between two well-matched cosmic forces, a conflict which will provide, at least in partial form, a demonstration of divine power. The loyal forces will finally triumph; of that we are never in doubt, not merely on theological grounds but also because the epic has begun by informing us of the outcome. Our surprise, though, is the very reverse, the discovery that their victory is by no means an easy one. Indeed, as we learn retrospectively, the claim of the rebel angels in Hell was not unfounded after all. The battle was, as they had said, genuinely 'dubious' until the final moment, and we learn that 'long time in even scale/The Battle hung'. There are even moments when the rebels are in the ascendancy, and the defenders need all their tenacity and ingenuity to withstand the onslaught.

In this connection, Milton has been censured for contriving to make the battle end in a 'stalemate' merely in order to accord the Son all the glory of leading them to final victory.[14] Such a reading misses, I think, both the purpose and the intrinsic quality of the scene. The term 'stalemate', with its connotations of immobility and paralysis, cannot be meaningfully applied to the tumultuous explosion of energy which marks the climax of the battle. In the baroque mode, as opposed to those which preceded and followed it, resolution is achieved only after powerful resistance, or a strenuous struggle of muscle and will. The cathedral weighs down massively upon the viewer before it offers the release of the well-lit dome interior or the elevation of the soaring angels painted on the ceiling, and without that massivity the subsequent sense of elation is lost. In the same way the dynamic but unresolved battle here functions not simply to reserve the honour of victory for the Son, but to create the conflict between 'ruinous assault' and 'inextinguishable rage' where the near infinity of each power ensures its ability to resist the might of its opponent.

As the authorial voice of the epic reminds us, each individual angel here, whether rebel or loyal, was alone capable of performing deeds on a cosmic scale. Multiply that force by millions of such angels all engaged in furious strife and the result is so cataclysmic

that God himself must eventually intervene in order to contain the
battle and protect the heavens from lasting harm:

> What wonder? when
> Millions of fierce encount'ring Angels fought
> On either side, the least of whom could wield
> These Elements, and arm him with the force
> Of all thir Regions: how much more of Power
> Army against Army numberless to raise
> Dreadful combustion warring . . . .

(VI, 219–25)

If this is a stalemate, it is a remarkably violent one.

There is a further purpose achieved here. From the beginning of
the epic we have watched Milton's 'building block' technique,
whereby each scene, from the tangibility of the setting in Hell, up
through the rugged masses of the planets, and on to the battle of the
angelic hosts, has step by step enlarged the reader's comprehension
of the cosmic magnitude of creation. Now at last we are to witness
the final stages in that ascent, leading as close as humanly possible to
God's own omnipotence, conceived not as a vague, theological
abstraction but as a multiple of visible and demonstrated power. In
the initial scenes, Satan has repeatedly described his army as
combatting God himself, defying the Omnipotent to arms, and
endangering his sovereignty. Now we learn that behind that limited
defending force, sufficient merely to match Satan on numerical
terms, there is a series of further powers—the remaining army of
God which he has never troubled to bring into battle, behind it the
figure of the Son clothed terribly in armour and accompanied by
'ten thousand, thousand Saints', and far, far beyond and above in
the distant Empyreal heights God himself with all his infinite
strength still untouched and untried. For all Satan's claim of
personal combat, God has never needed to stir from his throne and
he conquers merely by a word of command to his servants. In the
same way as a man attempting to ascend a mountain keeps
imagining that he is already scaling the topmost peak, but having
climbed to its summit discovers another peak much higher beyond
it, and yet another beyond that, so our sense of the power of God
becomes immeasurably enhanced as we watch the cosmic struggle
between two celestial armies, knowing that they are dwarfed by a
range of enormously greater powers beyond, leading in the infinite

distance to the inconceivably dazzling power of God himself. And that, as we have seen, was one of the major purposes Milton had set himself in writing the epic, to convey an image of the divine, proportionate to the new vastness of the heavens and yet expressed in physical and at least partially comprehensible terms.

Within the battle scenes this dual perspective is carefully preserved. On the one hand the rebel forces are genuinely intimidating in their strength and, at least from the military viewpoint, worthy rivals of God's angels. The two armies draw up opposite each other front to front 'in terrible array/Of hideous length'. Yet on the other hand we are from now on continually made aware of those immensely larger forces held in abeyance. Just as in an earlier book we learnt how God voluntarily withdraws his power in order to allow man, like the angels, freedom of choice, so here God has decided to withhold his hand in order to allow the loyal angels an opportunity to demonstrate their courage and trust. As Satan advances 'tow'ring, arm'd in Adamant and Gold', Abdiel acknowledges that the Grand Foe does seem 'to sight unconquerable', but he determines to test the latter's strength, finding courage in the knowledge that even if he himself should fail, the final outcome of the war can be in no doubt:

> . . . fool, not to think how vain
> Against th' Omnipotent to rise in Arms;
> Who out of smallest things could without end
> Have rais'd incessant Armies to defeat
> Thy folly; or with solitary hand
> Reaching beyond all limit, at one blow
> Unaided could have finisht thee, and whelm'd
> Thy legions under darkness; but thou seest
> All are not of thy Train; there be who Faith
> Prefer, and Piety to God . . . .

> (VI, 135–44)

The sense of actual warfare is maintained within the limited area of the battle, while the implications of the larger perspective are not forgotten.

There is nothing ethereal about the blow which Abdiel delivers on the crest of Satan, sending him staggering back ten huge paces to sink almost to his knees. The archangel Michael sounds the trumpet, and with 'horrid shock' the battle is joined. For those who interpret Book VI either as comedy or, in accordance with J. H. Hanford's reading, as a lesson in the futility of warfare,[15] there are counter-indications in the text which must on no account be ignored. If, as is claimed, Milton *intended* the scene to be amusing or ironic, how are we to explain those passages which can only have been inserted in order to persuade the reader of the serious, epic grandeur of the struggle? A device often resorted to in literature, when there is a danger of incredulity on the part of the reader, is the system of an outer and inner narrator, each reinforcing the story's persuasive power. *Wuthering Heights* offers a classic instance. Supernatural powers and transcendental passion become believable because of our gradual introduction into the weird events first through the unimaginative Lockwood and then through the commonsensical Nellie Dean. Conrad's *Heart of Darkness*, with its mysterious, symbolic journey into the jungle, adopts a similar technique. The enveloping scene on the Thames estuary establishes for us through the anonymous story-teller the bond of affection and trust between the four seafaring friends, waiting for the turn of the tide; only when they have fallen into a comfortable, contemplative silence, and our confidence has been won, does Marlow himself begin his reminiscences.

So it is here. In the opening invocation of the epic, the narrator, though announcing his intention to pursue things unattempted yet in prose or rhyme, remains within the convention of a bard requesting aid from the muse in relating his tale. He establishes the solemnity of the epic but remains an 'anonymous' narrator. However, as we leave the scene in Hell and are about to soar into the Empyrean heavens, he reappears, this time in a more personal form, with a moving lament for his own loss of sight (III, 21f.). It is neither a casual nor an unwarranted autobiographical digression. As John S. Diekhoff has shown, Milton was committed to the twofold principle that poetry must persuade and that it must persuade towards probity. In the tradition of classical rhetoric, with its firm opposition to sophistry, he maintained that the poet or orator must first be worthy in himself, inspiring confidence in his sincerity, as well as offering a moral message. The image created by the speaker is thus an essential part of the whole. This was at least one of the reasons for Milton's eagerness to defend himself against personal attack, arguing in the *Apology for Smectymnuus* that '. . . I thought it my duty, if not to my selfe, yet to the religious cause I had in hand, not to leave on my garment the least spot, or blemish in good name

so long as God should give me to say that which might wipe it off'.[16]
The lament for his blindness, then, is not a cry of self-pity. Any
potential compassion on the part of the reader is immediately
channelled into a positive literary direction, associating the narrative voice of the epic with such blind visionaries as Homer and
Teiresias, dedicated to the sacred task of prophecy. The fervour of
his invocation here goes beyond the conventions of the classical epic,
setting the tone of high seriousness for the scenes of heaven which are
to follow.

As we approach the War itself, the task of reinforcing the reader's
confidence now devolves upon the inner narrator who may be
expected to claim our fuller trust by virtue of being an archangel, as
opposed to the mortal bard of the epic. If there is to be any
intentional irony or farce in the subsequent scene, then he as
Milton's narrator must be party to it, warning us of the absurdities
of the rebel attempt. Yet his warnings are aimed precisely in the
opposite direction, stressing that however mighty the events may
appear in his recounting of them, they can never match the
immensely greater power of the original conflict. He is hesitant to
describe the battle at all (and reluctance on the part of a narrator is
a recognised device for authors wishing to increase his credibility)
and he agrees to do so only because it may be for Adam's good. In
other words, Milton here is making every effort to bolster our faith
in Raphael, as the latter informs us of the gravity of the scene he is
about to describe; and that very attempt by the poet, by marking
the seriousness with which Milton regards the coming account of the
battle, speaks strongly against Stein's theory of a consciously comic
intent. Raphael pauses, wondering whether he will be able to depict
the exploits of the warring spirits in any manner comprehensible to
man:

> . . . how shall I relate
> To human sense th' invisible exploits
> Of warring Spirits; how without remorse
> The ruin of so many glorious once
> And perfect while they stood; how last unfold
> The secrets of another World, perhaps
> Not lawful to reveal? yet for thy good
> This is dipens't . . . .

(V, 564–71)

Such is his introduction to the War at large; but as he begins the description of the duel between the two champions, Satan and Michael—the very duel which has been the object of so much adverse criticism or interpretation as farce—he pauses again as though in despair of ever finding words which could even approximate to its infinite might:

> They ended parle, and both address'd for fight
> Unspeakable; for who, though with the tongue
> Of Angels, can relate, or to what things
> Liken on Earth conspicuous, that may lift
> Human imagination to such highth
> Of Godlike Power: for likest Gods they seem'd,
> Stood they or mov'd, in stature, motion, arms
> Fit to decide the Empire of great Heav'n.
>
> (VI, 296–303)

To suggest, then, that Milton intentionally presented the scene in ironic disparagement is to ignore the careful framing of the narrative and his repeated attempts to stress both the magnitude and the solemnity of the battle. Moreover, the imagery he employs accentuates the seriousness of his intent. In Homer or Vergil the epic hero is for the most part dignified by similes drawn from the familiar world of nature. At the height of battle he is compared to a wild boar beset by hunters, a wounded lion, or '. . . as when ruinous fire falleth on dense woodland, and the whirling wind beareth it everywhere, and the thickets fall utterly before it, being smitten by the onset of the fire, even so beneath Agememnon son of Atreus fell the heads of the Trojans as they fled . . . '.[17] On the few occasions when the image is drawn from heavenly bodies, like the shield of Achilles whose 'brightness shone afar off as the moon's', the comparison is acknowledgedly from small to great, intended to elevate the hero in our estimation by the very fact that such a lofty comparison is possible. Here the situation is reversed. Raphael concedes that the conflict between the champions of good and evil is beyond description, 'unspeakable' even for the tongues of angels, and for want of an alternative he must resort to comparisons drawn from the *lesser* world of that cosmos visible to man. Now it is the planets which are small compared with the angelic protagonists, but there is nothing else which can serve to convey the immense dimensions of the celestial fight itself:

> . . . such as, *to set forth*
> *Great things by small*, if Nature's concord broke,
> Among the Constellations war were sprung,
> Two planets rushing from aspect malign
> Of fiercest opposition in mid Sky,
> Should combat, and thir jarring Sphere confound.
> Together both with next to Almighty Arm,
> Uplifted imminent one stroke they aim'd
> That might determine, and not need repeat . . . .
> (VI, 310–18)

Again, this description can scarcely be intended to ridicule or minimise the scene. The collision of two planets contributes here too to underscoring the physicality of Milton's celestial setting. The vastness of the physical universe, instead of dwarfing the biblical world, becomes a stepping-stone for comprehending the even greater power of the Creator.

The two champions here are perfectly matched; no odds, we are told, appear between them. Satan, after the earlier blow dealt by Abdiel, has recovered his prestige. He has shown 'prodigious power' on that day and met no equal in arms. As becomes a general in battle, he seeks out his counterpart Michael, before whose huge two-handed sword he opposes the rocky orb of his own adamantine shield. Here is the baroque clash between the insuperable and the apparently impregnable, with that slight advantage to the victor which will determine the conflict. The advantage held by Michael is in the divine origin of his sword which (in the tradition of Achilles' armour received from Pallas Athene), ensures his ultimate superiority, for 'neither keen/Nor solid might resist that edge', and Satan is sent temporarily humbled to the ground. The larger conflict, however, continues, with the rebels now gaining the upper hand. Having recovered from this second fall, Satan, misled by pride, incorrectly assumes once more that his survival has been in the face of an enemy force representing God's greatest strength ('What Heav'n's Lord had powerfullest to send'), and that victory lies within his grasp by means of the new weapon he introduces. Derisively he suggests they should 'briefly touch' on what they propose—that brief touch, as we learn a few lines later, being the 'touch' of the flame to the narrow vent of the cannon. The effect of the celestial cannon is gargantuan, with devilish glut of chained thunderbolts and hail of iron globes ravaging the ranks of the defenders who, as Milton explicitly informed us earlier, though impervious to pain, can be 'from their place by violence mov'd'. The response of the loyalists once they recover is to uproot whole mountains and hurl them at their foes—a scene based, of course, on Hesiod's *Theogony* and therefore dignified for Milton's contemporary reader by the classical epic tradition. This is the passage which, it is argued, constitutes 'custard-pie' farce and perhaps, for the last time, we should examine the text itself for signs of any humorous or farcical intent:

> Amaze,
> Be sure, and terror seiz'd the rebel Host,
> When coming towards them so dread they saw
> The bottom of the Mountains upward turn'd,
> Till on those cursed Engines' triple-row
> They saw them whelm'd, and all thir confidence
> Under the weight of Mountains buried deep,
> Themselves invaded next, and on thir heads
> Main Promontories flung, which in the Air
> Came shadowing, and opprest whole Legions arm'd.
>
> (VI, 646–55)

According to Milton, human war is, compared to this scene, only a 'civil game' and for the second time the battle is presented as potentially so cataclysmic that God himself must intervene to prevent the total destruction of heaven. After the demonstration of celestial might within the circumscribed area of the battle between the angels, his reappearance now affirms that larger perspective which, since Abdiel's speech, had been left unmentioned, the ultimate tranquillity and inviolability of Eternal Providence. God gazes down from his throne above, 'secure' and untouched by the fray; and Raphael reminds us that, so far from having endangered heaven, the entire conflict had been controlled, foreseen and permitted by God.

> . . . and now all Heav'n
> Had gone to wrack, with ruin overspread,
> Had not th' Almighty Father where he sits
> Shrin'd in his Sanctuary of Heav'n secure,
> Consulting on the sum of things, foreseen
> This tumult, and permitted all, advis'd:

That his great purpose he might so fulfil,
To honor his Anointed Son aveng'd
Upon his enemies . . . .

                                                    (VI, 669–77)

The time has come for the conflict to be brought to its end—'War weary hath perform'd what War can do'. This does not mean, as has been argued, that all warfare is futile. If so, why have the Son conquer in the role of a warrior clad magnificently in armour, when a bolt from heaven would have done as well? It is only in this specific battle, between the two vast but equally matched forces of angels, that warfare can do no more; for, as God says, had there been no intervention from above, the combatants, created equal, would have struggled on endlessly in 'perpetual' and indecisive fight.

                . . . sore hath been thir fight
        As likeliest was, when two such Foes met arm'd;
        For to themselves I left them, and thou know'st,
        Equal in thir Creation they were form'd . . . .

                                                    (VI, 687–90)

That intervention from above is carefully arranged to suit Milton's larger purpose. As so often in this epic, his innovation is integrated into the work so smoothly that its originality can easily be overlooked. In the tradition which Milton inherited, including that of the New Testament sources, the final victory had not been accorded to the Son. It belonged either to God, to an anonymous angel, or to Michael as the leader of the loyal forces. In the more recent versions, such as those by Du Bartas and Spenser, God himself casts the rebels down to Hell; in Valvasone's *L'Angeleida* and Vondel's *Lucifer*, Michael, after defeating Satan in single fight, leads waves of troops to overwhelm the rebels, and the Son plays no part. For Milton neither solution is satisfactory. On the one hand his enlarged vision of the divine invalidates the possibility of God's personal embroilment in the strife, while on the other hand, the angels and archangels have already served their turn in the epic. As participants in the indecisive celestial battle, they cannot function effectively as the final overwhelming victors. Were Milton to resort to the usual solution of the baroque mode, either implied or expressed, whereby the victor's final thrust just manages to overcome the apparently insuperable foe, the very smallness of that margin of victory, impressive though it may be for human heroes, would damage that sense of God's immeasurable superiority which it is Milton's purpose to convey. The solution can only be found in some emissary of God who ranks above the archangels and yet below God, and who, by virtue of his higher power, can sweep the Arch Antagonist's army before him without detracting from the impressiveness of their earlier resistance.

The only possible candidate for such a task is the Son—and then only because of Milton's personal belief that the Son was not an equal member of the Trinity but a lesser member, and hence hierarchically eligible for an intermediate role.[18] Even then a problem remained; for how was he to transform into so formidable a warrior the traditional Lamb led meekly to the slaughter, the turner of his cheek to the smiter, the heavenly patron of compassion and mercy, when these formed the primary attributes of Jesus? The source he found was in an allegorical scene in Revelation, containing a rare depiction of the 'wrath of the Lamb'. Although even there it is an angel, and not the Son, who actually binds Satan and casts him into the bottomless pit, the scene is still close enough to serve his purpose, with some little manipulation. The Son is depicted there symbolically as seated upon a white horse and named Faithful and True: 'And the armies which were in heaven followed him upon white horses, clothed in fine linen, white and clean. And out of his mouth goeth a sharp sword, that with it he should smite the nations: and he shall rule them with a rod of iron: and he treadeth the winepress of the fierceness and wrath of Almighty God' (Rev. 19:14–15). The allegory Milton quietly drops, so that the Word of God, described here as a sword which 'proceedeth out of his mouth', becomes a real sword girt upon his 'puissant Thigh'. In brief, the mild Son is transformed into an intimidating figure of martial vigour. Theology too is bent a little to suit his needs, this time without any biblical precedent, allegorical or otherwise. The attribute of vengeance belonging in Christianity exclusively to the Father ('Vengeance is mine, saith the Lord') is now modified. It becomes not only God's but is also '. . . whose he sole appoints' (VI, 808), in order to allow the Son to function as the avenger in his place. Appointed to that task, the Son ascends the divine chariot, 'mightiest in his Father's might', bearing in his right hand ten thousand bolted thunders, and clad in almighty armour. God's inviolable seclusion is thus preserved, yet his might is vicariously displayed.

If, earlier in the epic, Milton had aimed at gently drawing his reader away from the association of angels with translucent, gossamer-like creatures flitting weightlessly through space, here is the crowning accomplishment, a vision of the supposedly meek Jesus executing his terrible ire upon the rebel forces in the full panoply of war. He has become the symbol of celestial power next highest above the archangels, yet still infinitely below the ineffable might of the Supreme Creator. As the Son effortlessly routs the insurgents who, ironically, would now be only too relieved to be overwhelmed with mountains as protection from his wrath, we are again reminded how distant we are from witnessing the ultimate force of heaven. Even at this lower level of forces wielded by a deputy of God, the victory provides only a reduced and restrained exhibition of that lesser might:

> Yet half his strength he put not forth, but check'd
> His Thunder in mid Volley, for he meant
> Not to destroy, but root them out of Heav'n . . . .
>
> (VI, 853–5)

The fall of the defeated rebels—'Heav'n ruining from Heav'n'—afrighting Hell itself and confounding the wild anarchy of Chaos, completes the scene, and the Son returns triumphant to his saints, who '. . . silent stood/Eye-witnesses of his Almighty Acts'. The saints are, by extension, ourselves the readers, privileged through Milton's art to witness this demonstration of divine power in action.

Earlier in the chapter it was suggested that modern interpretations of the War in Heaven as farce or simply as epic failure may arise from a fault in the criteria by which it is judged. Taken out of its baroque context and scrutinised in a coldly logical light, the idea of ethereal spirits donning armour is indeed ridiculous, as Milton was the first to admit. Hence the warning that Raphael is measuring things in heaven by things on earth. It is the continuation of that warning, however, which suggests the real purpose of the scene, as Milton declares through Raphael that he has '. . . reveal'd/What might have else to Human Race been hid'. Like the great religious artists of the baroque, Milton's purpose is to go beyond the factual world and to provide for the willing spectator a vision of superhuman forces in tumultuous yet physically realised conflict, so that out of that compression of energy will erupt the imaginative release into the infinite, the upward surge of religious faith.[19]

Now, at the culmination of the War, the immense cosmic pressures built up by the two hosts locked in combat are suddenly resolved, and the reader's eye raised even higher. The victorious Son is escorted towards the throne above to take his assigned place at the right hand of God, as in one of those apotheoses painted on the ceiling of the nave by a Gaulli or Pozzo, in which the holy figure, surrounded by hosts of hymning angels, rises to the seat awaiting him in the distant heavens. The central figure here, however, is not a saint or martyr as in the Catholic versions but the Son himself, whose glory Milton can unhesitatingly depict. Here again the dazzling brilliance of the paintings is replaced by the verbal contrast of 'Shaded . . . . bright', and where poetry cannot depict directly the soaring upward movement of such apotheoses, Milton offers, as only a truly gifted poet can, the leap of the run-on lines, as the Son '. . . celebrated rode/Triumphant' through the heavens to '. . . his mighty Father Thron'd/On high':

> . . . as they went,
> Shaded with branching Palm, each order bright,
> Sung Triumph, and him sung Victorious King,
> Son, Heir, and Lord, to him Dominion giv'n,
> Worthiest to Reign: he celebrated rode
> Triumphant through mid Heav'n, into the Courts
> And Temple of his mighty Father Thron'd
> On high; who into Glory him receiv'd,
> Where now he sits at the right hand of bliss.
>
> (VI, 884–92)

Such a scene of victorious ascent would have lost all its effect if the Son had merely triumphed over some foolish spirits, ridiculously clattering about in armour—and no-one, I believe, would question the seriousness of Milton's intent in this final ascension scene. On the contrary, it marks the climax of the first part of the epic which has been animated throughout by his baroque concerns, his translation of spiritual conflict into tangible and spatial elements, whereby the implications of the new science can be absorbed and incorporated into his faith.

5 Adventurous Song

The din of battle subsides, the Son returns to his Father in triumph, and the first of Milton's self-appointed tasks, to assert Eternal Providence as the controlling force in the expanded universe has, in effect, ended. Some elements will remain, such as Adam's enquiry into the seventeenth-century theories concerning the planetary systems; but in the same way as our first view of Eden in the earlier part of the poem formed only an interlude in the major drama of the cosmic conflict between God and the Arch Antagonist, so from now on the primary interest of the poem will focus down from the distant heavens to a single garden situated on earth, and the ways of God to men.

This separation of the epic into two equal halves, corresponding to the two tasks defined at the beginning of the poem, may appear a little too neat, a structural division conveniently read into the poem to suit a critical theory; but that was Milton's own view. For him the end of Book VI marks the pivotal point of the poem. 'Half yet remains unsung', he now declares. He could not have meant, incidentally, merely that he had reached the mid-way mark in terms of length, for this statement appears even in the first edition of the poem, before the ten books of the epic were split into twelve, and in that original edition the end of Book VI did not constitute the half-way point of the epic. Quite apart from this technicality, however, the context of his statement makes it abundantly clear that Milton intended the distinction between his two major themes to be felt by the reader, emphasising as it does the overall symmetry of the poem, with the latter half echoing and expanding the theme of the first.

At the close of Book VI, Raphael had summarised the moral lesson which Adam must learn from the rebellion in heaven. With Janus-like effect Raphael's warning points both backwards and forwards, demonstrating that the part of the story related until now has formed a foreshadowing of the scenes about to be enacted. Although Adam in his innocence hopes that all may yet be well, the reader, with the hindsight of history and of his own reading of the Bible, cannot miss the full significance of the admonition which Milton places there. In the same way as Satan's pride has led in Heaven to his own disobedience and fall, so Eve's pride within the Garden will now lead to the disobedience and fall of all mankind:

> . . . let it profit thee to have heard
> By terrible Example the reward
> Of disobedience; firm they might have stood,
> Yet fell; remember, and fear to transgress.

> (VI, 909–12)

The structural balance of the epic is augmented by our knowledge that Man's fall will constitute Satan's revenge for his earlier defeat, with this moment marking the transition between the two themes.

The opening of Book VII sharpens the reader's awareness of this thematic change. The bardic narrator reappears, and touchingly laments his personal lot. He has fallen on evil days, dwells in darkness, and is surrounded by constant danger; but the lament contains a message which must not be missed. Within the mythological garb of an appeal to the muse, he announces to the reader that the change in theme is to be accompanied by a corresponding change in style. Isabel MacCaffrey has shown how effectively Milton exploits the spatial elements of his epic, winging up to heaven, plunging into hell, speeding through the skies, and using innumerable times through the poem such images as 'uprear'd', 'downcast', 'aspire', to reinforce this sense of animated movement.[1] Here, however, the initial phrase of the invocation 'Descend from Heav'n, *Urania* . . .' is more than spatial in its implications. It is a harmonic descent, suggesting a diminution in tone, like the closing of an organ-stop to reduce the volume from the thunder of massed chords to the quieter music appropriate to pastoral scenes and human intercourse. Until this point, the bard recalls, he has striven to soar above the flight of human voice, inspired by the celestial song of Urania herself. Now he begs her to lead him back to earth, to a poetic style more suited to his human abilities, and to the mortal themes which are now to occupy him:

> Up led by thee
> Into the Heav'n of Heav'ns I have presum'd,
> An Earthly Guest, and drawn Empyreal Air,

Thy temp'ring; with like safety guided down
Return me to my Native Element.

(VII, 12–16)

Appeals to the muse are not normally to be taken too seriously.
They are time-honoured conventions without which the epic
flavour of the poem would be lost. Milton himself had used similar
devices elsewhere. In *Lycidas* he pretends at one point that some
greater voice has taken command of the poem. After the 'higher
mood' of Phoebus' speech on fame, the poet apologises humbly for
resuming his own simpler oaten pipe, as though the reader did not
know that he was the author of Phoebus' lines too. When St. Peter
ends his rebuke of the false curates, again the poet assures the streams
and flowers that they can now come out of hiding, as the 'dread
voice is past'. The effect in our passage, however, is more sombre.
His call to Urania, while fulfilling the ritual requirements of the
epic, is directed to her not as the pagan muse but as the symbol of
divine inspiration, dwelling in the presence of God. His prayer is for
aid in adapting his verse to the needs of a changed theme, and it is a
way also of warning us that the transition from a cosmic to a
terrestrial theme is to be accompanied by an appropriate modulation in poetic tone:[2]

Half yet remains unsung, but narrower bound
Within the visible Diurnal Sphere;
Standing on Earth, not rapt above the Pole,
More safe I sing with mortal voice . . . .

This point has been acknowledged in very general terms.
Sensitive readers have long recognised that Milton's style in this
poem is not uniformly magniloquent and sonorous, and that within
the limits of the lofty rhyme, his verse possesses a flexibility allowing
him to adapt it from the tumult of celestial warfare to more gentle
scenes of love, and descriptions of the natural haunts of Paradise.[3]
There are bounds beyond which Milton, with his respect for epic
decorum, will not permit himself to go, however flexible his style
may be. When he describes the birds and beasts playing innocently
together in the prelapsarian world, he will not fall below the level of
grandeur required by the epic genre, and his preference even in
such scenes is for the weighty. To illustrate the 'frisking' of the first-
formed beasts of the earth, he offers, as though in parody of his own

massivity of style, the unwieldy elephant wreathing his lithe
proboscis to make them mirth. It was not that Milton was
temperamentally restricted to weightier verse. He was no Dr.
Johnson, provoking Goldsmith's justifiable retort, 'Sir, if you were
to make little fishes talk, they would talk like whales'.[4] On the
contrary, Milton had proved himself capable of writing with a
feather-like touch when he wished, and when the occasion demanded. A poet who could compose the lines 'Come and trip it as
you go/On the light fantastic toe' was clearly not restricted to organ
tones. There is, however, little trace of such lighter vein in the epic,
and understandably so. His choice since 'L'Allegro' had fallen on
the 'prophetic strain' as more suited to his graver theme.
Nevertheless, within the limits of the epic genre, the variety of his
style is still broad in range.

Fortunately, a discussion of Milton's poetry no longer has to
begin with an attempt to rebut the strictures of T. S. Eliot or F. R.
Leavis. If in 1958 Leavis complained with some justice that
members of the academic world had virtually ignored the case
made out against Milton as a poet even while they made a show of
discussing it, Christopher Ricks' penetrating and witty reply,
Milton's Grand Style, has, together with a number of other studies, by
now consigned the controversy to the annals of critical history.[5] He
has shown how invalid many of the criteria for disparagement really
were, tending as they did merely to prove that Milton was not
Donne nor had ever meant to be; and that many (if by no means all)
of the faults they had identified in his verse could be traced to
insensitivity or to mis-reading on the part of the critics. The
knowledge that even Milton nods is neither new (Addison had
argued it long ago) nor particularly damning, and the consensus
among scholars today is that his verse can stand up to the most
rigorous analysis, and emerge fully vindicated. Indeed, where
critical method appears to disqualify his verse, it is now the critical
method that comes under suspicion; as Empson remarked, one can
well sympathise with those reluctant to accept evidence that
Milton's poetry is bad, when it is so evidently not so.

Nevertheless, within the various studies which have restored
Milton's reputation as a poet, there is one aspect which has, I think,
been underplayed and which is particularly relevant here. The
variety within the Grand Style has been legitimately recognised by
the better critics, and the delicacy and suppleness of his verse
acknowledged in addition to its powerful sonority; yet the basic

difference of style between the scenes of Satan's fall and those of Adam and Eve, or broadly speaking between the first and second halves of the epic, has gone largely unnoticed. One would of course expect a tonal change as we move in subject-matter from the panic-stricken fall of the defeated angels to the idyllic calm of Eden. If there were not, Milton would be failing badly as a poet. Yet even when a scene in the latter half parallels thematically one of the earlier situations the difference in timbre is striking. Here, for example, are two descriptions of an identical scene, the Creation, the first a vigorous and rather splendid account as recalled by Uriel when Satan is making his way towards earth:

> Confusion heard his voice, and wild uproar
> Stood rul'd, stood vast infinitude confin'd;
> Till at his second bidding darkness fled,
> Light shone, and order from disorder sprung:
> Swift to thir several Quarters hasted then
> The cumbrous Elements, Earth, Flood, Air, Fire,
> And this Ethereal quintessence of Heav'n
> Flew upward spirited with various forms,
> That roll'd orbicular, and turn'd to Stars
> Numberless . . . .
>
> (III, 710–19)

This is the Grand Style which Sypher describes so well in baroque terms, when Milton '. . . puts his heaviest masses, his most plastic and monumental images into grandiose motion, releasing the bulk of his material into outflowing waves of energy'.[6] However, if this is the Grand Style of the epic as a whole, why is the next passage, taken from the latter part of the poem, so obviously muted and relaxed?

> Again, God said, let there be Firmament
> Amid the Waters, and let it divide
> The Waters from the Waters: and God made
> The firmament, expanse of liquid, pure,
> Transparent, Elemental Air, diffus'd
> In circuit to the uttermost convex
> Of this great Round: partition firm and sure,
> The Waters underneath from those above
> Dividing . . . .
>
> (VII, 261–69)

The restrained style here has usually been explained as resulting from Milton's fidelity to the biblical text; but that explanation merely shuffles the cards around. The scriptural source is identical for both passages, and we would need to know why Milton chose to remain faithful to the Bible just here, and not in the earlier description. Moreover, if one examines the latter passage closely, it is apparent that only the first three or four lines are faithful to the biblical text, and when he moves away into his own elaboration of the source, the 'expanse of liquid, pure . . .', there is no noticeable change in tone, no vibrant force or energised waves such as distinguish Uriel's earlier description.

What is really missing here stylistically is that very quality which has formed a focal point for our discussion of the baroque until this point—the challenge or powerful resistance which forces the visual and poetic muscles to bulge and strain. The burst of energy in so much of the more vigorous, exuberant art of the baroque period is achieved, as we have seen time and again, by means of an initial thwarting or blocking of force. There is an optical constriction, a hampering of free movement such as the enclosing of a triangular pediment within a semicircular one, the crowding of reiterated courses of cornice upon capitals and pillars, so that the release into the blaze of light above comes not as a quiet raising of the eyes as in a Gothic or Renaissance church, but as a rush of emotion, impelled by the need to overcome the obstacle. On Milton's larger canvas, Satan's rebellion becomes a means of displaying an enormous celestial force crushing the rebellious angels, and the technique is reflected on the smaller scale too. As one would expect in poetry at its best, this basic baroque theme finds its expression in the imagery, the prosody, and the syntactical forms employed in that part of the poem presenting the struggle, and these features disappear once the purpose or content of the verse has changed.

Accordingly, in the Uriel description quoted above, creation is depicted throughout as an imposition of will, the act of overcoming or dominating counter-forces. Confusion is *routed*, wild uproar is *quelled*, vast infinitude *confin'd*, darkness put to flight, and the 'cumbrous' elements compelled despite their weight to 'hasten' to their new abode. It is that surging victory which lends the passage its vigour. The second description from the latter part of the epic is altogether more restful, as no such opposition is assumed. There, if God commands the firmament to form or the waters to divide, they do so obediently and without fuss. There is no assertion here, no attempt to convince by demonstration nor to overwhelm imaginatively by vastness and infinitude. As a result, the potential impressiveness of the latter creation scene is transformed into a quiet recital of the order of events.

This is not, of course, to suggest that the second half of the epic is inferior. On the contrary, the story of the happiness, the fall and the eventual regeneration of man in Eden contains some of the finest and most moving passages in the entire poem; but they move us in a different way, in a manner more intimate and gentle. The account of man's fall draws its poetic strength from a different aspect of the baroque which has as yet scarcely been touched upon here, and accordingly it dispenses with those stylistic techniques aimed at evoking visions of enormous might and inconceivable energy.

The stylistic difference can be confirmed many times over by any random browsing through the epic. Here is a further illustration—again a comparison between two passages describing an essentially similar scene, but producing contrasting effects. Early in the epic, Belial visualises the possibility of God destroying the rebel angels if they persist in their opposition, while towards the end of the poem we are shown the Giants, or Sons of God, destroying their human victims. The theme of the mighty crushing the weak could have produced similar results, yet it is hard to realise, when the two passages are placed side by side, that they even belong to the same epic. Here is Belial's vision of the unimaginable force of divine wrath, *blowing* into rage, *plunging* into flames, *spouting* cataracts, *hurling* and *transfixing* on to rock all who have presumed to challenge him. It is a remarkable and awesome picture.

> What if the breath that kindl'd those grim fires
> Awak'd should blow them into sevenfold rage
> And plunge us in the flames? or from above
> Should intermitted vengeance arm again
> His red right hand to plague us? what if all
> Her stores were op'n'd, and this Firmament
> Of Hell should spout her Cataracts of Fire,
> Impendent horrors, threat'ning hideous fall
> One day upon our heads; while we perhaps
> Designing or exhorting glorious war,
> Caught in a fiery Tempest shall be hurl'd
> Each on his rock transfixt, the sport and prey

Of racking whirlwinds, or for ever sunk
Under yon boiling Ocean, wrapt in Chains . . . .

(II, 170–83)

Set beside this passage the later description of the Giants is closer to
the pastoral tradition. In contrast to the excited enjambement
above, where the emotional force crashes across the line-endings,
here the regular, predominantly end-stopped lines create an overall
distance and restraint. It offers a foretaste of the eighteenth-century
heroic couplet, with its conception of the poet as the detached, and
often sardonic spectator.[7]

> . . . scarce with Life the Shepherds fly,
> But call in aid, which makes a bloody Fray;
> With cruel Tournament the Squadrons join;
> Where Cattle pastur'd late, now scatter'd lies
> With Carcasses and Arms th' ensanguin'd Field
> Deserted: Others to a City strong
> Lay Siege, encampt; by Battery, Scale, and Mine,
> Assaulting; others from the wall defend
> With Dart and Jav'lin, Stones and sulphurous Fire;
> On each hand slaughter and gigantic deeds.

(XI, 650–9)

Where there is a run-on line, it is not a true enjambement suggesting
emotional involvement, but an after-thought, an addendum not vital
to the meaning. There lies '. . . th' ensanguin'd Field/Deserted'—
vastly different from '. . . this Firmament/Of Hell should spout her
Cataracts of Fire'. And when the battle does take place, the
squadrons do not clash with hideous shock, but simply 'join'. If this
is the Grand Style, it is a markedly modified form of it, and suggests
once again the need for some discrimination between the different
streams within that overall style.

We shall return later to this second, quieter variety, but before
doing so, a few last words about the dominant style of the earlier
cosmic episodes. Many of the poetic techniques employed in that
more vigorous mode have been identified by others, and I shall not
examine here in any detail what has already been so widely
acknowledged. There are the lengthy, complex sentences producing an effect of massivity, the 'foreign' idiom echoing the Tuscan
poets with whom Milton was familiar, and the inversion of word-

order which, by treating English as if it were an inflected tongue, gave him the freedom to organise his sentences in accordance with rhythm and emphasis rather than conventional syntax. Matthew Arnold recorded long ago how this freedom from the dictates of normal syntactical order allowed Milton in the opening lines of the poem to create the great rolling period 'Of Man's first Disobedience . . .', which sets the tone for the epic as a whole: 'So chary of a sentence is he, so resolute not to let it escape him till he has crowded into it all he can, that it is not till the thirty-ninth word in the sentence that he will give us the key to it, the word of action, the verb.'[8]

All these elements contribute to the 'monumental' quality of his verse; but it should be noted that they themselves are closely linked, in their weaknesses as well as their strengths, to stylistic changes occurring within the visual arts. Here too there can be no exact equivalents between word and picture, between epic and edifice, and it is not in stylistic detail that we should search for such affinities. Hence our appreciation of all the arts on their own merits, as indeed of each individual artist or writer, who must forge his own tools for his personal act of creation. It is, however, in the larger perspective, such as the changing attitude during this period towards the classics as model and source of inspiration, that one may find a shared concept which each poet or architect worked out in his own way.

One prominent attack on Milton, for example, was directed against the Latinism of his diction, which, it was charged, was the residue of his youthful classical training, and blurred the sharpness of his poetic vision. In recent years, that criticism has been substantially modified. In their less felicitous usage the Latinisms could indeed artificialise the natural scene, interposing a linguistic barrier between the reader and the vista described. The Vergilian balance of noun with adjective, particularly in the training which schoolboys received with the aid of a *Gradus ad Parnassum*, at times encouraged an adjectival redundancy which was to become the besetting sin of minor poets imitating Milton's style in a later era. And he himself is certainly guilty of setting a bad precedent on occasion. In the lines

Whether to deck with Clouds th' uncolor'd sky,
Or wet the thirsty Earth with falling showers . . . .

(V, 189–90)

the word 'uncolor'd' is singularly inept as a description of the ever-changing hues of the sky, and one wonders what insight is added to showers by the epithet 'falling'. On the other hand, such lapses are rare in Milton, and what has been recognised recently is the positive contribution of his Latinisms in elevating the poetry above the colloquialism of everyday speech. A Vergilian phrase such as 'spread his aery flight' does lend a poetic stateliness to the verse, raising it above the human scale as it enquires who will

> . . . find out
> His uncouth way, or spread his aery flight
> Upborne with indefatigable wings
> Over the vast abrupt?

(II, 406–9)

Such Latinisms can, then, be traced back to the Vergilian model. However, the manner in which Milton introduced them into his poem and the place they occupy in the epic as a whole deserve closer attention. For that, it is illuminating to watch how in architecture Vignola and others were responding to the Palladian revival of classicism.

In the mid-sixteenth century, Andrea Palladio had provided for the architects of the humanist age that classical model of elegance, harmony, and proportion which it had been seeking. Brunelleschi and Bramante had for some time been moving away from medieval forms towards such an ideal, but a higher sanction was needed to lend authority to the style. Palladio, by his rediscovery of architectural treatises written by the Roman Vitruvius, and by his own examination of ancient buildings (regarded as among the earliest of archaeological surveys) was able to supply his fellow architects with the basic principles of the Greek and Roman styles in his widely acclaimed *Quattro Libri dell' Architettura* (1570). It did much the same for his own branch of art as Castelvetro's popularising of Aristotle's *Poetics* in the same year, Jasper Heywood's *Seneca His Tenne Tragedies* (1560), and Arthur Golding's translation of Ovid (1567) were doing for European literature. The Greek and Roman classics became the new model, inspiring Ben Jonson to produce modern versions of Menander and Plautus, and Palladio himself to design his own famed and widely imitated Villa Rotunda, with the chaste simplicity of its temple-like porticos placed symmetrically on the four sides of the small building.

However, it was not to last. After its initial enthusiastic reception in Italy and through Inigo Jones in England, the classical ideal inaugurated by Palladio suffered a marked eclipse, and did not come fully into its own again until Lord Burlington reintroduced it as the style *par excellence* for the early eighteenth century. The reason for the eclipse is that during that intervening period the baroque took over the Palladian style, but introduced a drastic change. Instead of continuing the adulation and attempting to attain to the lofty classical ideal, it subordinated classicism to its larger needs. The columns and porticos there are no longer arranged to serve as the culminating achievement of the building, the source of its grace and charm. They are now reduced to the status of contributory motifs, reiterated throughout the structure in order to add cumulatively to the overall majesty and power of the building. The baroque no longer strives after the classical style but transcends it, not least, perhaps, because of its secular origins and the need for paganism now to become symbolically subservient to the Christian ethos.

There is an echo of this in Milton. The aim of *Paradise Lost*, as he repeatedly informs us, is not humbly to imitate the classical epic, but to soar beyond. He admires its greatness as literature, but the Aonian Mount or the heights of Olympus are for him only stepping-stones to the higher biblical heaven. The theme of man's fall and God's mercy is in his view 'Not less but more Heroic than the wrath/ Of stern Achilles', and he announces from the first his determination to pursue things unattempted yet in prose or rhyme—unattempted, that is, in classical literature as well as English. As Professor T. J. B. Spencer has pointed out, for all Milton's indebtedness to Greece and Rome, he writes at times in sardonic disparagement of the classical epic upon which it has so often been assumed he modelled his own poem.[9] Like the architects of his own era, he incorporates such epic devices as the invocation to the Muse, the occasional Homeric metaphor, or the Latinate idiom but only as derivative features intended to be evocative of the genre; and that subordination to a higher purpose is largely responsible for the difference in effect between Milton's Latinisms and those of the eighteenth-century poets. The ultimate praise for which Swift or Pope strove was to be recognised as the new Juvenal or Horace of their eras, capturing for their own age the wit and satire of their admired predecessors.[10] The same might perhaps be said of Milton in his earlier phase, conscious in *Lycidas* of writing in the tradition of the classical, pastoral elegy, and attempting to echo in English the mood and tone of Theocritus. By the time of *Paradise Lost*, however, he had changed. There the texture of his verse is very rarely, and then only momentarily, evocative of Homer or Vergil, as critics have begun recently to note, and the Latinisms serve only as smaller units or motifs in the larger structure. In the following passage, *neighbouring Arms, opportune excursion, unvisited of* are immediately recognisable Latinisms, like the triangular pediments and Ionic pillars in a baroque church, but the passage as a whole is, like that church, very far from classical in its final effect:

> . . . perhaps in view
> Of those bright confines, whence with neighboring Arms
> And opportune excursion we may chance
> Re-enter Heav'n; or else in some mild Zone
> Dwell not unvisited of Heav'n's fair Light
> Secure, and at the bright'ning Orient beam
> Purge off this gloom . . .
>
> (II, 394–400)

One has only to compare Milton's terrifying plummeting of the rebel angels with Vergil's urbane and balanced description of the Titans' fall to sense the difference in timbre between them:

> hic genus antiquum Terrae, Titania pubes,
> fulmine deiecti fundo volvuntur in imo.
>
> (*Aeneid* VI, 580–1)

Even at the most gripping moments of the *Aeneid*, as when the aged Priam strikes out helplessly against the brutal invaders, we never lose, and are never intended to lose, our appreciation of the literary skill, the sophisticated delight in a well-turned phrase or 'golden' Latin line where noun is echoed by noun, adjective by adjective, and the caesura acts as a central pivot. This is perhaps the basic contrast between the Helleno-Roman view of life and the Hebraic, where for the classics artistic form was a praiseworthy end in itself, while for the scriptural prophet literature was always primarily didactic, a tool for impressing upon man the enormity and urgency of his moral tasks in the universe.[11] The pastoral idyll both of Theocritus and of Vergil presents a genteel literary competition between two shepherds, while a third adjudicates the prize not for the fervour of the shepherd's passion but for the artistry whereby he transmutes it into poetry; and writers produced treatises on poetics, or composed poems on the art of poetry. In contrast, the biblical prophet never ceased to regard his poetry as an instrument for a higher ethical purpose. Milton, needless to say, had in *Paradise Lost* donned the mantle of the prophet, identifying himself with the moral impetus of the biblical tradition; and in this respect, too, his major purpose is reflected in the detailed features of his prosody. Where Pope gives prominence to his Vergilian circumlocutions, relishing them for their own sake as evidence of his own poetic wit and elegance, Milton inserts them unobtrusively, catching their epic associations but proceeding to dwarf them as the passage surges towards its visionary power. In his well-known description of an angler, Pope offers us the 'scaly breed' and 'bending reed' as highlights of the verse, teasing the reader with their clever side-stepping of banal words considered inappropriate for poetry:

> With looks unmoved, he hopes the scaly breed,
> And eyes the dancing cork, and bending reed.
> Our plenteous streams a various race supply,
> The bright-eyed perch with fins of Tyrian dye.[12]

For Milton, however, such Vergilian phrases as 'steers his flight' and 'incumbent on', while they serve by their un-English idiom to evoke associations with the Latin epic, remain only minor touches, as we are swept into the excitement of a grander vision far removed from the conscious artistry and more detached narration of the classical epic:

> Then with expanded wings he steers his flight
> Aloft, incumbent on the dusky Air
> That felt unusual weight, till on dry Land
> He lights, if it were Land that ever burn'd
> With solid, as the Lake with liquid fire
> And such appear'd in hue; as when the force
> Of subterranean wind transports a Hill
> Torn from *Pelorus*, or the shatter'd side
> Of thund'ring *Aetna*, whose combustible
> And fuell'd entrails . . . .

(I, 225–34)

What holds true for the prosody is repeatedly expressed more directly in the text. His allusions to classical myth demonstrate this 'stepping-stone' technique, whereby he exploits the established dignity and splendour of the classics to reach beyond, or, as Vignola's Il Gesù had done with the Palladian style, to subordinate it to a higher end. The hosts assembled at the famous epic battles in Thebes or Troy, where gods had fought side-by-side with men, become reduced here to pygmy proportions before the awesome might of Satan's army:

> For never since created man,
> Met such imbodied force, as nam'd with these
> Could merit more than that small infantry
> Warr'd on by Cranes: though all the Giant brood
> Of *Phlegra* with th' Heroic Race were join'd
> That fought at *Thebes* and *Ilium*, on each side
> Mixt with auxiliar Gods . . . .

(I, 573–9)

Milton's association with the biblical tradition, where necessary at the expense of the classical, sheds light also on his use of word-play, which has formed another reason for critical attack, on the grounds that his punning detracts from the seriousness of the message. 'O Eve, in evil hour . . .' is a well-known instance. In fact, Milton was better acquainted with the biblical tradition than his critics. He had the added advantage of knowing the original Hebrew, where solemn word-play of this kind is fully authenticated by the prophets. Inevitably, the English version loses all trace of it in translation, and with it much of the rhetorical force of such passages. When Isaiah complained bitterly that God 'had . . . looked for judgment, but behold oppression; for righteousness, but behold a cry', in the Authorised Version the pointed contrast of the original has disappeared: 'He looked for *mishpat* but behold *mispah*; for *tzedakah* but behold *tze'akah*' (Is. 5, 7). Christopher Ricks is again right when he recognises the play of *Eve* and *evil* as a solemn knell rather than a jingle, even though he may not have known of this biblical tradition on which Milton relied. The Bible had always assumed there to be a metaphysical quality in people's names, linked, often obscurely, to some aspect either of their character or their destiny. Hence the command that Jacob's name ('the deceiver') be changed to Israel ('he who wrestled with God') after his struggle with the angel, for it marks a turning-point in his inner development and in the role he is to play henceforth in his people's destiny.[13] In the blessing he delivers to his sons before his death (Gen. 49), their names repeatedly offer hints of the future in store for the tribes descended from them. This is the tradition behind Adam's taunting of Eve in *Paradise Lost*, that she has proved only too true to the warning of evil concealed in her name. The biblical consciousness of a divine destiny unifying all aspects of creation, and reflected even in the names of objects as well as people, lends a deeper resonance to Milton's perception of such ironies in his own account of the biblical story. The epic opens with his description of man's mortality as the 'Fruit' of that forbidden Tree, and there is no trace of humour in such irony. The right to pursue such metaphysical word-play even when names of people and objects had been translated from their Hebrew originals into another tongue had, incidentally, long been accepted within the Church, on the grounds that God was responsible at Babel for having formed these other languages too, and hence could transfer the subtler associations to them when he wished. Witness the long-established assumption that the verbal identity in English of *Son* and *Sun* (in an age unbothered by spelling) had implications far beyond coincidence. Donne could take that initial identity for granted in developing it into one of his most brilliant images of the Crucifixion:

> There I should see a Sunne, by rising set,
> And by that setting endlesse day beget.[14]

To assume, therefore, that word-play of this kind in Milton detracts from the seriousness of his message, is to ignore that consciousness of an all-pervasive destiny permeating language as well as history, such as had animated the biblical and prophetic tradition in which he wrote.

In addition to the foreign-sounding Latin idioms which Milton introduced to evoke epic associations, there is a further stylistic device which, in the earlier part of the epic, is of major importance in creating the powerful effect of his lines. Although the adjectives most commonly used by Milton are, surprisingly enough, such simple words as *good, high, fair, bad, happy*, and *sweet* (as a statistical survey has established[15]), the adjectives which reverberate in the memory and seem most distinctly Miltonic in those cosmic scenes are such heavier epithets as *immeasurable, intractable, irremediable*.

Their massivity contributes obviously enough to the weight of the line, but there is, I think, a far more important reason for the lasting impact they produce. Style is, at its best, not an extraneous element joined to content. Ideally it grows organically out of the subject-matter, as an integral part of it, corroborating in its smallest details the theme, mood, or tone of that content, and hence reinforcing the final, overall effect of the central message. Within these early books, the central baroque theme is, as we have seen, that of infinite strength overcoming powerful resistance in order to demonstrate its might. These epithets introduced so often into the cosmic scenes as to become characteristic of them in fact convey wonderfully in miniature that very theme in action. In place of a simple adjective such as *pure*, with its associations of quietness and passivity, Milton conjures up a powerful epithet such as *incorruptible*. A negative prefix thrusts against the active verb *corrupt* to create an energised tension. The suffix then expands *uncorrupted* into *incorruptible*, enlarging the term into one of eternal supremacy, for ever crushing all attempts at seduction in the future as well as in the past. Into one word he has compressed the image of a supreme power overcoming all opposition and achieving infinite and dynamic dominion.

It is a device reiterated throughout the early books of the poem. *Unextinguishable* fire, *insatiable* in pursuit, *indissolubly* firm. The gates of Hell are not merely strong but *impenetrable*, the loss of Heaven *irreparable*, and the forces of God *irresistible, unconquerable, invincible*. The merely human heroism traditional in the classical epic is thereby elevated to cosmic proportions by the superlative and crushing might implicit in such epithets:

> Far otherwise th' *inviolable* Saints
> In Cubic Phalanx firm advanc'd entire,
> *Invulnerable, impenetrably* arm'd:
>   . . . in fight they stood
> *Unwearied, unobnoxious* to be pain'd . . . .
>
> (VI, 398–404)

The effect created is what Wölfflin long ago defined in the visual art of this period as the 'atectonic' style, when a scene refuses to be contained within the limits of the canvas and seems to burst out of its frame.[16] Milton applies this technique to space as well as military prowess. Adjectives defying spatial restriction together create a vista of unimaginably expanded size, the *illimitable, boundless, infinite, bottomless, immeasurable* abyss. One might imagine such words to be the inevitable concomitant of celestial space, but as usual we have only to look back to the Renaissance to perceive how specifically Miltonic and baroque the usage is. Spenser's heavens in contrast seem scarcely larger than man-size. There, the fall of the entire rebel host only creates an emptiness in the 'wyde Pallace' of God:

> But that eternall fount of loue and grace,
> Still flowing forth his goodness unto all,
> Now seeing left a waste and emptie place
> In his wyde Pallace, through those Angels fall,
> Cast to supply the same . . . .[17]

There is nothing immeasurable, limitless, or vast in that description.

In *Paradise Lost* these adjectives are often given augmented force by being placed at the beginning of a line as the culmination of an enjambement. There they bring the sentence to a rumbling halt, like some locomotive meeting the terminal buffers:

> The Tow'rs of Heav'n are fill'd
> With Armed watch, that render all access
> Impregnable . . . .

(II, 129–31)

> Thir armor help'd thir harm, crush't in and bruis'd
> Into thir substance pent, which wrought them pain
> Implacable.

(VI, 666–8)

> Nor did they not perceive the evil plight
> In which they were, or the fierce pains not feel;
> Yet to thir General's Voice they soon obey'd
> Innumerable.

(I, 335–8)

> Hell at last
> Yawning receiv'd them whole, and on them clos'd,
> Hell thir fit habitation fraught with fire
> Unquenchable.

(VI, 874–7)

The final word in these instances echoes away into space, reinforcing the sense of boundless range and defiant assertion which these earlier books seek to convey.

Milton held no monopoly over such words as *immeasurable* or *inextinguishable*, characteristic as they are of his style. They do occur in the works of other poets. Yet there is something specifically Miltonic both in the frequency with which they appear in that part of the epic and, most of all, in the prominence which such positioning accords them. Wordsworth, in one of those sonnets written when he was much under Milton's influence and an admirer of his magniloquent tones, does echo the style; but as a romantic poet not aiming at the full reverberating baroque effect, his lines are quieter and more meditative:

> In our halls is hung
> Armoury of the invincible knights of old:
> We must be free or die, who speak the tongue
> That Shakespeare spake; and the faith and morals hold
> Which Milton held.

The word *invincible* appears there, evocative of heroism and national pride, but one can imagine that slight yet profound change which Milton would have made had he composed the line. Instead of

> In our halls is hung
> Armoury of the invincible knights of old:

he would have written

> . . . the armoury of ancient knights
> Invincible.

suggesting by that not a historical fact but a stirring challenge to anyone daring to question their supremacy. Indeed, there is a close instance in God's command to his archangel:

> . . . thou in Military Prowess next,
> Gabriel, lead forth to Battle these my Sons
> Invincible.
>
> (VI, 45-7)

The theme of resisted might is to be seen stylistically not only in these adjectival forms, but also in the imagery and texture of the longer passages. The scene of Satan rising from the lake after his fall from heaven could have been presented even in Milton's enlarged terms as that of a warrior gradually recovering from a staggering blow and eventually regaining his feet in order to resume the fight. Instead, in both language and imagery, the poetry creates the tensions of continual thrust and counterthrust. There is an architectonic stress as vigorous insurrection struggles up against the crushing downward force of divine authority. He lies bound down by heavy chains, against which he 'heaves' his head only to heap on himself destruction. His rebellion results in infinite goodness and grace from God to man, but on him will pour treble confusion, wrath, and vengeance. Accordingly, Satan does not just rise, but '*rears* from off the Pool/His mighty Stature', against the huge forces working in opposition. The scene in effect foreshadows the magnitude of the conflict to be fought:

> So strecht out huge in length the Arch-fiend lay
> Chain'd on the burning Lake, nor ever thence
> Had ris'n or heav'd his head, but that the will
> And high permission of all-ruling Heaven
> Left him at large to his own dark designs,
> That with reiterated crimes he might
> Heap on himself damnation, while he sought
> Evil to others, and enrag'd might see
> How all his malice serv'd but to bring forth
> Infinite goodness, grace, and mercy shown
> On Man by him seduc't, but on himself
> Treble confusion, wrath and vengeance pour'd.
> Forthwith upright he rears from off the Pool
> His mighty Stature . . . .

(I, 209–22)

This is the spatial dialectic of the epic in which the forces of rebellion struggle upwards against the ultimately unconquerable powers of the heavens above, the conflict being reflected in the very movement of the verse.

In a stimulating discussion of *Paradise Lost*, Roy Daniells has rightly singled out as major baroque themes the concepts of unity, power, and will which dominate the epic. They characterise

Milton's God, whose absolute unity and power find their expression in absolute will, in a demand for total obedience from his creatures. In the same way, he argues, as Bernini's piazza at St. Peter's does not so much invite as visually compel the spectator to ascend the steps to the basilica, so Milton's God, though allowing his creatures freedom of choice, in fact imposes his will upon them by threatening with destruction all who dare to disobey. Satan too, as the Idol of Majesty Divine, incorporates those qualities, if in modified form. He draws the forces of rebellion into 'Union Irresistible' under his control, his insurrection is a brazen act of will directed against God, and even after his defeat he is motivated in his seduction of man by the 'unconquerable Will and study of revenge'.

It is tempting to carry the argument further and to assume, as Daniells does, that in Eden too we witness '. . . man's rebellious will thrusting up against the will of God'.[18] Such a reading would establish a single axis for the entire epic; but, attractive as the theory may be, the poem as Milton wrote it will not conform to that pattern. If the fall of Satan foreshadows the fall of man as an act of disobedience against divine will, there is nevertheless a profound qualitative difference between them; for Satan's rebellion is depicted throughout as a trial of strength, while man's is at all times seen as the outcome of weakness. Satan needs no encouragement to be strong, as Adam constantly does. On the contrary, the Arch Antagonist is animated by an excess of self-confidence, by a proud conviction that he can attain to equality with God, and he un-hesitatingly exerts all his power to achieve it. His is a wilful revolt. Adam, on the other hand, is from the first presented to us as 'innocent, frail man', created, it is true, sufficient to stand but also created vulnerable and infirm, requiring repeated injunctions and exhortations to be on his guard and to stand fast against temptation. Even before the Fall, he admits that he feels '. . . weak/Against the charm of Beauty's powerful glance', and once the serpent begins his task, guile finds 'too easy entrance' into Eve's heart, and Adam in his turn is 'fondly overcome with Female charm'.[19] They succumb through infirmity, not audacity, and at no point can either of them be legitimately described as thrusting a rebellious will against the will of God. Indeed, the only resolution Adam makes in the entire scene is to die with Eve—not in defiance of God, but sadly, in full knowledge of his guilt, reluctantly 'Submitting to what seem'd remediless'.

This contrast between the cosmic vigour of Satan's disobedience and the weakness of man's surrender to temptation accounts to no small extent for the change in poetic tone which the bardic narrator has announced. The poet is descending not only from celestial heights to more familiar ground, but also from the dynamic vortex of clashing forces and conflicting wills to the quiet garden where two vulnerable creatures are about to relinquish eternal happiness in exchange for a mere apple. Satan, at least, had had the prospect of supreme kingship before him as he determined to revolt, but mankind has fallen for the most trivial of reasons. As Satan gleefully reports on his return:

> Him by fraud I have seduc'd
> From his Creator, and the more to increase
> Your wonder, with an Apple . . . .
>
> (X, 485–7)

The change in prosody is marked. The powerful 'implosive' adjectives disappear, architectonic stress is relaxed, the rolling periods contract, and the verse as a whole now inspires tenderness and compassion rather than awe. At the climactic moment of this second Fall, as Eve is finally tempted and mankind doomed, the modulation in tone is striking. So simple is the description there, so lacking in the magniloquent 'Grand Style', that one might miss its significance entirely were it not for the response of Earth and Nature. Even they, instead of cataclysmic thunderbolts or earth-quakes, respond only with a wound and a sigh:

> So saying her rash hand in evil hour
> Forth reaching to the Fruit, she pluck'd, she eat;
> Earth felt the wound, and Nature from her seat
> Sighing through all her Works gave signs of woe
> That all was lost.
>
> (IX, 780–4)

How different in poetic strategy, as well as mood, from the energised vision of Satan at the corresponding moment of the earlier Fall, his own act of defiant rebellion:

> High in the midst exalted as a God
> Th' Apostate in his Sun-bright Chariot sat

Idol of Majesty Divine, enclos'd
With Flaming Cherubim, and golden Shields . . .
Satan with vast and haughty strides advanc'd,
Came tow'ring, arm'd in Adamant and Gold.

(VI, 99–110)

While examining the cosmic struggle of Milton's opening books, we have inevitably, in our search for parallels, been looking towards the more vigorous aspects of baroque art, exemplified in the battle scenes by Rubens or the straining biceps of his wrestling heroes; but there is another side even to his art. The rich mellowness of his *Château de Steen* or his *Landscape with a Cart at Sundown*, the languid, buxom nudes of his *Judgement of Paris* or *Diana Bathing* offer scenes entirely free from the tumult and conflict which characterise his more violent canvases; and yet they are no less intrinsic to the baroque. As has been recognised, the quality unifying all his work, vigorous and tranquil alike, is his delight in the superabundance of a nature freely pouring forth its wealth and power with assurance of unlimited supplies to come. His landscapes and serener scenes present, in fact, a second aspect of the baroque impulse to celebrate divine creation. Instead of the kinetic force and brilliance of the heavens, his admiration turns here to the rich variety and vitality on earth, both in the natural world surrounding man and in the natural beauty of man and woman themselves.

Hence that element in Rubens' work which has so often puzzled subsequent eras and at times has seemed even blasphemous, that his exuberant delight in the flesh animates his religious canvases no less than his pagan. He himself was a devout Catholic, and despite his enormously busy life, is said never to have missed attending morning Mass. Yet he rejected out of hand the deep-rooted tradition in Christianity which despised the flesh as merely the temporary, mortal 'rags' clothing the soul. Instead he regarded that flesh as vibrant evidence of the beauty and vigour which God had chosen in his bounty to bestow on mankind. There is no place in his art for a medieval *contemptus mundi* such as the Mannerist painters of his own age had revived, with monks gazing at skulls to remind them of the ephemerality of this world. The commandment to which he responds most readily is God's first commandment to man, to be fruitful and multiply. His ideal female is not, as for so many other artists, a slim young maiden coyly waiting to be initiated into the rites of love, but a mature woman in the full bloom of maternity, with a plump child or two seated on her lap, and ample breasts that have given and will again give suck to the young. Accordingly even the weight of his females (one has only to recall the captors in *The Rape of the Daughters of Leucippus* struggling to lift their heavy prizes off the ground) symbolises for him the promise of health and fecundity; and everything his brush touches becomes suffused with warm, glowing hues suggestive of opulence in a world filled with mass, energy, and colour.

In baroque architecture, this amplitude is reflected not only in the multiplication of plinths, columns, cornices, and architraves, together with the wealth of gold-leaf, onyx, and porphyry that create the overall richness of a church or palace interior, but even in the minor decorative features. There is an astonishing profusion of motifs in the stucco ornamentation characteristic of that style. In one small area of Cortona's ceiling decoration for the Sala di Giove in the Palazzo Pitti (Plate 12) can be discerned more shapes, figures, and decorative devices than one would have thought could be crowded into so small a space, and all executed with an extraordinary wealth of detail. Two human figures are linked by garlands to a shell-shaped image, which is supported by two chubby putti. They in turn bestride an elaborate medallion representing in relief a charioteer being struck down by one of Jove's thunderbolts. The medallion is held in place by a pair of mythological creatures suggestive of mermaid and merman, and all this is set against an ornate background of cornucopias, shells, horns, grapes, and a lion's head, the entire feature resting on a cornice composed of at least ten courses of variegated decorative motifs, one of which alone contains a whole series of theatrical masks.

Such is the richness and profusion which lends a baroque sumptuousness to the quieter scenes of Eden in *Paradise Lost*:

> . . . a circling row
> Of goodliest Trees loaden with fairest Fruit,
> Blossoms and Fruits at once of golden hue
> Appear'd, with gay enamell'd colors mixt:
> On which the Sun more glad impress'd his beams
> Than in fair Evening Cloud, or humid Bow,
> When God hath show'r'd the earth; so lovely seem'd
> That Lantskip: And of pure no purer air
> Meets his approach, and to the heart inspires

Vernal delight and joy, able to drive
All sadness but despair: now gentle gales
Fanning thir odoriferous wings dispense
Native perfumes, and whisper whence they stole
Those balmy spoils.

(IV, 146–59)

The natural world in Milton's epic is distinguished by its warm
and teeming fecundity. He presents not 'painted' or static scenes but
an earth continually sprouting and burgeoning, impregnated with
showers and blessed with blossoms and ripe fruits. This image of
fertility he applies retrospectively to the first act of creation, which
becomes for him a process of insemination and birth. In the
scriptural account, there is no hint of this—God speaks, and at his
word the world comes into being, as at the wave of a conjuror's
wand. In Milton, the opening lines of the epic appeal to the Spirit
that sat 'brooding' on the vast abyss and made it pregnant. From a
host of medieval and rabbinic commentaries on the hovering of
God's spirit over the abyss, Milton, as usual, selects the one most
suited to his own poetic needs and quietly incorporates it into his
epic structure as though no other were possible.[20] When Raphael, at
Adam's request, recounts the story of Genesis in more detail, the
dominant images of impregnation and birth, of gestation and
incubation, inform the verse with the plenitude associated with
abundance of growth and propagation. Beginning with that
moment alluded to in the invocation, when the Spirit of God spread
its wings on the watery calm, Raphael describes how it proceeded to
infuse its 'vital warmth' throughout the fluid mass:

. . . in the Womb as yet
Of Waters, Embryon immature involv'd
Appear'd not: over all the face of Earth
Main Ocean flow'd, not idle, but with warm
Prolific humor soft'ning all her Globe
Fermented the great Mother to conceive,
Satiate with genial moisture . . . .

(VII, 276–82)

Once impregnated, the waters 'generate/Reptile with Spawn
abundant', and the tepid caves and fens 'Thir Brood as numerous

hatch, from th' Egg that soon/Bursting with kindly rupture forth
disclos'd/Thir callow young'. Then the earth is commanded to
bring forth its living insects and beasts, and 'straight/Op'ning her
fertile Womb teem'd at a Birth/Innumerous living Creatures'. The
process of proliferation continues with infinite ramifications until
earth swarms with bees and drones building their waxen cells stored
with honey, and the multitude of fish and fowl in a nature yielding
numbers and variety without end. Here is God's boundless
creativity conceived no longer in terms of immeasurable space, but
as the vitality of propagation here on earth:

> . . . each Creek and Bay
> With Fry innumerable swarm, and Shoals
> Of Fish that with thir Fins and shining Scales
> Glide under the green Wave, in Sculls that oft
> Bank the mid Sea . . . .
>
> (VII, 399–403)

The Garden of Eden shares this quality of copious increase. The
vegetation there is thick and luxuriant; and the plentiful fruit,
which is satisfying also to sight and smell, provides flavours sufficient
for the most discriminating palate. Eve is told to 'bring forth and
pour/Abundance' in a meal fit for their honoured guest.
Accordingly '. . . for drink the Grape/She crushes, inoffensive must
and meaths/From many a berry, and from sweet kernels prest/She
tempers dulcet creams' (V, 344–47). The richness of the Garden is
acknowledged too in the tasks that Adam and Eve must perform.
From the Bible's simple command that man should 'work' the
ground, we might have assumed that he and his helpmate would be
employed in encouraging the plants to grow.[21] Since there were no
weeds before the Fall, we would expect to see them watering the
shrubs or tending the seeds in preparation for transplanting. In
Milton's Eden, however, no such aid is required, for everything
grows spontaneously and in profusion. As for the fruit, 'abundance
wants/Partakers, and uncropt falls to the ground' (IV, 730). The
task which keeps the gardeners busy from morn to eve is not fostering
growth but pruning or clipping away the continually proliferating
plants. Whatever they cut back by day sprouts again by night, when
Nature 'multiplies/Her fertile growth, and by disburd'ning grows/
More fruitful' (V, 318), and they realise that there are needed

'More hands than ours to lop thir wanton growth' (IV, 629). Like the stucco motifs which luxuriantly spill over into each other's domain, so here the overwoody trees reach out their pampered boughs too far, needing to be checked, while the Vine entwines her marriagable arms about the Elm, bringing as her dowry the clusters of grapes to adorn his leaves (V, 213).

As that last image suggests, the setting of the garden is in many ways a paradigm for Adam and Eve's own natural condition. Barbara Lewalski has revealed to us how far Eden here parallels the 'paradise within', where wanton desires need constantly to be curbed.[22] Even in their innocent state, their Mind and Fancy are only too apt 'to rove/Uncheckt' (VIII, 188). They must prune and lop back their own impulses to 'mazy error', in order to prevent their natures from returning, like an untended garden, to the pristine condition of chaos. For them too there can be no one-time pruning, and whatever restraints they impose today must be reapplied with no less rigour tomorrow when those same wanton desires grow back with renewed strength. When their vigilance is momentarily relaxed, Eve does reach forth her pampered hand too far, and all is lost.

Like the fruit of the Garden, Eve too is rich in the mature sensory satisfaction she can offer. She has a softness and a sweet attractive grace inspiring love and amorous delight, and Milton rejoices in her opulent beauty. From any other Puritan one might have expected a decorous veiling of her charms. Even though the nakedness of man and woman before the Fall was an integral part of the original story, in a literary as opposed to a visual depiction of the scene, a passing allusion would have sufficed. Yet here Eve's nakedness is repeatedly given prominence as the culmination of the joys offered by the Garden. Without lasciviousness, but also without prudery, he describes in that first scene in Eden how ' . . . her swelling breast/ Naked met his under the flowing Gold/Of her loose tresses hid' (IV, 495–7). Like those naked figures surrounded in the stucco decorations by cornucopias and luscious bunches of grapes, so here the 'youthful dalliance' of the pair is placed within the luxuriant natural scene where all flowers, fruits, streams, and banks join in offering them the fulfilment of their every desire. After their pleasant labours, they come with wholesome thirst and appetite to their evening meal:

> Nectarine Fruits which the compliant boughs
> Yielded them, side-long as they sat recline
> On the soft downy Bank damaskt with flow'rs:
> The savory pulp they chew, and in the rind
> Still as they thirsted scoop the brimming stream;
> No gentle purpose, nor endearing smiles
> Wanted, nor youthful dalliance as beseems
> Fair couple, linkt in happy nuptial League . . . .
>
> (IV, 332–9)

The sensuousness of Milton's Garden has appeared to some readers inconsistent with his Puritanism. Eve, it is said, becomes for him a seductive image of fleshly desires towards which his own warm sexuality unconsciously draws him. As a result, he himself succumbs to her attractions at the very moment when he intends the reader to condemn Adam for that sin.[23] The fact that the Puritans had rejected celibacy as an ideal and condoned marital intercourse does not really answer the charge. William Gouge might maintain that physical union is '. . . one of the most proper and essential acts of marriage', and William Whately warn the contemporary Puritan that neither partner can 'without grievous sinne deny it' to the other,[24] but that is not the same as the voluptuous descriptions of Eve in naked beauty entering a blissful bower endowed with fragrant plants, verdant walls, and rich inlay of violet, crocus, and hyacinth, where Love waves his purple wings and revels as the happy pair enjoy the rites of their nuptial bed. The answer must be sought elsewhere.

To suggest that Milton unconsciously sympathised with views he thought he was condemning recalls the assumptions behind the so-called 'Satanist fallacy'—that his suppressed passions surfaced against his will to contradict his declared purpose. Here, too, the suggestion underestimates his independence of spirit and his determination to desert convention when he believed the truth lay elsewhere. There is more than a grain of truth in Tillyard's wry comment that, had Milton been in Eden in place of Adam, he would probably have eaten the fruit himself and then written a treatise to justify his act.[25] Milton had always been a rebel, even within his own party. He had managed to combine his dedication to a prophetic task—to scorn delights and live laborious days—with a full aesthetic appreciation of Renaissance humanism at its best. At the time of the most virulent Puritan attacks on the contemporary stage, he had imperturbably attended the theatre both at Cambridge and London, and written openly in praise of Ben Jonson and Shakespeare as dramatists.[26] Music he loved; and the classics, for all their pagan idolatry, were for him a perpetual and acknowledged source of inspiration.

Even more relevant, however, to this charge of unconscious identification is the fact that no-one was more aware of his own unorthodoxies than Milton himself. There is clear evidence of this within the area of his theology. When his *Christian Doctrine* was discovered and first published in 1825, the treatise shocked many of his admirers. Until then, he had been popularly regarded as an orthodox champion of the Christian cause whose poems could safely be placed on the shelf of any family library. Now those passages which had been hesitantly suspected by some as not conforming completely to official doctrine, and whose non-conformity had been attributed to inattention on Milton's part or to an unconscious shifting away from a strictly orthodox standpoint, were suddenly seen as expressing firmly-held heretical beliefs, arrived at after long study and reflection. In that prose tract he openly denied such basic principles as the three-personed Trinity and the *creatio ex nihilo*, accepted the doctrine of 'mortalism', and condoned Old Testament polygamy. His arguments, buttressed with learned quotations drawn from scriptural and hermeneutical sources, showed that, both as Protestant and as humanist, he insisted on substituting for the theological authoritarianism of the church his own personal examination of the original texts; and he unhesitatingly espoused those conclusions to which his reading led him. As Maurice Kelley has shown, the beliefs expressed in his *Christian Doctrine* formed the ideological basis for *Paradise Lost*, written at about the same time. There can therefore be no doubt now that the divergences from official church doctrine in his epic were placed there deliberately and that he was perfectly aware of the implications when he incorporated them into the poem.

In matters less strictly theological, such as his unconventional depiction of Satan or of Eve, we have no prose treatise to prove that his unorthodoxies were deliberate, but there are signposts pointing to his intentions. In the same way as a baroque reading of his work suggests that the theory of an unwitting identification with Satan as rebel is unfounded, and that Milton had, with full cognisance, aggrandised the devil in the early books in order to enlarge the conflict.and hence the ultimate concept of God's might, so here his celebration of Eve's nakedness and of the sensuous joys of the Garden should be seen not as a suppressed passion erupting through his religious restraint, but as an integral part of his baroque vision. Like Rubens, he regarded an appreciation of the opulent vitality of the material world as a positive religious experience. As with music and drama, he rejected the more ascetic vein of Puritanism with its frowning upon pleasure. For him the beauty of the physical world, the 'fragrance of the fertile earth/After soft showers', the trees 'hung with copious fruit', were proof of the bounty of divine creation; and within that bounty the crowning blessing of all was the fulfilment of love, without which all other joys lost their savour:

> But neither breath of Morn when she ascends
> With charm of earliest Birds, nor rising Sun
> On this delightful land, nor herb, fruit, flow'r,
> Glist'ring with dew, nor fragrance after showers,
> Nor grateful Ev'ning mild, nor silent Night
> With this her solemn Bird, nor walk by Moon,
> Or glittering Star-light without thee is sweet.
>
> (IV, 650–6)

So far from being 'seduced' by his vision of Eve, Milton, in his admiration of her naked beauty, remains in perfect accord with the central message in this section of the epic. Although the fruit of one specific tree is prohibited to Adam, the fruits of the permitted trees are to be enjoyed to the full, and of them he is commanded to 'eat freely and with glad heart'. In the same way, love between man and woman has its permitted and its forbidden forms. Harlotry and extra-marital intercourse are anathema for the Puritan, as is mere carnal lust within marriage. But in the setting of true wedded love, the epic not only sanctions the rites of marriage, but gives full baroque endorsement to them as among the most valued gifts of God to mankind. Accordingly, Milton's own warm and unembarrassed descriptions of Eve's feminine beauty form a natural and fitting aspect of his broader tribute to the splendours of the created world, and are far from being an unconscious surrender to illicit passion.

The hymn to wedded love which Milton inserts here as the two retire to their bower should dispel any lingering doubt of his intent. He rebuts any charge of prurience on his part on the grounds that such conjugal joy is the command of God, the pure means of ensuring fertility and increase. As one might expect, the verse itself is redolent of the serene richness which characterises the Garden. Soft, simple words such as *pure*, *fair*, and *true* replace those stirring epithets associated with Satan's revolt, the *uncontaminated* and *incorruptible*, which had charged the cosmic scenes with vigour and spaciousness. Instead, all is gentle and calm:

> into thir inmost bower
> Handed they went . . .
>   nor turn'd I ween
> *Adam* from his fair Spouse, nor *Eve* the Rites
> Mysterious of connubial Love refus'd:
> Whatever Hypocrites austerely talk
> Of purity and place and innocence,
> Defaming as impure what God declares
> Pure, and commands to some, leaves free to all.
> Our maker bids increase, who bids abstain
> But our Destroyer, foe to God and Man?
> Hail wedded Love, mysterious Law, true source
> Of human offspring . . . .
>
> (IV, 739–52)

In an analysis of Milton's poetic techniques, then, it does seem justifiable not merely to note the broad range of versification included under the term 'Grand Style' but also its separation into two main styles, corresponding to the two main themes of the poem. Once the declared purpose of the epic is perceived to be twofold, in its message both of celestial might and of human frailty, the timbre of the verse is seen to adjust itself to these themes even when the local subject-matter, such as a scene from Creation or a military skirmish, is potentially similar. For the architectonic magnificence and vastness of the cosmic battle he employs massive, rolling periods, implosive adjectives conveying in miniature the larger conflict portrayed, and a stress and tension in the forward movement of the passage to reflect that struggle of forces. When, as Milton informs us bardically, he descends from the soaring flight above the Olympian hill, he modulates the verse to suit man's earthly habitation, relating now in mortal voice 'What nearer might concern him'. The reason there is no falling off in that modulated descent is that the vigour and spatial range of the cosmic scenes is replaced there by the enriching quality of plenitude and luxuriance associated both with Eden and with the natural world at large. In their different ways, both form an integral part of the baroque Grand Style, for the theme they share is the hymn to God as Creator, the desire ' . . . the more / To magnify his works.'[27]

That theme – '*Ad majorem gloriam Dei*' – had provided the motto and the inspiration for the builders of the great baroque churches established throughout Europe, with their architectural response to the expanded view of the heavens and their symbolic representation in a wealth of marble and onyx of the abundance prevailing on man's earthly habitation. That purpose had animated Milton's epic too, in its display of cosmic might under divine dispensation and its placing of the Fall within the setting of a proliferating and ever-burgeoning nature, in order by that presentation to offer what

> . . . best may serve
> To glorify the Maker.

> (VII, 115–16)

Notes

NOTES TO CHAPTER I

1. Benedetto Croce, *Storia della età barocca in Italia* (Bari, 1929), p. 23. Jacob Burckhardt's *The Civilization of the Renaissance in Italy* (1860) had long established the view that the baroque was a dissolution of healthier Renaissance forms, but both his work and Heinrich Wölfflin's influential *Renaissance and Baroque* (1888), which attempted to rectify the bias, suffer as critical works from the fact that in that period little attempt was made to distinguish between the baroque and what we today identify as mannerism. For other important studies, see T. H. Fokker, *Roman Baroque Art*, 2 vols. (Oxford, 1938), Emil Mâle *L'Art religieux après le Concile de Trente* (Paris, 1932); W. Stechow, 'Definitions of the Baroque in the Visual Arts' as well as 'The Baroque: a critical summary', in *Journal of Aesthetics and Art Criticism*, 5 (1946), 109 and 14 (1955), 171; and, more generally, Victor L. Tapié, *The Age of Grandeur: Baroque Art and Architecture* (New York, 1966), in addition to other works listed below. For the use of the term 'baroque' in literature, René Wellek's 'The Concept of the Baroque', together with his Postscript of 1962, are indispensable. They appear in his *Concepts of Criticism*, ed. S. G. Nichols Jr. (New Haven, 1965).

   I have found the two main books on Milton's relationship to the baroque extremely helpful, and if I do not always accept their conclusions, I am sincerely grateful for the many insights they offered. They are, of course, Wylie Sypher, *Four Stages of Renaissance Style* (New York, 1955) and Roy Daniells, *Milton, Mannerism and Baroque* (Toronto, 1963). Frank J. Warnke, *Versions of Baroque* (New Haven, 1972), is a stimulating book but he too fails to distinguish between mannerism and baroque, and accordingly leaves the latter term too vague for my purposes. Roland M. Frye's valuable study *Milton's Imagery and the Visual Arts* (Princeton, 1978) appeared when this present book was already written, but in fact there are few points of contact. Frye's purpose, which he achieves with impressive skill, is to reveal the wealth of iconographic traditions in European art *prior* to Milton, on which the poet could have drawn for the imagery in his epics; but the author specifically excludes from his study any exploration of Milton's relationship to the contemporary baroque mode.

2. Carl J. Friedrich, *The Age of the Baroque, 1610–1660* (New York, 1965), pp. 44–5.

3. Carl J. Friedrich, 'Style as the Principle of Historical Interpretation', *Journal of Aesthetics and Art Criticism*, 14 (1955), 143.

4. Rudolf Wittkower, *Gian Lorenzo Bernini* (London, 1966), pp. 7–8.

5. Rudolf Wittkower, *Art and Architecture in Italy 1600–1750* (Harmondsworth,

1973), p. 25. T. H. Fokker, *Roman Baroque Art*, i, 34 had expressed similar views much earlier but with less documentation. The case for the Counter-Reformation origins of the baroque was presented in its clearest form by Werner Weisback, *Der Barock als Kunst Gegenreformation* (Berlin, 1921).

6. J. Donne, 'The First Anniversary', 205–15. For the suggestion that Copernicanism was less revolutionary in its impact than is generally believed today, see A. O. Lovejoy, 'Plenitude and the New Cosmology', in his *The Great Chain of Being* (New York, 1960), where he maintains that the medieval geocentric universe did not give man a sense of dignity and importance. The only evidence he offers for this supposedly medieval view is, strangely enough, from Montaigne and seventeenth-century writers who, he says, 'continued' an earlier tradition.

7. A. O. Lovejoy, *op. cit.*, p. 108.

8. 'Nihil aliud habet illa demonstratio quam indefinitam coeli ad terram magnitudinem. Ad quousque se extendat haec immensitas minime constat.' The recognition that the heavenly bodies were composed of physical matter is discussed in A. R. Hall, *The Scientific Revolution* (Boston, 1962), p. 108.

9. See Marie Boas, *The Scientific Renaissance* (New York, 1962), p. 98.

10. Thomas Digges, *A Perfit Description of the Celestiall Orbes* (1576) appended to his edition of Leonard Digges, *Prognostication Everlasting*. The work was rediscovered earlier in this century by F. R. Johnson and S. V. Larkey, who published an account in the *Huntington Library Bulletin*, 5 (April, 1934). A few years later F. R. Johnson, in his *Astronomical Thought in Renaissance England* (New York, 1968, orig. 1937), argued that the intellectual challenge posed by the new cosmology, including man's relationship to the enlarged universe, was not felt in England until the mid-seventeenth century. Yet the evidence adduced in his own book militates against that thesis. He acknowledges, for example, that the Englishman Thomas Digges was in 1576 '. . . the pioneer in decisively shattering the outer wall of the old cosmology and incorporating into the Copernican system the conception of an infinite universe' (p. 291), while in Donne he sees a writer learned in astronomy whose discussion of the new cosmology in 1611 is of outstanding importance in indicating '. . . the immediate influence of the new astronomical discoveries on English literature' (p. 244). Certainly the initial concern with the New Philosophy received an added boost at the time of Galileo and Kepler and continued to grow through the seventeenth-century, but Copernicanism had its impact even on England long before the 1650s. See also Paul H. Kocher, *Science and Religion in Elizabethan England*, (New York, 1969).

11. C. S. Lewis, *The Discarded Image* (Cambridge, 1964), p. 100.

12. Quoted in Hiram Haydn, *The Counter-Renaissance* (New York, 1960), p. 157, which provides one of the most interesting discussions of the implications of the New Philosophy for the sixteenth and seventeenth centuries.
    There are passing hints at the possibility of some connection between the baroque and Copernicanism in Nikolaus Pevsner, *Studies in Art, Architecture and Design* (London, 1969), i, 42 and Arnold Hauser, *The Social History of Art* (New York, 1951), ii, 180, but they were never developed.

13. The philosopher Crescas, for example, in his *Or Adonai* (1410) firmly challenged Aristotle's statement that no other worlds exist.

14. The discussion of mannerism here is little more than a brief nod, as it formed a

central theme of my recent *The Soul of Wit: a study of John Donne* (Oxford, 1974). There seemed little point in repeating the material here.

15. Augustine, *The City of God*, V, x, in the translation by G. G. Walsh, D. B. Zema, and G. Monahan (New York, 1950). The 'pantocrator' in medieval art is sometimes Jesus (for example, over the entrance to a cathedral to recall the verse 'I am the door, by me if any man enters he shall be saved') and sometimes the Father, as in the passage quoted here from the Chester play. C. A. Patrides makes the important comment that in *Paradise Lost* '. . . Milton differentiates between the Father and the Son *only* during their verbal exchanges in the various councils that took place in Heaven, but as soon as these councils end and the Godhead acts beyond the confines of Heaven the distinction between the two persons is abruptly dropped. Thus during the council before the creation of the universe the Father and the Son are clearly differentiated (VII, 131ff.) but once the Creator embarks on his mission outside Heaven he is specifically termed "God".' See his *Milton and the Christian Tradition* (Oxford, 1966), p. 25. For that reason one may legitimately speak of Milton's baroque concern with the Almighty as Creator of the universe even though in the poem it is the Son who issues from Heaven to perform the task.

16. The dedicatory epistle to Giordano Bruno's *Of the Infinity of the Universe* (1584). See also Alexander Koyré, *From the Closed World to the Infinite Universe* (Baltimore, 1957), p. 42. That Bruno was condemned by the inquisition mainly for his non-astronomical heresies is argued in Frances A. Yates, *Giordano Bruno and the Hermetic Tradition* (London, 1971), particularly pp. 355–6.

17. Copernicus and Kepler responded differently to such writers as Lactantius who had condemned the heliocentric theory on scriptural grounds. Copernicus maintained that his opponents were perverting the true meaning of the biblical texts, while Kepler argued more boldly that there was one truth for theology and another for the physical sciences. See Grant McColley, '*Paradise Lost*': an account of its growth and major origins (New York, 1963), p. 229.

18. The interpretation of baroque arches as symbolic orbits cannot, of course, be applied to St. Peter's, since most of the High Baroque features were added to the interior after it had been completed structurally.

19. In the Middle Ages, the sun had been equated both with Christ and with royalty. Within some Carolingian and early Romanesque churches, a circular window was placed behind a balcony or *solarium* to symbolise the majesty of Christ throned. The device was soon replaced by the so-called 'rose-window', which seems to have been associated not with the sun but with the wheel of fortune. At all events, the *solarium* as such had disappeared from church architecture for many centuries at the time of its revival in an entirely new form within the baroque church. For the early history of the tradition see H. J. Dow, 'The Rose Window', *Journal of the Warburg and Courtauld Institutes*, 20 (1957), 248.

20. Donne, 'First Anniversary', 268–78. Donne's knowledge of Kepler is indicated in *Ignatius His Conclave*. For the importance of this shift in concept, and its reflection in the poetry of the time, see Marjorie H. Nicolson, *The Breaking of the Circle* (New York and London, 1965).

21. Cf. R. Wittkower, *Art and Architecture*, p. 198, where the elliptical dome is described as one of Borromini's bizarre 'mannerist' forms.

22. S. Andrea al Quirinale was begun in 1658, a little late for the theory presented here; but in fact Bernini had preceded Borromini by constructing in 1634 a church with an oval plan in the Palazzo di Propaganda Fide. Unfortunately, that church was later pulled down, and I have therefore discussed here S. Andrea instead, which still stands today as testimony to his introduction of the ellipse into every aspect of its planning and execution.

23. Emile Mâle, *Religious Art from the Twelfth to the Eighteenth Century* (New York, 1965), p. 152.

24. There is an earlier cupola fresco by Correggio, *The Assumption of the Virgin*, in Parma Cathedral (1526–30), which might be thought to belong to this category. It anticipates the angle of the later paintings by presenting the scene as viewed from directly below, but it has none of the infinitude and spaciousness which characterise the post-Copernican frescoes. In fact, the view of the angels from beneath in the Correggio fresco was unkindly described by one of the canons present at its unveiling as a mere 'hash of frogs' legs'.

25. Maurice Kelley, *This Great Argument: a study of Milton's 'De Doctrina Christiana' as a Gloss upon 'Paradise Lost'* (Princeton, 1941).

26. Roy Daniells, for example, who does not question the Counter-Reformation source of the baroque, is forced reluctantly to admit (p. 101) that for all their similarities there remains a basic conflict between Milton's aims and those of the baroque. M. M. Ross, *Poetry and Dogma* (New Brunswick, 1954), pp. 185–7, objects in principle to the identification of Milton's baroque qualities with the Catholic tradition.

27. William Haller, *The Rise of Puritanism* (New York, 1957), pp. 131 and 140. See also G. Wilson Knight, *The Chariot of Wrath* (London, 1942), p. 26.

28. Continental authors such as Du Bartas were, of course, moving in this direction before Milton, but none of them achieves the cosmic range and energy of his epic.

29. Cf. W. Kerrigan, *Prophetic Milton* (University of Virginia, 1974).

30. E. N. S. Thomson, 'A Forerunner of Milton', *Modern Language Notes*, 33 (1917), 479.

31. A. O. Lovejoy, 'Milton's Dialogue on Astronomy', in J. A. Mazzeo, ed., *Reason and Imagination* (New York and London, 1962), p. 135. Dame Helen Gardner, in *A Reading of 'Paradise Lost'* (Oxford, 1965), p. 51, suggests interestingly that Milton vacillates between the two systems in order to create by means of the contradictions a universe which 'surmounts the reach of human sense'.

32. *Areopagitica* in M. Y. Hughes' edition of the *Complete Poems and Major Prose* (New York, 1957), p. 737.

33. K. Svensden, *Milton and Science* (Cambridge, Mass., 1956), p. 48. See also Lawrence Babb, *The Moral Cosmos of 'Paradise Lost'* (Michigan, 1970). For the theory that Milton leaned heavily on John Wilkins, *Discovery of a World in the Moone* (1640) and *A Discourse that the Earth May be a Planet* (1646), see Grant McColley, pp. 217f.

34. L. B. Alberti, *De re aedificatoria*, bk. vi, chapter 2, tr. J. Leoni (London, 1755).

35. H. Wölfflin, *Renaissance and Baroque*, tr. Kathrin Simon (Ithaca, New York, 1967), particularly pp. 38 and 67.

36. See Jean Seznec, *The Survival of the Pagan Gods* (New York, 1953).

37. Spenser, 'An Hymne of Heavenly Love', 64–70. Cf. Kathleen Williams,

'Milton, Greatest Spenserian', in J. A. Wittreich, ed., *Milton and the Line of Vision* (Madison, 1975), pp. 25–55.

38. See especially Sears Jayne, 'The Subject of Milton's Ludlow Mask', *Publications of the Modern Language Association of America*, 74 (1959), 533 and John Arthos, 'Milton, Ficino, and *Charmides*', *Studies in the Renaissance*, 6 (1959), 261.

39. Robert M. Adams, *Ikon: John Milton and the Modern Critics* (Ithaca, New York, 1955), p. 5.

40. Sypher, *Four Stages*, p. 175 and Daniells, pp. 37f.

41. Cf. J. H. Hanford, 'The Pastoral Elegy and Milton's *Lycidas*', *PMLA*, 25 (1910), 403.

42. F. T. Prince, *The Italian Element in Milton's Verse* (Oxford, 1969), pp. 109 and 128.

43. J. H. Hanford, *John Milton, Englishman* (New York, 1949), p. 97. Also Marjorie B. Garber, 'Fallen Landscape and the Art of Milton and Poussin', *English Literary Renaissance*, 5 (1975), 96.

44. John Arthos, *Milton and the Italian Cities* (London, 1968), pp. 81–6, supplies a lengthy note discussing whether this musical evening took place at the Barberini palace or elsewhere under Barberini patronage. After a careful examination of the evidence, he concludes that the evening was held at the palace, but see also J. M. Bottkol, 'The Holograph of Milton's Letter to Holstenius', *PMLA*, 68 (1953), 625, which originally raised the doubt. The letter itself appears in the Columbia edition of Milton's works, xii, 41.

NOTES TO CHAPTER 2

1. For valuable discussions of this relationship, see R. Wellek and A Warren, *Theory of Literature* (Harmondsworth, 1966), pp. 125f., and Mario Praz, *Mnemosyne: the parallel between Literature and the Visual Arts* (Washington and London, 1970).

2. A. J. A. Waldock, *Paradise Lost and its Critics* (Cambridge, 1961), p. 143.

3. The references are to Dryden's *Dedication of the Aeneis* (1697), Blake's *Marriage of Heaven and Hell* (1793), and Shelley's *The Defence of Poetry* (1821).

4. E. M. W. Tillyard, *Milton* (Harmondsworth, 1968), p. 234, and R. J. Z. Werblowsky, *Lucifer and Prometheus: a study of Milton's Satan* (London, 1952), p. xvi. Robert M. Adams, *op. cit.*, pp. 35f., denies this Jungian interpretation.

5. Waldock, pp. 79–83. John Peter follows a similar line of argument in his *A Critique of Paradise Lost* (New York, 1960) but with less sympathy for Milton's positive achievements. More recent discussions of Satan's heroic qualities may be found in Joan Bennett, 'God, Satan and King Charles: Milton's Royal Portraits', *PMLA*, 92 (1977), 441, and the subsequent correspondence in *PMLA*, 93 (1978), 118f., in which Empson participated.

6. Bernard Bergonzi, 'Criticism and the Milton Controversy', in *The Living Milton*, ed. Frank Kermode (London, 1967), p. 168, argues the case very effectively, and also offers a helpful summary of the main lines of critical argument in recent years.

7. C. S. Lewis, *A Preface to Paradise Lost* (London, 1960), p. 100.

8. Stanley E. Fish, *Surprised by Sin: the Reader in Paradise Lost* (Berkeley, 1971),

especially the opening chapter. See also J. Summers, *The Muse's Method* (Harvard, 1962) and Ann Ferry, *Milton's Epic Voice: the Narrator in Paradise Lost* (Harvard, 1963).

9. Waldock, pp. 77–8.

10. Note the contrast with Pollaiuolo's *Hercules and Antaeus* (1480), a small bronze statue seventeen inches high, in which a lean Hercules has already succeeded in lifting Antaeus off the ground.

11. There are remarkably few battle scenes depicted in the Renaissance itself. Uccello's early series on the *Battle of San Romano* are exercises in the art of perspective with no real attempt to capture the dynamism of the scene. Perhaps the only painting of the High Renaissance approaching this baroque interest is Leonardo Da Vinci's *Battle of Anghiari* which has not survived. The only sketch of it (apart from the copies of small details by Michelangelo and Raphael) is, significantly, by Rubens, and it is obviously impossible at this stage to determine how much of that copy is Rubens' own interpretation after he had filtered the scene through his own baroque sensibility. The original painting was in any case known in its day for the individual facial studies of human and animal fury rather than for its depiction of the clash of forces. For reproductions of copies and engravings of Titian's *Battle of Cadore*, see Harold E. Wethey, ed., *The Paintings of Titian* (London, 1974), figs. 52–6.

12. Many readers have assumed that the word 'Providence' here means 'foresight' (*pro-videre*), pointing to God's foreknowledge that the Fall would lead to the coming of the Messiah and hence justify his decision not to prevent man's corruption. In fact, even in classical times the word had almost lost that meaning of foreknowledge in favour of its modern sense to *provide for*, or 'oversee', (cf. *deorum providentia mundum administrari*, Cicero, *De. Div.*, i, 51). The evidence from within Milton's poem is perhaps more relevant. If the epic begins with this determination to assert Eternal Providence, it concludes with the sad pair leaving Eden, the world before them '. . . and Providence thir guide', where Providence can only mean the divine power which watches over all.

Dame Helen Gardner, in *A Reading*, p. 22 is, I believe, the only critic who has perceived that the purpose stated in the invocation is twofold. One should add, however, that the dual purpose takes on a greater significance when the assertion is seen within this baroque context as Milton's attempt to resist the nihilistic implications of a mechanistic universe.

13. Arthur Sewell, *A Study in Milton's Christian Doctrine* (London, 1939), p. 78.

14. C. S. Lewis, *A Preface*, p. 76.

15. Arnold Stein writes very well on this passage in his *Answerable Style: essays on Paradise Lost* (Seattle and London, 1967), p. 124, arguing for its dramatic effectiveness in depicting the inner struggle of Satan.

16. Dryden, *Dedication of the Aeneis* (1697).

17. John M. Steadman, *Milton and the Renaissance Hero* (Oxford, 1967). His more recent *The Lamb and the Elephant* (San Marino, 1974), offers some helpful insights into the artistic background of the era.

18. Sir Philip Sidney, *An Apology for Poetry*, in *Elizabethan Critical Essays*, ed. G. G. Smith (Oxford, 1904), i, 171.

19. *The Reason of Church Government* in Hughes ed., p. 668.

20. The list appears in the Columbia edition of Milton's *Works*, xviii, 231–2.

21. See H. J. C. Grierson, *Milton and Wordsworth* (Cambridge, 1937), pp. 126–7. Phillips, in his own life of Milton, merely states that these lines were written 'some years' before the poem itself, but John Aubrey's biography quotes Phillips as recalling that they were written 'fifteen or sixteen years before ever his Poem was thought of', which would place their composition at about 1642.

22. A. H. Gilbert, 'The Cambridge Manuscript and Milton's Plans for an Epic', *Studies in Philosophy*, 16 (1919), 172, makes the valid point that the fortuitous survival of the Trinity manuscript listing themes of projected tragedies is not conclusive evidence that he was then planning only a drama, since a similar list for possible epics may have existed and not survived. On the other hand, the lines the poet showed to Edward Phillips prove beyond doubt that he had at an early date already begun work on a projected tragedy, and that his final choice of the epic genre came at a later date.

23. Merritt Y. Hughes' comment in his edition of Milton's work, p. 173.

24. Sir Arthur Quiller Couch, *Studies in Literature: second series* (Cambridge, 1923), p. 140. Masson had made the same suggestion, though with greater reservation, in his *Life of Milton* (London, 1880), vi, 663.

25. A. H. Gilbert, *On the Composition of Paradise Lost* (Chapel Hill, 1947), p. 159.

NOTES TO CHAPTER 3

1. This tendency to present noble characters as Christianly perfect is closely paralleled by the heroines of Restoration drama, and reaches its fullest expression in the sentimental plays of the eighteenth century. Paul E. Parnell has shown how in such plays these figures epitomise, in their lack of humility and charity, the very reverse of the Christian ideal, and he attributes to that contradiction much of the mawkishness of the drama itself. See his 'The Sentimental Mask', *Publications of the Modern Language Association of America*, 78 (1963), 529.

2. Joseph Mede, *The Apostasy of These Latter Times*, in *Works* (London, 1677), p. 626. Also Andrew Willet, *Synopsis Papismi* (London, 1614), II, viii, 385.

3. Cf. 'The Apotheosis of St. Ignatius Loyola' in the church of Il Gesù, Rome. The original solid-silver statue was later melted down by Pope Pius VI to pay his debts to Napoleon, and replaced by a less expensive substitute.

4. Wittkower, *Art and Architecture*, p. 140. For the didactic elements in baroque art, see H. J. Jensen, *The Muses' Concord* (Bloomington, 1976), especially pp. 39f.

5. Richard Crashaw, 'In Memory of the Virtuous and Learned Lady Madre de Teresa', 118–32.

6. Cf. D. Saurat, *Milton, Man, and Thinker* (London, 1964), pp. 112f.

7. Donne's 'Aire and Angels' is a perfect example of this concept expressed in verse.

8. Max Weber's essay, 'The Protestant Ethic and the Spirit of Capitalism', was later developed in R. H. Tawney, *Religion and the Rise of Capitalism*, (London, 1926). For a criticism of the theory, see H. R. Trevor-Roper, 'Religion, the Reformation, and Social Change', *Historical Studies*, 4 (1963), 18.

9. *The Christian Doctrine*, trans. Charles R. Sumner, in Hughes ed., p. 976. The problem of 'Milton and the Mortalist Heresy' and its implications for his

validation of matter have been examined in G. Williamson's article of that name in *Studies in Philology*, 32 (1935), 553. Also W. B. Hunter, 'Milton's Materialistic Life Principle', *Journal of English and Germanic Philology*, 45 (1946), 68. I speak here deliberately of the Italian baroque, as Rubens was a Flemish artist, more exposed to Protestant influences by his location in the Low Countries.

10. Donald Davie, 'Syntax and Music in *Paradise Lost*', in *The Living Milton*, p. 70. The number nine is, of course, borrowed from Hesiod's *Theogony*, where the Titans fell from heaven to earth in nine days and nights, and then from earth to Tartarus in another nine.

11. Spenser, 'An Hyme of Heavenly Love', 83–8.

12. Letter dated 13 March, 1610.

13. Kester Svenden, *Milton and Science*, p. 74, quotes evidence to suggest that the discovery of the moon's cavities was not so impressively new. The evidence he cites, however, is merely the earlier belief that there might be scratches or marks on the mirror-like surface of a perfect sphere, and that is entirely different from a recognition that it was a craggy mass with a rutted surface of mountains and gorges, similar to that of the earth.

14. Walter Curry, *Milton's Ontology, Cosmogony, and Physics* (Lexington, 1966), p. 81.

15. See, for example, the commentary of Rashi on Isaiah 6:2.

16. Merritt Y. Hughes, 'Milton and the Symbol of Light' in his *Ten Perspectives on Milton* (New Haven, 1965), p. 63. Also D. C. Allen, *The Harmonious Vision* (Baltimore, 1954), pp. 95f.

17. Marjorie H. Nicolson, 'Milton's Hell and the Phlegraean Fields', *University of Texas Quarterly*, 7 (1958), 500, which quotes the description by the Jesuit priest Athanasius Kircher in his *Mundus Subterraneus* (1638). The area of Sulfatara remains today more or less as Kircher then described it.

18. Edward Fairfax's translation of 1600, entitled *Godfrey of Bulloigne*, IV, 8.

19. W. Kirkconnell, *The Celestial Cycle* (New York, 1967), p. 89, translation by the editor.

20. The comparison of Satan to a rising sun seen through the mist, and shorn of its beams (I, 595) is, of course, a view of dawn seen from the earth, and remains within the classical tradition.

21. Du Bartas, *Divine Weekes and Workes*, tr. Joshua Sylvester (London, 1621). G. C. Taylor, *Milton's Use of Du Bartas* (Cambridge, Mass., 1934), examines similarities in words or phrases to argue for Milton's indebtedness to Du Bartas, but it underplays the differences between the two works.

22. Henry More, *An Explanation of the Grand Mystery of Godliness* (London, 1660), I, iii, 6. Robert H. West, *Milton and the Angels* (Athens, Georgia, 1955), offers a useful history of angelology in this period.

23. M. M. Mahood, *Poetry and Humanism* (London, 1950), p. 200, used this same passage of Satan's ascent to argue that Milton's heaven is free from gravitational forces, but the text does not support her interpretation.

24. Interestingly enough, in the latter part of the epic, where the poet is no longer concerned with the theme of heavenly battle or celestial might, he returns to a more traditional view. As the Son descends to Eden, he comments that '. . . the speed of Gods/Time counts not, though with swiftest minutes wing'd' (X, 90–1).

25. Kirkconnell, p. 234.
26. Galileo, *Sidereus Nuncius* (The Sidereal Messenger), tr. E. S. Carlos (London, 1880), pp. 42–3.
27. Marjorie H. Nicolson, 'Milton and the Telescope', *Journal of English Literary History*, 2 (1935), 1, and 'The Microscope and the English Imagination', *Smith College Studies in Modern Languages* (1935), both republished in her *Science and Imagination* (Ithaca, 1956). See also Jackson I. Cope, *The Metaphoric Structure of Paradise Lost* (Baltimore, 1962), and Thomas M. Greene, *The Descent from Heaven: a study in epic continuity* (New Haven, 1963), p. 378.
28. John Donne, 'The First Anniversary', pp. 278–82.
29. Dedicatory epistle to his *On the Infinity of the Universe* (1584), quoted in Alexander Koyré, *From the Closed World*, p. 42.

NOTES TO CHAPTER 4

1. J. B. Broadbent, *Some Graver Subject: an essay on Paradise Lost* (New York, 1960), p. 223.
2. Samuel Johnson, *Lives of the Poets* (London, 1968), i, 108.
3. Arnold Stein, *Answerable Style*, especially pp. 23f.
4. Very occasionally the word appears in the Bible in the more general sense of 'happiness' ('Let your laughter be turned to mourning' James 4; 9). For other uses of laughter as an expression of mockery see *PL*, VII, 78 and XII, 59. Milton, incidentally, did have a sense of humour, if a rather heavy one (witness his early sonnets on Hobson, and the wit that sometimes emerges in the Sixth Elegy), but he had a much stronger sense of propriety.
5. The images of belching and defecation in VI, 585f., which have often been regarded as humorous by modern critics, were in fact an accepted part of the devil tradition. See, for example, the bird-headed devil in Hieronymus Bosch's painting *The Garden of Delight*, consuming human souls and defecating them into the hole of hell below.
6. S. E. Fish, *Surprised by Sin*, p. 178.
7. Cf., Harold Fisch, 'Hebraic Style and Motifs in *Paradise Lost*', in *Language and Style in Milton*, ed. R. D. Emma and J. T. Shawcross (New York, 1967), p. 40.
8. J. M. Evans, '*Paradise Lost*' *and the Genesis Tradition* (Oxford, 1968), pp. 34f. Grant McColley, '*Paradise Lost*: *an account of its growth and major origins* (New York, 1963) provides a detailed survey of the development of this tradition.
9. *Ludus Coventriae*, ed. K. S. Block, Early English Text Society (Oxford, 1960), p. 18.
10. Vondel, *Lucifer* in Kirkconnell, p. 413.
11. Wayne Shumaker, *Unpremeditated Muse: feeling and perception in Paradise Lost* (Princeton, 1967), p. 22 makes the excellent point that in literature reason works best not, as is often thought, when it is divorced from aesthetic sensibility, but when both are engaged simultaneously.
12. B. Rajan, '*Paradise Lost*' *and the Seventeenth Century Reader* (London, 1966), p. 96, writes interestingly of the 'illusion of equality' created at the opening of the poem. He suggests, however, that Satan is at once reduced in stature and never regains his splendour; and there we part ways. See also Geoffrey Hartman, *Beyond Formalism* (New Haven, 1970), pp. 115f., for a contrast between God's

divine imperturbability and the vigour of Satan's rebellion.

13. Cf. *PL* II, 692, and V, 710.

14. John Peter, *Critique*, pp. 79–80. In *Milton's God* (London, 1965), p. 41n., William Empson argues rather strangely against the view that God divides his army into two on the grounds that the phrase 'equal in number' is often used to mean 'not less than': but he offers no evidence to support that statement. Certainly to be 'equal to the challenge' means to be not less than the required level, but that is not the same as 'equal *in number*', which can only be used for a strict mathematical equation.

15. J. H. Hanford, 'Milton and the Art of War', *Modern Philology*, 18 (1921), p. 232. The idea is echoed by Joseph Summers, 'The Embarrassments of *Paradise Lost*', in *Approaches to Paradise Lost*, ed. C. A. Patrides (London, 1965), p. 69.

16. John S. Diekhoff, *Milton's 'Paradise Lost': a commentary on the argument* (New York, 1963). On the prologues and invocations, see also E. M. W. Tillyard, *Milton*, pp. 207f., and, on the problem of Milton as narrator, Arnold Stein, *The Art of Presence* (Berkeley, 1977).

17. *Iliad*, XI, 160–3 tr. Lang, Leaf, and Myers (London, 1935), p. 185.

18. In the *Christian Doctrine* I, v, Milton argues at length that the statement in John 14, 28, '. . . my Father is greater than I', refers not only to Christ in his human form, but also as risen.

19. That imaginative release after powerful unresolved pressures occurs also in the final scene of *Samson Agonistes*, where

> . . . straining all his nerves he bow'd;
> As with the force of winds and water pent
> When mountains tremble, those two massy Pillars
> With horrible convulsion to and fro
> He tugg'd, he shook, till down they came, and drew
> The whole roof after them with burst of thunder
> Upon the heads of all who sat beneath . . . .

Here again, the baroque struggle between the irresistible and the immovable remains in doubt as Samson heaves to and fro with horrible convulsions, until the moment when the massy pillars come crashing down. I have preferred not to include a discussion of *Samson Agonistes* in this present work but am preparing a lengthy article for publication elsewhere on the implications of certain theories advanced here for an analysis of the play.

NOTES TO CHAPTER 5

1. Isabel G. MacCaffrey, *'Paradise Lost' as Myth* (Cambridge Mass., 1967), p. 64.

2. See J. B. Broadbent's perceptive article, 'Mortal Voice and Omnific Word', in C. A. Patrides, ed., *Approaches*, p. 99, and John Wain, 'Strength and Isolation', in *The Living Milton*, p. 1, for a recognition of the difference between Milton's 'lofty' and 'plain' style, although neither essay relates these styles to the two main themes of the epic. Northrop Frye, *The Return to Eden* (Toronto, 1965), p. 13, notes that the classical epic was often split into two fairly equal sections, the quest and the settling of society.

3. Pope remarked that '. . . he is not lavish of his exotic words everywhere alike, but employs them more where the subject is marvellous, vast, and strange'. *Postscript to the Odyssey* (1723).

4. James Boswell, *The Life of Johnson* (Oxford, 1946), i, 497.

5. Christopher Ricks, *Milton's Grand Style* (Oxford, 1963). Also Bernard Bergonzi, 'Criticism and the Milton Controversy', in *The Living Milton*, p. 162, and B. Rajan, *The Lofty Rhyme* (London, 1970). The letters by Leavis and Empson appeared in the *Times Literary Supplement*, 19 September and 3 October, 1958. There is a useful summary of the controversy in Patrick Murray, *Milton, the Modern Phase: a study of twentieth-century criticism* (London, 1967).

6. *Four Stages*, p. 205.

7. R. D. Havens, *The Influence of Milton on English Poetry* (New York, 1922), although often unsatisfactory, remains the major study of this topic. For a deeper understanding of eighteenth-century poetic modes not in relation to Milton's verse, see James Sutherland, *A Preface to Eighteenth Century Poetry* (Oxford, 1948), and Geoffrey Tillotson *Augustan Studies* (London, 1961).

8. Matthew Arnold, *On Translating Homer* (London, 1861).

9. T. J. B. Spencer, '*Paradise Lost*: the Anti-epic' in *Approaches*, p. 81.

10. Cf. Caroline M. Goad, *Horace in English Literature of the Eighteenth Century* (New Haven, 1918).

11. For supporting evidence that Milton's poem is non-Vergilian in texture, see Donald R. Pearce, 'The Style of Milton's Epic', *Yale Review*, 52 (1963), 427, and R. D. Emma, 'Grammar and Milton's English Style', in *Language and Style in Milton*, p. 233. The latter article is aimed at rebutting Janette Richardson, 'Virgil and Milton Once Again', *Comparative Literature*, 14 (1962), p. 321. D. P. Harding, *The Club of Hercules* (Urbana, 1962) also examines Milton's relationship to Homer and Vergil.

12. Pope, 'Windsor Forest', 139–42.

13. Cf. 'Is he not rightly named Jacob, for he has supplanted me these two times?' Gen. 27, 36.

14. John Donne, 'Goodfriday 1613: Riding Westward', 11–12.

15. Josephine Miles, *Major Adjectives in English Poetry*, (Berkeley, 1946), p. 308.

16. Heinrich Wölfflin, *Principles of Art History*, tr. M. D. Hottinger (New York, 1950), pp. 141f., originally published in German in 1915.

17. Spenser, 'An Hymne of Heavenly Love', 99–103.

18. Roy Daniells, p. 79.

19. The quotations are from IV, 11; VIII, 530; IX, 734; and IX, 999.

20. D. Daiches, 'The Opening of *Paradise Lost*', in *The Living Milton*, p. 66, lists some of the commentators on which he could have drawn.

21. The translation of the Authorised Version, '. . . to dress and keep it', is an inaccurate rendering of the Hebrew which Milton, of course, knew at first hand: yet he chose, despite this knowledge, to adopt the version of pruning and cutting away excess rather than that of their working the soil.

22. Barbara K. Lewalski, 'Innocence and Experience in Milton's Eden', in Thomas Kranidas, ed., *New Essays on 'Paradise Lost'* (Berkeley and Los Angeles, 1969), p. 86.

23. W. Sypher, *Four Stages*, pp. 194 and 200, presents this argument, even though his knowledge of the baroque might have been expected to lead him away from such a view.

24. William Gouge, *Of Domesticall Duties* (London, 1634), p. 224 and William Whately, *A Bride-bush* (London, 1619), p. 14, both quoted in Roland M. Frye's helpful article 'The Teachings of Classical Puritanism on Conjugal Love', *Studies in the Renaissance*, II (1955), 148. See also C. A. Patrides *Milton and the Christian Tradition* (Oxford, 1966), especially chapter IV. For the importance of the Creation theme as a contrast to the theme of the Fall, see M. Lieb, *The Dialectics of Creation: Patterns of Birth and Regeneration in 'Paradise Lost'* (Boston, 1970), especially, pp. 42f.

25. E. M. W. Tillyard, *Milton*, p. 239, published originally in 1930. A retraction appears in his *Studies in Milton* (London, 1964), pp. 67f., published originally in 1951.

26. 'L'Allegro', 131-4. In his 'Elegia Prima', addressed to Charles Diodati, he relates with enthusiasm how, when wearied of his books, '. . . the magnificence of the arched theatre diverts me and the chattering actors invite me to applaud them'. Much later, in his *Apology for Smectymnuus* (1642) he answered the charge of having frequented playhouses by neatly sidestepping the matter, without explicitly denying his earlier attendance.

27. *Paradise Lost*, VII, 96-7.

Index

190 *Index*

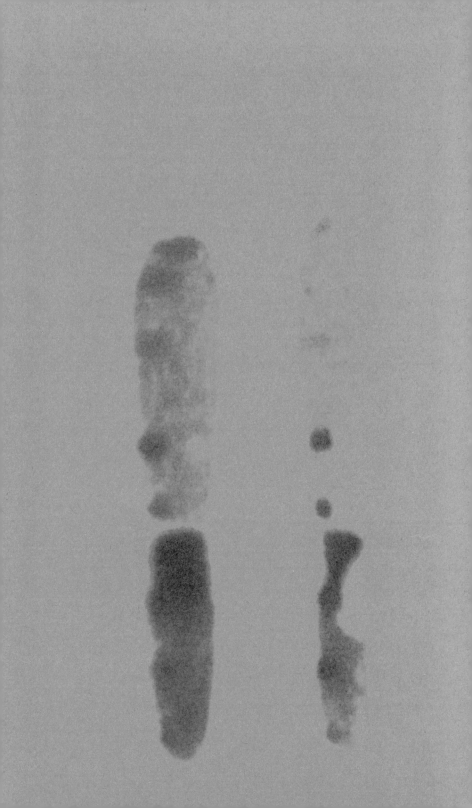